Referring in a Second Language

The introduction and tracking of reference to people or individuals, known as referential movement, is a central feature of coherence, and accounts for "about every third word of discourse". Located at the intersection of pragmatics and grammar, reference is now proving a rich and enduring source of insight into second language development. The challenge for second language (L2) learners involves navigating the selection and positioning of reference in the target language, continually shifting and balancing the referential means used to maintain coherence, while remaining acutely sensitive to the discourse and social context.

The present volume focuses on how L2 learners meet that challenge, bringing together both eminent and up-and-coming researchers in the field of L2 acquisition. The chapters address a range of problems in second language acquisition (SLA) (e.g., form-function mapping, first language [L1] influence, developmental trajectories), and do so in relation to various theoretical approaches to reference (e.g., Accessibility Theory, Givenness Hierarchy). The global outlook of these studies relates to the L2 acquisition of English, French, Japanese, Korean, and Spanish and covers a diverse range of situational contexts including heritage language learning, English as a medium of instruction, and the development of sociolinguistic competence.

Jonathon Ryan is a principal academic staff member at Wintec in Hamilton, New Zealand, with the Centre for Languages and the Master of Applied Innovation programme. He is also Head of Materials Development for Chasing Time English. His research interests include reference, practitioner research, L2 pragmatics, and Conversation Analysis for language teaching.

Peter Crosthwaite is a senior lecturer in the School of Languages and Cultures at the University of Queensland, Australia (since 2017), having formerly been an assistant professor at the Centre for Applied English Studies (CAES), University of Hong Kong, China (since 2014). His areas of research and supervisory expertise include second language acquisition, reference to person, the use of corpora for language learning (known as "data-driven learning"), and English for General and Specific Academic Purposes.

Routledge Studies in Applied Linguistics

Language Management and Its Impact
The Policies and Practices of Confucius Institutes
Linda Mingfang Li

Multiliteracies, Emerging Media, and College Writing Instruction
Santosh Khadka

Cantonese as a Second Language
Issues, Experiences and Suggestions for Teaching and Learning
Edited by John Wakefield

The Social Lives of Study Abroad
Understanding Second Language Learners' Experiences through Social Network Analysis and Conversation Analysis
Atsushi Hasegawa

Defining and Assessing Lexical Proficiency
Agnieszka Leńko-Szymańska

Global Perspectives on Project-based Language Learning, Teaching, and Assessment
Key Approaches, Technology Tools, and Frameworks
Edited by Gulbahar H. Beckett and Tammy Slater

Referring in a Second Language
Studies on Reference to Person in a Multilingual World
Edited by Jonathon Ryan and Peter Crosthwaite

Aspects of Language Development in an Intensive English Program
Alan Juffs

For more information about this series, please visit: https://www.routledge.com/Routledge-Studies-in-Applied-Linguistics/book-series/RSAL

Referring in a Second Language

Studies on Reference to Person in a Multilingual World

Edited by Jonathon Ryan and Peter Crosthwaite

LONDON AND NEW YORK

First published 2020 by Routledge

2 Park Square, Milton Park, Abingdon, Oxon OX14 4RN
605 Third Avenue, New York, NY 10017

Routledge is an imprint of the Taylor & Francis Group, an informa business

First issued in paperback 2021

Coyright © 2020 selection and editorial matter, Jonathon Ryan and Peter Crosthwaite; individual chapters, the contributors

The right of Jonathon Ryan and Peter Crosthwaite to be identified as the authors of the editorial material, and of the authors for their individual chapters, has been asserted in accordance with sections 77 and 78 of the Copyright, Designs and Patents Act 1988.

All rights reserved. No part of this book may be reprinted or reproduced or utilised in any form or by any electronic, mechanical, or other means, now known or hereafter invented, including photocopying and recording, or in any information storage or retrieval system, without permission in writing from the publishers.

Notice:
Product or corporate names may be trademarks or registered trademarks, and are used only for identification and explanation without intent to infringe.

Publisher's Note

The publisher has gone to great lengths to ensure the quality of this reprint but points out that some imperfections in the original copies may be apparent.

British Library Cataloguing-in-Publication Data
A catalogue record for this book is available from the British Library

Library of Congress Cataloging-in-Publication Data
A catalog record for this title has been requested

ISBN: 978-0-367-20894-3 (hbk)
ISBN: 978-1-03-217284-2 (pbk)
DOI: 10.4324/9780429263972

Typeset in Galliard
by Deanta Global Publishing Services, Chennai, India

Contents

List of figures vii
List of tables ix
List of contributors xi
Foreword xiii
List of abbreviations xvii
Acknowledgements xviii

1 Referring in a second language: Introduction to the volume 1
   PETER CROSTHWAITE AND JONATHON RYAN

2 Referent accessibility marking and referent's social status in Japanese as a second language 16
   JO LUMLEY

3 Use of demonstratives in oral narratives by Japanese learners of English 39
   BONNIE SWIERZBIN

4 Do referential marking styles transfer to L2 story retelling? 56
   YUKO NAKAHAMA

5 Referential movement in L2 vs. Heritage Korean: A learner corpus study 75
   PETER CROSTHWAITE AND MIN JUNG JEE

6 Under-explicit and minimally explicit reference: Evidence from a longitudinal case study 100
   JONATHON RYAN

7   Anaphora resolution in topic continuity: Evidence from L1
    English–L2 Spanish data in the CEDEL2 corpus   119
    FERNANDO MARTÍN-VILLENA AND CRISTÓBAL LOZANO

8   Using the Givenness Hierarchy to examine article use in
    academic writing: A case study of adult Spanish-speaking
    learners of English   142
    JENNIFER KILLAM

9   Referent introducing strategies in advanced L2 usage: A
    bi-directional study on French learners of Chinese and
    Chinese learners of French   164
    LUDOVICA LENA

10 Nominal reference in L2 French: How do adult learners
    manage to understand the multifunctionality of
    determiners and their discourse counterparts?   184
    EWA LENART

11 Afterword: New directions in L2 reference research   203
    JONATHON RYAN AND PETER CROSTHWAITE

    Index   211

Figures

5.1	Reference annotation scheme	82
7.1	Annotation scheme used in the software UAM Corpus Tool	125
7.2	Production of RE forms (frequency and %) by group in topic continuity	127
7.3	Production of pragmatically (in)felicitous forms by group	129
7.4	Production of null pronominal subjects (Ø) in topic continuity by group according to the syntactic environment of the RE	130
7.5	Form of the antecedent for null pronominal subjects in topic continuity by group	132
7.6	Overt material REs (overt pronouns and NPs) produced in topic continuity according to number of potential antecedents (1, 2, 3, 3+) by group	133
7.7	Production of overt pronouns in topic continuity with two potential antecedents according to gender (same vs different gender) by group	135
7.8	Production of NPs in topic continuity with two potential antecedents according to gender (same vs different gender) by group	135
8.1	The six cognitive statuses of the Givenness Hierarchy	143
8.2	The relationship between cognitive statuses of the Givenness Hierarchy and the English articles	144
8.3	The relationship between the six cognitive statuses of the Givenness Hierarchy and the English and Spanish articles	146
8.4	Definite article distribution by cognitive status	152
8.5	Indefinite article use by cognitive status	156
8.6	Zero article use by cognitive status	158

10.1 Types of reference markers used by Polish learners of L2 French and by French speakers: reference to garçon (boy) 196
10.2 Types of reference markers used by Polish learners of L2 French and by French speakers: reference to chien (dog) 196
10.3 All reference markers used by beginners 197
10.4 All reference markers used by advanced learners 197
10.5 All reference markers used by native speakers 198

Tables

2.1	Summary of role-play tasks	18
2.2	The number of referring expressions produced	19
2.3	Coding for discourse pragmatic variables of distance and competition	19
2.4	Interactions between discourse pragmatic variables and referent social status	20
2.5	Referring expressions used by referent social status, use of deferential expressions for higher-status referents and referring expressions used on a narrative task (group level)	23
2.6	Interactions between referent social status and form choice (group level)	24
2.A1	Participant information for learners of Japanese (L) and Japanese native speakers (JA)	32
2.A2	Referent social status and form choice for individual learners at both stages	35
3.1	Participant profiles	44
3.2	Frequency of demonstratives by category and proficiency level	45
3.3	Type of referents of discourse deictic demonstrative pronouns by proficiency level	47
3.4	Type of referents of discourse deictic demonstrative determiners by proficiency level	47
3.5	Temporal and causal relations with discourse deixis by proficiency level	48
3.6	Situational use by proficiency level	48
4.1	Referential forms of English within discourse contexts	57
4.2	Low-intermediate level learner results in L2 English	61
4.3	High-intermediate level learner results in L2 English	63
4.4	Advanced level learner results in L2 English	63
4.5	Results in L1 Japanese	65
4.6	Marked syntactic structures (MSS)	70

x   Tables

5.1	Corpus size across subcorpora	81
5.2	Distribution of reference across learner corpora	83
5.3	Forms used for specific discourse-new reference	84
5.4	Forms used for generic reference	86
5.5	Forms used for given reference by type	89
5.6	Forms used for coreferential reference	90
5.7	Forms used for switch-role reference	93
5.8	Forms used for switch-reference	94
6.1	Accessibility coding in English (based on Ryan, 2012, 2015)	105
6.2	RE types used in referent tracking	106
6.3	Distribution of pronouns by accessibility context (Yoona)	107
6.4	Yoona's system of accessibility marking	108
7.1	CEDEL2 corpus sample	124
A7.1	Learners' biodata	138
8.1	The Spanish definite and indefinite articles	146
8.2	Participant demographics and course enrollment	149
8.3	Total article NPs by frequency and percent of total NPs	151
8.4	Distribution of the definite article across cognitive statuses	153
8.5	TLU for each of the articles by participant and task	154
8.6	Distribution of the indefinite article across cognitive statuses	157
8.7	Distribution of the zero article across cognitive statuses	158
9.1	Distribution of the syntactic structures linked to referents introduction in the L1s and L2s	168
9.2	The structures associated to the introduction of each character in the L1s	172
9.3	The structures associated to the introduction of each character in the L2s	174
10.1	Types of reference markers in L1 French and L1 Polish	192

Contributors

Peter Crosthwaite is a senior lecturer in the School of Languages and Cultures at the University of Queensland, Australia (since 2017), having formerly been an assistant professor at the Centre for Applied English Studies (CAES), University of Hong Kong, China (since 2014). His areas of research and supervisory expertise include corpus linguistics and the use of corpora for language learning (known as "data-driven learning"), as well as English for General and Specific Academic Purposes.

Henriette Hendriks is a reader in language acquisition and cognition at the University of Cambridge, UK. She is known internationally for her research in the area of cognitive linguistics, and she researches the relationship between language and cognition through work in child first and adult second language acquisition. Dr Hendriks studied at Leiden University, the Netherlands, and then started her career at the Max-Planck Institute for Psycholinguistics. In 1998, she moved to the University of Cambridge, where she has since been lecturing and researching.

Min Jung Jee is a lecturer in Korean at the University of Queensland, Australia. She completed a PhD in foreign language education at the University of Texas at Austin and taught Korean language courses there before she joined the Korean program at the University of Queensland. Her research interests are technology-assisted language learning and teaching (esp. Web 2.0 tools), learner differences (esp. affective factors), intercultural communication (esp. telecommunication), and heritage Korean language learners.

Jennifer Killam is an assistant professor of English for Academic Purposes at Broward College in Pembroke Pines, Florida, USA. She received an MA in ESL from Hamline University in Saint Paul, Minnesota, and is a doctoral student in Composition and Applied Linguistics at Indiana University of Pennsylvania.

Ludovica Lena is a PhD candidate in linguistics (CRLAO – Paris/"La Sapienza" – Rome) and has benefited from numerous research grants (in particular at Academia Sinica, Taiwan, and Xiamen University, China). Ludovica has been teaching Chinese (Paris VI University) and linguistics (Tours University). Her research mainly focuses on the linguistic means used to express referential movements in French and in Chinese, both L1 and L2. She is also interested in corpus linguistics and the pragmatic analysis of informal spoken Chinese.

Ewa Lenart is an associate professor in Linguistics at the University of Paris 8, France, and in the laboratory *Structures Formelles du Langage* (CNRS). Her main research concerns L1 and L2 acquisition of nominal reference in French and Polish. She is also interested in the early L2 acquisition at school.

Cristóbal Lozano received his PhD from the University of Essex, England, and is an associate professor in Applied Linguistics (Second Language Acquisition) at the Universidad de Granada, Spain. His research interests are Second Language Acquisition, Bilingualism, and Learner Corpus Research. He is currently interested in the acquisition and processing of anaphora resolution (ANACOR project) and is director of the CEDEL2 corpus (http://learnercorpora.com).

Jo Lumley is a member of academic staff in the School of East Asian Studies, University of Sheffield, UK, with research interests including person reference and pragmatic development in Japanese as a second language.

Fernando Martín-Villena holds a BA in English Studies and an MA in English Linguistics from the Universidad de Granada, Spain. He is currently a PhD student supervised by Dr Cristóbal Lozano and Prof. Antonella Sorace and a member of the ANACOR project. His main research interests are SLA and L1 attrition at the syntax–discourse interface.

Yuko Nakahama is a professor of Applied Linguistics at Keio University, Japan. She received her PhD in Linguistics from Georgetown University, USA. Her study interest lies in examining L2 use in natural contexts. Her research has appeared in books and journals such as *Modern Language Journal* and *TESOL Quarterly*.

Jonathon Ryan is a principal academic staff member at Wintec in Hamilton, New Zealand, with the Centre for Languages and the Master of Applied Innovation programme. He is also Head of Materials Development for Chasing Time English. His research interests include reference, practitioner research, L2 pragmatics, and Conversation Analysis for language teaching.

Bonnie Swierzbin is an unabashed grammar geek captivated by the myriad ways to create meaning in English. As an ESL teacher and language teacher educator, she helps her students view grammar as a resource for making meaning instead of dry rules to be memorized. Dr Swierzbin is the co-author (with Elaine Tarone) of *Exploring Learner Language* (OUP, 2009).

Foreword

Occasionally I get asked as a linguist: "What is it really that you study?" And when I answer that I study language, I may then be asked: "And what's so fascinating about language that you have been studying it all your life, and still don't seem to be finished with it?" And I have found myself pondering over that question in some depth many times during my career. In my view, language is one of the most fantastic tools that humanity has been given. From the individual words that allow us to name objects and events, to the full sentential structures that allow us to ask, direct, query, express ideas and emotions, and many more things. Language makes it possible for us to communicate. And if we can do more with language than just thread a few words together, it allows us to tell our story: our personal story, the story of our families, our cultures, or even our histories.

In order to thread words together in a coherent fashion, and hence communicate, one needs more than just nouns and verbs to label objects and events. One needs linguistic elements that indicate to the listener or reader how the words and how the sentential structures link together. And to make our communication not just coherent but also cohesive, one needs to know how to use language in such a way that there is never any doubt about who, what, or where one is referring to. For this purpose, we use reference.

How does reference work? Nouns may be embedded in noun phrases that have determiners that indicate what is new or given information, reference to objects and protagonists may be maintained by other, lighter forms such as pronouns, or zero anaphora, and verbs may carry information about the time in which the event took place, or if it is an important event in the story or rather one that happened in the background. In other words, all the linguistic means available to us have multiple functions: a purely referential function, where the object of the reference is in the external reality that we are speaking of, but also a discourse referential function through which expressions in one's discourse, text, or narrative are linked. The fact that language has these multiple functions makes it an infinitely more subtle and versatile tool than if one could just name things with it.

It seems obvious that learning a form that has multiple functions might be harder than learning forms that only have one. And possibly, this might lead to a learner picking up such functions one after another, possibly taking some time to acquire the further functions once a first function is acquired. And indeed, we seem to find this in child first language acquisition: Children very early on can use nouns and (somewhat later) verbs to describe, or label objects and events, as in: "Look! A duck!" However, careful studies of children's narrative discourse as conducted by Bamberg (1987), Karmiloff-Smith (1979), and Hickmann (2003) show that the text-internal cohesive functions of these linguistic means are acquired relatively late in the child's acquisition process. For example, Hickmann (2003) shows that children only acquire the appropriate use of referential expressions in narratives around the age of seven, whereas children can label items before they are three years old. In other words, children seem to acquire the linguistic means for reference one function at the time.

It has been argued that one of the reasons for this slower development is that children have to learn to understand what the function actually beholds. What does it mean when a form can indicate if something is "new" or "given" information in one's discourse? What does it mean when a form indicates that an event is part of the foreground or the background of the narrative or text? Indeed, quite intricate knowledge is required to use these markers appropriately. First of all, for the given-new distinction, the child has to understand that listeners and speakers may not share all the knowledge the speaker has, and that they may bring different perspectives to the exchange of information. Second, they have to come to an understanding that these forms that they have happily been using in order to refer to objects and events outside of the text can also be used to message to the listener that information is thought to be shared (or not), that some events are more or less important, temporally linked or not, etc., and, thirdly, they have to come to grips with the fine details of which forms do what exactly. In other words, they have to have acquired some level of theory of mind, a large scale of different forms, as well as a fine-grained understanding of the multiple functions of each of the forms.

In the past, it was thought (partly based on Piaget's work and his assumption of ego-centrism) that the child might take a long time to understand that their interlocutor might not share the same information they have access to. However, in more recent times, Tomasello and colleagues, and also Baillargeon and colleagues (amongst others) have amply shown that this is not the case, and that even the very young child very quickly has some understanding of the intentions and wishes of the individuals around them. The explanation for why these linguistic means are acquired late, therefore, has to lie in the fact that the child is confronted with linguistic forms that have multiple functions, some of which are more obvious to acquire, whereas others are more opaque and more in flux.

Imagine then a learner who already knows that language is multifunctional, that language allows the speaker to indicate to the hearer what information they already share or what information might be new to them, and who already knows that some forms are likely being used for these purposes. In other words, imagine an adult acquiring a new language. Interestingly, at the time I started looking into referential expressions in L2 learners, little had been written on the topic in this area. But logically, adults should bring a huge advantage to the task of language learning: they already know a lot about language, including the fact that language is multifunctional. One could therefore argue that they should have an easier task acquiring referential systems in a new language. This was indeed the assumption I made myself when I started to compare child first and adult second language acquisition of referential means.

But of course, the problem for the adult second language learner is not as self-evident as suggested here: as they already know another language, they will have potentially acquired very different linguistic forms for these functions, or the use of deceptively similar forms for slightly different functions. For example, where English provides its speakers with nouns, pronouns, and zero anaphors, the latter form is relatively infrequent and restricted to specific syntactic (as well as semantic) contexts of use. In Chinese, a similar range of forms is available (for the differences between the Chinese and English forms, see Hickmann and Hendriks, 1999), but the zero anaphor is used in very high frequency, and almost considered the default form once shared knowledge of the entity or protagonist has been established. At the same time, however, all languages seem to show a similar progression of fuller (noun + determiner or article) to lighter (pronoun or zero anaphor) forms along a scale which negatively correlates with how familiar the intended referent is to the hearer/in the discourse. In other words, the adult should be familiar with the principle, but will, of course, have to establish what forms are available, and how they are distributed across the scale.

Findings when looking at the comparison were interesting: Adults showed clear knowledge of the fact that (a lack of) shared knowledge can be marked linguistically (they marked new information relatively consistently, regardless of the forms needed to do so), but did not seem to mark different levels of given information equally clearly or systematically. In particular, when maintaining reference, adult learners seem to use over-explicit forms, i.e., nouns instead of pronouns, pronouns instead of zero anaphors. I have called this "a seeming contradiction" in earlier works (Hendriks, 2003). Similar findings have been found by many others also looking at adult L2 acquisition of referential marking in discourse. And various explanations have been offered: I personally proposed that it might be because adults understand the importance of shared knowledge so well that they try and avoid any ambiguous reference, leading them to use full noun phrases in cases of potential ambiguity because of gender or case markings (i.e., if one does not know if a cat is feminine or masculine in the target language, using the pronouns he versus she (which indicate that the information is given) might actually be more confusing than simply using a noun "the cat" (which may be confusing in terms of it being new or given information but is absolutely clear in terms of the designated referent). Hence a "seeming" contradiction only. Others, such as von Stutterheim have suggested that the problem lies with the fact that when producing spoken discourse, there might be a cognitive overload, such that learners, who will be trying to get the message right at the utterance level, might lose oversight of the structure of the full discourse, and hence marking of cohesion. Finally, yet other explanations have offered specific typological differences and a higher likelihood of over-explicitness in some languages than in others (i.e., languages with multiple genders and case might be more prone to over-explicit markings than those that do not have gender and case). Note that most of these data are production data, all involving mostly some type of narration or description of static pictures, picture sequences, or movies.

In other words, although some interesting and relatively similar findings have been reported across a small variety of tasks, and plausible explanations have been suggested, we need more studies on a larger variety of source and target languages, more diversified populations, and probably we also need more varied elicitation techniques. This book promises to do all of the above across a range of new studies, and is, therefore, a very welcome addition to the literature, promising to shed some further and much needed light on the issues surrounding reference as acquired and used by (adult) L2 learners.

Henriette Hendriks, University of Cambridge

References

Bamberg, M. (1987). *The acquisition of narratives*. Amsterdam, the Netherlands: Mouton de Gruyter.

Karmiloff-Smith, A. (1979). *A functional approach to child language: A study of determiners and reference*. Cambridge, UK: Cambridge University Press.

Hendriks, H. (2003). The use of nouns in reference maintenance: the seeming contradiction in adult second language acquisition. In A. Giacalone Ramat (Ed.), *Typology and second language acquisition* (pp. 291–326). Berlin, Germany: Mouton de Gruyter.

Hickmann, M. (2003). *Children's discourse: Person, space and time across languages*. Cambridge, UK: Cambridge University Press.

Hickmann, M., & Hendriks, H. (1999). Cohesion and anaphora in children's narratives: A comparison of English, French, German, and Chinese. *Journal of Child Language*, 26(2), 419–452. doi:10.1017/S0305000999003785

Abbreviations

Ø	zero
AT	Accessibility Theory
BV	Basic Variety
CEFR	Common European Framework of Reference for Languages
CLI	cross-linguistic influence
det.	determiner
EFL	English as a foreign language
ESF	European Science Foundation
ESL	English as a second language
FA	Functional Approach
FL	foreign language
GH	Givenness Hierarchy
HAM	high accessibility marker
HL	heritage language
HLS	heritage language speakers
L1	first language
L2	second language
L3	third or subsequent language
LAM	low accessibility marker
Lit	literal
MAM	medium accessibility marker
N	noun
NNS	non-native speaker
NP	noun phrase
NS	native speaker
PPVH	Pragmatic Principles Violation Hypothesis
RE	referring expression
SL	source language
SLA	second language acquisition
SVO	subject–verb–object
TLU	target-like use
VP	verb phrase
V–O	verb–object
V–S	verb–subject

Acknowledgements

We would like to thank Katie Peace and ShengBin Tan and the team at Routledge and the anonymous reviewers for their enthusiastic support of this project, and the chapter contributors for their inspired work and their prompt responses to reviewer feedback and editorial feedback. We would also like to extend our thanks to Dr Youngah Doh of the University of Hong Kong who provided early assistance with Chapter 5 of this volume. Finally, a special mention to Ludovica Lena, who gave birth to her first baby, Ondina, shortly before the submission date and yet still managed to find time for us.

1 Referring in a second language
Introduction to the volume

Peter Crosthwaite and Jonathon Ryan

During the production of any discourse, one must use language to *refer* to people, places, objects or ideas under discussion. While there are few genuine typological universals that hold across all languages, the ability to introduce and maintain *reference* is a feature common to every language, and, as with the ability to discuss concepts such as space, causation and time, reference is a feature relevant to the coherence of any discourse produced, resolving the central question of "who did what (to whom)?".

While, for reasons of space, we must necessarily eschew discussion of the various conceptual definitions of reference in the literature (e.g. Frege, 1892), in this volume we define reference as realised in the use of *referring expressions*, including zero, pronominal and nominal forms, to refer to entities under discussion. These expressions are then organised through such means as *information structure*, *substitution* and *word order*. The appropriate selection, position and marking of these referring expressions allow speakers and listeners (and writers/readers) to know when *new* information is being introduced into discourse, and when continued reference to *old* information is updated. This process of referential "movement" affects "about every third word of discourse (sometimes even more than that)" (Kibrik, 2001, p. 1124). Moreover, the complexity involved in managing reference across extended discourse and multiple referential targets is astounding, and in the face of such complexity, "the fact that people actually manage to understand one another most of the time *seems almost magical*" (Fretheim & Gundel, 1996, p. 7). Yet, the ability to introduce and maintain reference is one that is acquired by most children from a very young age (Serratrice & Allen, 2015).

The focus of the present volume is on how second language (L2) learners refer in their target language. Despite the apparent ease with which children acquire the ability to produce and maintain coherent reference in their first language as noted previously, research into second language acquisition has repeatedly shown that L2 learners struggle to acquire the means to make consistently accurate and felicitous reference in the target language. Rather, they are prone to producing reference that is ambiguous, erroneous, under-informative or overexplicit (or all of these), with serious implications for the coherence of any discourse that L2 learners are attempting to produce.

As pointed out by Hendriks in the foreword, while studies on L2 reference have revealed a range of findings explaining the difficulties involved in producing coherent reference in the L2, the time is now right to expand upon previous findings through new methodological advances, data from previously underexplored L1/L2 pairs and alternative theories of L2 reference acquisition and use. In the rest of this introduction, we explore how L1 reference has been characterised in the (applied) linguistics literature, before providing a brief overview of previous L2 treatments of reference in the field. We then discuss in more detail the need for this volume before introducing the individual contributions.

Approaches to L1 reference

There have been various treatments of reference in the (applied) linguistics literature over the past 40 years, each of which has sought to account for the conditions governing the speakers' (or writers') selection and positioning of referring expressions. Given considerations for space, we cannot hope to account for all of these, but have attempted to select treatments from those existing in only one domain (e.g. syntax) to those that take a more integrated (e.g. discourse-pragmatic) account of this phenomenon.

One of the most influential early syntactic treatments of reference is Chomsky's (1981/1993) government and binding theory, developed to account for the positioning and coreference of pronouns to their antecedents (i.e. John saw his mother), although the syntactic binding component of this theory was modified in the later Minimalist approach to include semantic and phonological elements (Lasnik & Lohndal, 2010). Similarly, early typological accounts of coreference have focused on relative clause formation, such as the Noun Phrase Accessibility Hierarchy (Keenan & Comrie, 1977). These approaches took the view that there were *universal* grammatical principles dictating the conditions for reference in natural languages. However, there has been a great wealth of research in linguistics to challenge this view (which we do not attempt to cover here), and, ultimately, these theories did not seek to address reference as performed across greater units than the sentence.

Early functional treatments went beyond the sentence level to categorise reference as an underlying semantic property of the complete text, under the notions of *cohesion* and *coherence* (Halliday & Hasan, 1976; Hasan, 1984). Halliday and Hasan suggested that the cohesion of a given discourse text was formed through the presence of cohesive "ties" between presupposed referential, spatial, temporal or causal elements. These included a general notion of "reference" in the form of antecedent-anaphor relations (e.g. definite articles and demonstrative noun phrases (NPs)), alongside "substitution" (including pronouns and ellipsis). Hasan (1984) claimed that the coherence of a text could then be determined by the frequency of the cohesive "ties" within it, although this theory was subsequently determined to be overly superficial and did not hold up to empirical scrutiny (Carrell, 1982).

More recent accounts of reference have (quite rightfully) determined that reference cannot be placed within the sole domain of syntax or semantics, but that reference is subject to a range of conditions and constraints at the intersection of syntax, semantic, pragmatic and discourse interfaces. Reference cannot be treated simply a feature of the text, but is now thought of as (minimally) a two-way exchange between speaker/hearer (or writer/reader) realised in the "common ground" (following Chafe, 1974; see also Clark, 2015), with reference to entities within a given discourse held in "in two collaborating minds" (Gernsbacher & Givon, 1995, p. viii) in real time, as shown in examples (1) and (2) below:

(1) A: I just got back from Paris last week.
    B: That must have been an interesting trip.
(2) A: Did you talk to Kate yesterday?
    B: Yes, I told her about the arrangements

(Clark, 2015, p. 330).

The speakers' (or writers') specific use of a shorter NP such as the demonstrative pronoun (1) or personal pronoun (2) at that particular moment (rather than the use of a fuller NP form) is designed to allow the listener (or reader) to resolve the reference with as minimal effort and maximal efficiency as possible (Hawkins, 2004). Under such accounts, either an *incorrect* (i.e. an error at the syntax/semantics level) or – for the first time – an *infelicitous* NP (at the pragmatics/discourse level) are both likely to result in the listeners/readers' inability to appropriately resolve the reference, potentially leading to miscommunication with an accompanying breakdown of overall coherence (Ryan, 2012).

Once researchers had realised the central importance of pragmatics and discourse to the realisation of reference, a range of syntax-pragmatic scales/hierarchies of referring expressions were then proposed in the literature to account for the felicitous selection of referential NP forms according to particular discourse-pragmatic contexts. A particularly influential account under this paradigm is that of Gundel, Hedberg, and Zacharski's (1993) *Givenness Hierarchy*, where the speakers'/writers' selection of referring expressions depends on the relative "cognitive status" of the referential target, depending on their relative "givenness" in the discourse as it unfolds (a more detailed account of this framework is provided in **Jennifer Killam's** chapter within this volume). An alternative account is that of Givon's (1995) *Topicality Scale*, where the selection of referring expressions signals the "topicality" of a referent according to its level of "activation," as calculated by such measures as the relative distance between references to said referent. In other words, zero or anaphoric pronouns may be used for "continued [coreferential] activation," while indefinite nouns, demonstrative NPs, definite NPs (including relative clause modifiers), L-dislocation and grammatical role/voice change are used for "discontinued [non-coreferential] activation," with these forms listed in order of their relative level of activation. While not without their flaws, the strength of these accounts was their ability to account for reference beyond the sentence level and to account for variation in referential forms used according to contextual/discourse-related factors shared between both speaker and listener (or reader/writer) during production.

Probably the most influential account of reference along discourse/pragmatic lines is that of Ariel's (1991, 2008, 2010) Accessibility Theory (AT), which is used in **Jonathon Ryan's**; **Jo Lumley's**; **Peter Crosthwaite** and **Min Jung Jee's**; and **Ewa Lenart's** chapters in this volume. Ariel's scale of referring expressions as organised according to the relative level of "accessibility" they denote are shown in this Accessibility Scale (Ariel, 2008, p. 44):

Full name > *long definite description* > *short definite description* > *last name* > *first name* > *distal demonstrative* > *proximate demonstrative* > *stressed pronoun* > *unstressed pronoun* > *cliticised pronoun* > *verbal person inflections* > *zero*

According to Ariel, referring expressions are used to "encode" (Ariel, 2008) the level of inference required to resolve any reference at a given moment, taking into consideration the target referent(s)' relative distance between discourse-old and repeated mentions, competition between referents of similar types, degree of salience of the referent, and the unity (breaks in continuity) of reference within a given discourse sequence. Interestingly, in a way, Ariel's hierarchy of referring expressions hearkens back to the universalist position taken by Chomsky et al. in that the configuration of forms along the hierarchy is believed to hold cross-linguistically.

Most recently, corpus-based and computational accounts of reference (mostly in the form of algorithms for coreference resolution) have become increasingly prominent, given the potential benefits of successful coreference resolution for machine translation and automated essay scoring, among other applications. While computational linguistics-based accounts of reference lie outside the scope of this volume, the history of these accounts has also followed a trajectory from mainly syntax-led approaches to those incorporating semantic and discourse information as key components of successful coreference resolution across a variety of languages (e.g. Poesio, Stevenson, Eugenio, & Hitzmann, 2004; Lee, He, Lewis, & Zettlemoyer, 2017).

Approaches to L2 reference

Like L1 reference, work on L2 reference has been conducted within the domains of syntax, semantics, discourse-pragmatics and the intersection of each. If we are to take the distinction between these domains at face value, the second language learner will have already internalised the kind of language-universal syntax-semantic-pragmatic tendencies of linguistic form and referential function (e.g. the NP hierarchies such as Ariel's AT) during the course of acquiring their first language. We should also consider that if typological universals [of the type predicted by AT] are universal to natural human languages, "then they should also hold for interlanguages" (Callies, 2009, p. 107). The challenge for L2 learners, therefore, is to first acquire a *new* set of referential forms in the target language, before mapping form to function according to the new syntax-semantic-pragmatic configuration required for coherent production of reference in that target language. They must do all this while avoiding any influence or transfer from their L1 into their L2 production, all during the performance of often cognitively and linguistically complex activities such as narratives or essay writing. Clearly, this is not a simple task, but it is a crucial one that – in our opinion at least – often takes a back seat to form-focused instruction on temporal, causal or spatial language in most L2 teaching and learning contexts (see the **Afterword** for further discussion).

Accounts of L2 reference must therefore consider the relative developmental states of the L2 learner, the typological configurations of L1 source/L2 target languages (and this is not always easy to work out in the case of L3, multilingual or heritage language learners, see **Peter Crosthwaite** and **Min Jung Jee's** chapter for further discussion) and the difficulties involved in both acquiring and managing L2 production at the syntax–semantics–pragmatic interfaces given the limited linguistic and processing means at L2 learners' disposal. One of the earliest influential accounts of L2-specific reference along these lines is sourced in the functional approach as part of Klein and Perdue's (1997) investigation of the "Basic Variety," a characterisation of low proficiency L2 production. This was summarised in Watorek, Benazzo, and Hickmann (2012) as "a simple linguistic organisation that is nonetheless well structured around a set of system-internal principles that are universal in the sense that they are shared by learners of different source and target languages during a certain period of time in the acquisition process" (p. 3). Reference under the Basic Variety (BV) is restricted via a "controller-first" agent-patient semantic constraint on most utterances combined with a "focus-last" pragmatic constraint on information structure, while referential forms themselves lack inflection for number and person or are frequently ambiguous due to the use of zero anaphora where pronominal or full-NPs may be required. Many L2 learners (for a variety of reasons) do not progress beyond the BV, and the coherence of the reference produced by such learners is strongly impacted by these limitations.

Beyond the BV, L2 learners are required to complete more complex linguistic tasks with the limited amount of L2 forms they have acquired, or need to increase their range of L2 forms to more accurately complete familiar tasks. It is at this point in an L2 learners' development where the L1/L2 configuration plays a more prominent role in the task of acquiring and managing L2 reference, and there have been a wealth of studies investigating particular referential forms and functions across different L1/L2 pairs. For example, there has been much work on the acquisition of grammatical articles such as the English indefinite and definite articles across different L1/L2 pairs (e.g. Ekiert, 2010; Crosthwaite, 2014), as well as a number of contrastive studies on L2 zero anaphora production (e.g. Tao & Healey, 2005; Nakahama, 2009), L2 demonstrative use (e.g. Ionin, Baek, Kim, Ko, & Wexler, 2012) as well as transfer of topic/focus information structure into subject/object languages (e.g. Sasaki, 1990; Yuan, 1995).

However, even when the form/function mappings across L1/L2 appear to have been acquired, the difficulty involved in maintaining coherent reference across complex linguistic tasks such as narratives have often resulted in accurate yet pragmatically infelicitous (and therefore less coherent) discourse. For example, Hendriks (2003) notes a "seeming contradiction" in L2 discourse where L2 learners are typically overexplicit in full-NP production compared with native speakers, in part because they are unable to produce the discourse conditions for felicitous use of high accessibility forms (i.e. zero or pronouns). However, even advanced L2 learners have been shown to face significant difficulties in fully mastering information organisation in the target language (von Stutterheim, 2003).

Explanations of these difficulties from SLA theory range from arguments related to linguistic relativity (e.g. Slobin, 1996), functional/typological accounts (e.g. Hendriks, 2003), processability/relevance-based accounts (e.g. Filipovic & Hawkins, 2013), frequency/contingency-based accounts (e.g. Ellis, 2006a, 20006b) and accounts involving learnability issues across the syntax/semantics and pragmatics/discourse interfaces (e.g. Sorace, 2011; Sorace & Filiaci, 2006). Certainly, aspects of each of the above theories can help researchers to interpret the considerable challenges faced by L2 learners during the course of acquiring L2 reference. We do not explicitly seek to support or challenge any one particular account through this volume *per se*, although a few chapters in this volume are designed to provide support in favour of individual accounts (see **Ewa Lenart's** and **Martín-Villena** and **Lozano's** chapters in this volume).

Need for the current volume

The present volume brings together a range of studies that both consolidate and advance established research agendas, alongside others with a more exploratory focus. For instance, the chapter by **Martín-Villena** and **Cristóbal Lozano** is among the latest work from the ANACOR research team, the largest-scale research project yet conducted on L2 reference. Headed by Lozano and based in the University of Granada, Spain, this is a major ongoing SLA investigation currently involving 15 collaborators using large-scale corpus data and experimental designs in multiple L1–L2 pairings. Their chapter here is characteristic of the methodological rigour and well-established SLA approaches of the ANACOR work in examining anaphoric reference (referent tracking) among higher-level bilinguals. Similarly, **Ewa Lenart's** chapter builds on a strong tradition of research from a functional perspective, employing the *quaestio* model of text organisation, and detailed consideration of the referential features of the source and target languages, while **Yuko Nakahama's** chapter is a relatively rare – and welcome – replication study in L2 pragmatics. Despite increasingly urgent calls for more replication studies (e.g. Porte & McManus, 2019), a recent review by Marsden et al. (2018) estimated that these account for only 1 in 400 papers published in applied linguistics journals, raising the possibility that flawed findings remain unchallenged and eventually become conventional wisdom within the field. One reason for the lack of replication is researchers' concerns that their findings may lack originality and newsworthiness (Porte, 2012, p. 12), leading to initiatives to ease this concern such as *Language Learning*'s adoption of Registered Reports. In any case, Nakahama's partial replication of Jarvis (2002), using a new source language group, reveals unexpected findings and demonstrates the solid contributions to theory that can be made through replication. Thus, the present volume achieves an important function in building upon well-established research agendas through new studies by some of the key researchers in the field.

The volume also fulfils an important role in broadening the research focus. For instance, to date, studies of L2 reference have overwhelmingly focused on referent tracking (anaphoric reference). This is largely true also of the present volume and is probably also a fair indication of the practical and theoretical importance of this area. There is, however, much of interest to be learned about L2 performance in other aspects of reference, as this volume demonstrates. **Jo Lumley's** chapter, for instance, explores the interaction between referent accessibility and social status, with highly intriguing results. **Ludovica Lena's** chapter is one of the few studies to have focused exclusively on referent introductions, and also reports on the seldom-examined area of bridging inference (see Crosthwaite, 2014). **Peter Crosthwaite** and **Min Jung Jee's** chapter is the first corpus-based study to explore reference in the context of heritage language learning, while **Jennifer Killam's** chapter is one of a very small number to have adopted the Givenness Hierarchy framework (see also Swierzbin, 2004). Similarly, while studies of reference in L2 English have overwhelmingly reported on the use of pronouns and articles, **Bonnie Swierzbin** is one of the few to explore the acquisition of demonstratives.

A further strength of the volume is the range of L1–L2 pairings and the comparisons enabled through complementary studies. These pairings (L1 listed first) are English–Japanese and Japanese–English; Chinese–French and French–Chinese; Spanish–English and English–Spanish; Korean–English and English–Korean; also represented are Polish learners of French- and English-speaking heritage learners of Korean. While some of these build on previous research into these pairings, little has been previously reported about the pairings of Chinese and French and of Polish and French. Thus, the volume as a whole contributes to the ever-growing breadth and depth of language pairings that have been researched, with relevance to discussions relating to universal and non-universal aspects of reference, evidence of developmental trajectories, and evidence of crosslinguistic transfer and other acquisitional processes.

A further need for the present volume arises from methodological considerations. The referential phenomena sought by SLA researchers usually requires discourse with a combination of some or all of the following features. There will be references to a range of third-persons, both male and female (with perhaps some inanimate), some of whom will be previously known and others unknown to the interlocutor. Among those who are previously known, some will be readily identifiable, while others will be recalled only with greater effort. Individuals will variously occupy central and peripheral roles in the discourse, with some mentioned only in passing, others lapsing from focus only to be reintroduced, while still others will be tracked across long anaphoric chains. These chains may involve maintenance in either topic or focus position or switch between the two, and there will be times when tracking involves distinguishing between multiple individuals, perhaps with similar characteristics such as gender. Narrative data has proven the most reliable source for eliciting these features, particularly through tasks which provide an information gap in which the interlocutor has previous knowledge of some of the referents. Indeed, Ryan (2012) surveyed approximately 30 studies of L2 reference, finding just two that did not use narrative data and only a handful that supplemented narrative with a second or third source. Most widely used have been retellings involving the silent Chaplin film *Modern Times*, many of which utilise the specific task instructions pioneered in a major European Science Foundation (ESF) project (Perdue, 1984, 1993). The widespread use of *Modern Times* has undoubted advantages arising from ready cross-study comparisons, and is represented in the present volume in the chapters by **Ludovica Lena**; **Bonnie Swierzbin**; and **Yuko Nakahama**, while **Ewa Lenart** similarly used a silent cartoon. However, there are also grounds for encouraging broader data exploration, particularly due to the performance variability associated with different types of communicative purpose (Lantolf & Ahmed, 1989) and degrees of task complexity (Foster & Skehan, 1996). More specifically in relation to reference, Schiffrin (2006) has demonstrated ways in which L1-referring practices are sensitive to genre. While not addressing the issue of genre directly, the present volume does include several chapters reporting alternatives to narrative data, and in so doing, presents findings that suggest new research directions. In particular, **Jo Lumley's** use of role-plays has enabled examination of the influence of social distance on the selection of referring expressions (REs), while **Jonathon Ryan's** use of interview data reveals extensive minimal- and under-explicitness.

In further broadening the research agenda, the present volume includes four chapters – those by **Yuko Nakahama**; **Jennifer Killam**; **Fernando Martín-Villena** and **Cristóbal Lozano**; and **Peter Crosthwaite** and **Min Jung Jee** – focusing on reference in L2 writing, complementing the more numerous studies into L2 oral production. While there have been previous studies focusing on written production, renewed focus in this area is welcome, particularly given evidence of substantial differences between L1 referring behaviour in spoken and written modes in both Japanese (Clancy, 1982) and English (Fox, 1987).

Contributions to the volume

The volume starts with three chapters involving Japanese–English language pairings. **Jo Lumley's** chapter breaks new ground in exploring the interaction between social status and the use of more explicit RE forms in L2 Japanese. Drawing on both Accessibility Theory (Ariel, 1990) and Politeness Theory (Brown & Levinson, 1987), he proposes that Japanese speakers use more explicit RE types to show deference. His study then presents longitudinal data from English-speaking learners of Japanese before and after a sojourning (study abroad) experience and compares this with data from L1 Japanese performance of the same role-play and narrative data. His findings reveal a counter-intuitive developmental trajectory, whereby participants were more target-like pre-sojourn in terms of the interaction between social status and RE explicitness. This was particularly so in terms of students in the post-sojourn phase using more non-target-like null forms for higher-status individuals. These findings are in contrast to those found under conditions where social status is not a factor. Lumley argues that this may be due to the additional complexity of contexts in which learners have to attend to social relations in the selection of REs.

Bonnie Swierzbin's chapter builds on the very limited number of studies to closely examine the use of demonstrative forms in L2 speech. She adopts Himmelmann's (1996) taxonomy of cross-linguistic uses of demonstrative forms, distinguishing between discourse deixis, text reference, extended reference and situational use. Her focus is the use of the English singular forms *this* and *that* by L1 speakers of Japanese across three proficiency groups in the completion of a narrative task. Her findings reveal that learners across all three groups were largely felicitous in their demonstrative usage, but that their use becomes substantially more frequent with increasing proficiency and that the range of uses expands, with the recognitional function and indefinite *this* only recorded at the high proficiency level. Swierzbin notes that some of these uses were unlikely to have been explicitly taught, raising the question of how exactly were they acquired. Her discussion considers the likely roles of crosslinguistic transfer and of incidental input in the classroom and wider community.

Yuko Nakahama's chapter is a partial replication of an earlier study of topic continuity by Jarvis' (2002), examining referential forms used in L2 writing across a number of discourse contexts. The contexts examined are introductions, continuation/maintenance and reintroductions, with distinctions made between use in topic and comment position. The initial study by Jarvis had provided strong evidence of crosslinguistic influence through his comparisons of Swedish and Finnish learners of English. Like Finnish, Japanese uses postpositional particles for functions associated with the English articles system and thus appears suitable for confirming Jarvis' findings, while also providing a point of difference in its more restricted distribution of third-person pronouns. Nakahama reports both positive and negative evidence of crosslinguistic influence. Most surprising are participants' relatively accurate use of articles and the relatively target-like use of pronouns even at low-competency levels. The findings and their divergences from Jarvis (2002) are discussed in terms of scales of acquisitional difficulty as well as possible task effects and sampling factors.

The following two chapters involve Korean–English pairings. **Peter Crosthwaite** and **Min Jung Jee's** chapter is another corpus-based contribution to our understanding of L2 referential movement, this time comparing the discourse-new, generic and given reference produced by foreign and heritage learners of Korean at beginner and intermediate levels of proficiency. In recent times, the dichotomy between native speakers and L2 language learners is becoming blurred as the global movement of people and a trend towards increasingly multilingual societies in the twenty-first century have led a rise in what is known as heritage language learning. Heritage language learners are acquiring a minority language (the language typically spoken at home) together with a majority language (typically English). Studies comparing the production of specific referential forms such as zero article use between foreign and heritage learners are now common, although there are fewer studies that have looked at reference more broadly to encompass new, genetic and given referential contexts. Using a corpus of almost 100 written texts divided into beginner and intermediate foreign/heritage learners, significant effects of heritage vs. foreign language status as well as proficiency were found regarding the forms used for reference introduction and maintenance. The findings suggest heritage learners' knowledge of and ability to produce reference in the target language therefore differs from that of foreign learners at equivalent levels of proficiency, with potential implications for future instruction in the target language for both groups.

Jonathon Ryan's chapter presents a longitudinal case study of references by one Korean user of English in interview data over the course of her mainstream academic studies. Drawing on an AT (Ariel, 1990) framework, references were analysed in terms of RE type and accessibility coding system, allowing conclusions to be drawn regarding longitudinal development of a RE system and their deployment in context. The most unexpected finding was the speaker's consistent and extensive use of pronouns at the expense of zero anaphora, names and lexical NPs, with this being a stable feature over the length of the study. In contrast to the widely reported phenomenon of over-explicitness, the speaker overwhelmingly tended towards minimal- and at times under-explicitness. Despite this, Ryan reports that miscommunications and hearer-initiated repairs were rare, with the speaker appearing well attuned to the interlocutor's ability to resolve references. Ryan argues that the combination of successful and economical reference likely accounts for the stability of the speaker's referring behaviour over the two-and-a-half years of the study.

The next two chapters relate to Spanish–English pairings. **Fernando Martín-Villena** and **Cristóbal Lozano's** chapter looks at reference used for topic continuity produced by L1 English–L2 Spanish learners from a corpus-based perspective. Previous research has shown L1 English–L2 Spanish learners (even at advanced proficiencies) produce infelicitous forms including redundant overt pronouns and full noun phrases (NPs) when null pronouns are expected in topic continuity contexts due to processing difficulties at the syntax-discourse interface and the influence of the L1. To investigate further, the authors analyse written compositions of L1 English–L2 Spanish at three proficiency levels (beginner, intermediate, advanced) vs. a Spanish native control subcorpus from the CEDEL2 corpus (Lozano & Mendikoetxea, 2013) (http://cedel2.learnercorpora.com). Anaphoric reference was annotated for pragmatic (in)felicity; the syntactic patterns in which it occurred; and the chains created between the anaphoric form and their antecedent(s). The results show that L1 English–L2 Spanish learners are initially overexplicit in topic continuity contexts, gradually reducing overt forms in favour of native-like null pronoun use as proficiency increases. However, data from the advanced learners suggests they cannot attain full native-like pragmatic competence. Thus, while pragmatic felicity is acquired gradually with increasing proficiency, difficulties at the syntax-discourse interface remain problematic for L2 learners even at the highest proficiency levels.

Jennifer Killam's chapter presents an investigation into L1 Spanish–L2 English learners' production of definite, indefinite and zero article use in written academic essays, using the Gundel et al. (1993) Givenness Hierarchy (GH) to account for their distribution. In particular, the chapter seeks to determine whether zero and indefinite articles share "referential" or "type identifiable" cognitive statuses of the GH, which, in turn, would suggest the GH can be used to describe the distribution of definite, indefinite and zero articles in L2 English writing. Collecting multiple essay drafts from upper-intermediate to advanced L2 proficiency learners and analysing these submissions for article use, the results suggest that the learners exhibited near native-like use of indefinite and definite articles, despite occasionally transferring L1-Spanish-like syntactic constraints to their use. In addition, zero articles were most frequently associated with referents that have cognitive statuses of type identifiable and referential, as with the indefinite article, potentially indicating that zero articles in English and Spanish may potentially share the same distribution across cognitive statuses. As errors in article use are often heavily penalised in writing rubrics, these findings increase our understanding of how L2 English learners use such articles in written composition across indefinite, definite and generic referential contexts.

Ludovica Lena's chapter explores the impact of bi-directionality within L1/L2 pairs on L2 reference production, in this case determining whether the presence of similar form-function mappings for referent introductions necessarily leads the speaker to use the "corresponding" form in the L2. Focusing on French learners of L2 Chinese and Chinese learners of L2 French, Lena performs a video-retelling task across L1 French, L1 Chinese, Chinese-speaking L2 French learners and French-speaking L2 Chinese learners, investigating a range of referent introductions by character type. For the L2 learners, referent introductions are marked by overuse of certain forms (e.g. presentative constructions) and avoidance of others (e.g. V–S word order). However, similar form/function pairings across L1 source languages did not always predict use of the corresponding form in the target language, with learners tending to use a simpler inventory of structures than those employed by L1 native speakers, and with L2 learners' preference for certain referent introduction types tending to reflect individual L1-like principles.

Ewa Lenart's chapter explores the acquisition trajectory of reference by Polish adult learners of L2 French at two levels of proficiency (beginners and advanced) through an examination of the interaction of phrasal and communicative rules in the process of referring to entities in a film-retelling task, using Ariel's Accessibility Theory as the framework for analysis of high, mid and low accessibility markers used to maintain and switch reference to the protagonists of the story. The findings suggest that while Polish L2 French learners were overall able to construct coherent and cohesive discourse reference as a result of knowledge of how to produce such discourse in their L1, such learners experience difficulties with French determiners at beginner levels, as well as over-specification of reference at both the beginner and advanced levels. As a potential strategy to avoid referential ambiguity, the learners also tended to use high accessibility markers more than native speakers. This suggests that despite universal tendencies in information organisation, the L1 is a strong mediating factor on the acquisition of reference maintenance in the L2, and that even advanced L2 learners often experience a cognitive overload when trying to maintain cohesive and coherent reference in the L2.

Finally, we would like to acknowledge a planned contribution that was unable to be completed. In drawing up our initial "wish-list" of contributors, an obvious selection was **Marina Chini**, Professor of Sociolinguistics at the University of Pavia, whose published output included several important works on person reference (published mostly in Italian). Marina was enthusiastic about the project but ultimately declined due to ill health. We were saddened to hear of her passing in July 2018.

References

Ariel, M. (1990). *Accessing noun phrase antecedents*. London, UK: Routledge.
Ariel, M. (1991). The function of accessibility in a theory of grammar. *Journal of Pragmatics, 16*, 443–463. doi:10.1016/0378-2166(91)90136-L
Ariel, M. (2008). *Pragmatics and grammar*. Cambridge, UK: Cambridge University Press.
Ariel, M. (2010). *Defining pragmatics*. Cambridge, UK: Cambridge University Press.
Brown, P., & Levinson, S. C. (1987). *Politeness: Some universals in language usage*. Cambridge, UK: Cambridge University Press.
Callies, M. (2009). *Information highlighting in advanced learner English: The syntax-pragmatics interface in second language acquisition*. Amsterdam, the Netherlands: John Benjamins.
Carrell, P. L. (1982). Cohesion is not coherence. *TESOL Quarterly, 16*(4), 479–488. doi:10.2307/3586466
Chafe, W. L. (1974). Language and consciousness. *Language, 50*, 111–133. doi:10.2307/412014
Chomsky, N. (1993/1981). *Lectures on government and binding: The Pisa lectures (No. 9)*. Berlin, Germany: Walter de Gruyter.
Clancy, P. M. (1982). Written and spoken style in Japanese narratives. In D. Tannen (Ed.), *Spoken and written language: Exploring orality and literacy* (pp. 55–76). Norwood, NJ: Ablex.
Clark, E. V. (2015). Common ground. In B. MacWhinney & W. O'Grady (Eds.), *The handbook of language emergence* (pp. 394–412). Oxford, UK: Blackwell.
Crosthwaite, P. (2014). Definite discourse-new reference in L1 and L2: A study of bridging in Mandarin, Korean, and English. *Language Learning, 64*(3), 456–492. doi:10.1111/lang.12062
Ekiert, M. (2010). Linguistic effects on thinking for writing: The case of articles in L2 English. In Z. Han & T. Cadierno (Eds.), *Linguistic relativity in SLA: Thinking for speaking* (pp. 125–153). Bristol, UK: Multilingual Matters.
Ellis, N. C. (2006a). Language acquisition as rational contingency learning. *Applied Linguistics, 27*(1), 1–24. doi:10.1093/applin/ami038

Ellis, N. C. (2006b). Selective attention and transfer phenomena in L2 acquisition: Contingency, cue competition, salience, interference, overshadowing, blocking, and perceptual learning. *Applied Linguistics*, *27*(2), 164–194. doi:10.1093/applin/aml015

Filipović, L., & Hawkins, J. A. (2013). Multiple factors in second language acquisition: The CASP model. *Linguistics*, *51*(1), 145–176. doi:10.1515/ling-2013-0005

Foster, P., & Skehan, P. (1996). The influence of planning and task type on second language performance. *Studies in Second Language Acquisition*, *18*(3), 299–323. doi:10.1017/S0272263100015047.

Fox, B. A. (1987). *Discourse structure and anaphora: Written and conversational English*. Cambridge, UK: Cambridge University Press.

Frege, G. (1892). On sense and reference. In P. Geach & M. Black (Eds.), *Translations from the philosophical writings of Gottlob Frege* (pp. 56–78). Oxford, UK: Blackwell.

Fretheim, T., & Gundel, J. K. (1996). Introduction. In T. Fretheim & J. K. Gundel (Eds.), *Reference and referent accessibility*. Amsterdam, the Netherlands: John Benjamins.

Gernsbacher, M. A., & Givón, T. (1995). *Coherence in spontaneous text*. Amsterdam, the Netherlands: John Benjamins.

Givón, T. (1995). Coherence in text, coherence in mind. In T. Givón & M. A. Gernsbacher (Eds.), *Coherence in spontaneous text* (pp. 59–115). Amsterdam, the Netherlands: John Benjamins.

Gundel, J. K., Hedberg, N., & Zacharski, R. (1993). Cognitive status and the form of referring expressions in discourse. *Language*, *69*(2), 247–307. doi:10.2307/416535

Halliday, M. A. K., & Hasan, R. (1976). *Cohesion in English*. London, UK: Longman.

Hasan, R. (1984). Coherence and cohesive harmony. In J. Flood (Ed.), *Understanding reading comprehension* (pp. 181–219). Newark, DL: International Reading Association.

Hawkins, J. A. (2004). *Efficiency and complexity in grammars*. New York, NY: Oxford University Press.

Hendriks, H. (2003). Using nouns for reference maintenance: A seeming contradiction in L2 discourse. In A. G. Ramat (Ed.), *Typology and second language acquisition* (pp. 291–326). Berlin, Germany: Mouton de Gruyter.

Himmelmann, N. (1996). Demonstratives in narrative discourse: A taxonomy of universal use. In B. Fox (Ed.), *Studies in anaphora* (pp. 205–254). Amsterdam, the Netherlands: John Benjamins.

Ionin, T., Baek, S., Kim, E., Ko, H., & Wexler, K. (2012). That's not so different from the: Definite and demonstrative descriptions in second language acquisition. *Second Language Research*, *28*(1), 69–101. doi:10.1177/0267658311432200

Jarvis, S. (2002). Topic continuity in L2 English article use. *Studies in Second Language Acquisition*, *24*(3), 387–418. doi:10.1017/S0272263102003029

Keenan, E. L., & Comrie, B. (1977). Noun phrase accessibility and universal grammar. *Linguistic Inquiry*, *8*(1), 63–99.

Kibrik, A. A. (2001). Reference maintenance in discourse. In M. Haspelmath, E. König, W. Oesterreicher, & W. Raible (Eds.), *Language typology and language universals: An international handbook* (Vol. 2) (pp. 1123–1137). Berlin, Germany: Walter De Gruyter.

Klein, W., & Perdue, C. (1997). The basic variety (or: Couldn't natural languages be much simpler?). *Second Language Research*, *13*(4), 301–347. doi:10.1191/026765897666879396

Lasnik, H., & Lohndal, T. (2010). Government–binding/principles and parameters theory. *Wiley Interdisciplinary Reviews: Cognitive Science*, *1*(1), 40–50. doi:10.1002/wcs.35

Lantolf, J. P., & Ahmed, M. K. (1989). Psycholinguistic perspectives on interlanguage variation: A Vygotskyan analysis. In S. Gass, C. Madden, D. Preston, & L. Selinker (Eds.), *Variation in second language acquisition: Psycholinguistic issues* (pp. 93–108). Clevedon, UK: Multilingual Matters.

Lee, K., He, L., Lewis, M., & Zettlemoyer, L. (2017). End-to-end neural coreference resolution. *arXiv Preprint*, arXiv:1707.07045.

Lozano, C., & Mendikoetxea, A. (2013). Learner corpora and second language acquisition: The design and collection of CEDEL2. In A. Díaz-Negrillo, N. Ballier, & P. Thompson (Eds.), *Automatic treatment and analysis of learner corpus data* (pp. 65–100). Amsterdam, the Netherlands: John Benjamins.

Marsden, E., Morgan-Short, K., Thompson, S., & Abugaber, D. (2018). Replication in second language research: Narrative and systematic reviews and recommendations for the field. *Language Learning*, *68*(2), 321–391. doi:10.1111/lang.12286

Nakahama, Y. (2009). Cross-linguistic influence on referent introduction and tracking in Japanese as a second language. *The Modern Language Journal*, *93*(2), 241–260. doi:10.1111/j.1540-4781.2009.00859.x

Perdue, C. (Ed.). (1984). *Second language acquisition by adult immigrants: A field manual*. Rowley, MA: Newbury House.

Perdue, C. (Ed.). (1993). *Adult language acquisition: Cross-linguistic perspectives* (Vol. 1 Field Methods). Cambridge, UK: Cambridge University Press.

Poesio, M., Stevenson, R., Eugenio, B. D., & Hitzeman, J. (2004). Centering: A parametric theory and its instantiations. *Computational Linguistics*, *30*(3), 309–363. doi:10.1162/0891201041850911

Porte, G. (2012). Introduction. In G. Porte (Ed.), *Replication research in applied linguistics* (pp. 1–17). Cambridge, UK: Cambridge University Press.

Porte, G., & McManus, K. (2019). *Doing replication research in applied linguistics*. New York, NY: Routledge.

Ryan, J. (2012). *Acts of reference and the miscommunication of referents by first and second language speakers of English* (PhD doctoral thesis). University of Waikato, Hamilton, New Zealand.

Sasaki, M. (1990). Topic prominence in Japanese EFL students' existential constructions. *Language Learning*, *40*(3), 337–368. doi:10.1111/j.1467-1770.1990.tb00667.x

Schiffrin, D. (2006). *In other words: Variation in reference and narrative*. Cambridge, UK: Cambridge University Press.

Serratrice, L., & Allen, S. E. (Eds.). (2015). *The acquisition of reference*. Amsterdam, the Netherlands: John Benjamins.

Slobin, D. I. (1996). From "thought and language" to "thinking for speaking." In J. Gumperz & S. Levinson (Eds.), *Rethinking linguistic relativity* (pp. 70–96). Cambridge, UK: Cambridge University Press.

Sorace, A. (2011). Pinning down the concept of interface in bilingualism. *Linguistic Approaches to Bilingualism*, *1*(1), 1–33. doi:10.1075/lab.1.1.01sor

Sorace, A., & Filiaci, F. (2006). Anaphora resolution in near-native speakers of Italian. *Second Language Research*, 22(3), 339–368. doi:10.1191/0267658306sr271oa

Swierzbin, B. (2004). *The role of cognitive status in second language acquisition of English noun phrase referring expressions* (PhD Doctoral dissertation). University of Minnesota, Minneapolis, MN.

Tao, L., & Healy, A. F. (2005). Zero anaphora: Transfer of reference tracking strategies from Chinese to English. *Journal of Psycholinguistic Research*, 34(2), 99–131. doi:10.1007/s10936-005-3634-5

Von Stutterheim, C. (2003). Linguistic structure and information organisation: The case of very advanced learners. *EuroSLA Yearbook*, 3(1), 183–206. doi:10.1075/eurosla.3.11stu

Watorek, M., Benazzo, S., & Hickmann, M. (2012). New comparative perspectives in the study of language acquisition – Clive Perdue's legacy. In M. Watorek, S. Benazzo, & M. Hickmann (Eds.), *Comparative perspectives on language acquisition: Tribute to Clive Perdue*. Bristol, UK: Multilingual Matters.

Yuan, B. (1995). Acquisition of base-generated topics by English-speaking learners of Chinese. *Language Learning*, 45(4), 567–603. doi:10.1111/j.1467-1770.1995.tb00455.x01023493000

2 Referent accessibility marking and referent's social status in Japanese as a second language

Jo Lumley

Introduction

Reference to people is a process in which speakers respond to both the informational context of the discourse and the social relationships involved. This duality is captured in Enfield's (2009) proposal of two motivations underpinning communicative choices: informational and affiliational. According to the former, speakers seek to make themselves understood as far as is necessary for communication to be successful; and to the latter, they seek at the same time to be 'appropriately managing the social consequences of any interaction [they] happen to be in' (Enfield, 2009, p. 72). Person reference represents a particularly clear intersection of these dual imperatives. An expression referring to a person is chosen to allow the hearer to identify that person, and the same expression serves social functions such as giving deference.

Expressed in terms of these dual imperatives, a body of research on reference in second languages examines how learners deal with the informational imperative when referring – in other words, how aspects of informational context lead learners to select more or less explicit referring expressions. My aim in this chapter is to supplement this with a consideration of how social relationships influence the same choice when referring. This means I focus on how the referent's social status relative to the speaker affects accessibility marking (Ariel, 1990) of third-person referents rather than on management of social relationships through the choice of specific forms, such as using a name with or without a title attached. I consider the case of English-speaking learners of Japanese, using longitudinal spoken data from role-plays and a narrative task from six learners at two stages of development, with comparison data from six Japanese native speakers. The learners' accessibility marking patterns are shown to be somewhat different depending on whether the third-person referent is of a similar or higher social status. In this longitudinal study, accessibility marking of higher-status persons changes over time, and is distinctly different from the 'neutral' case of reference to characters in a fictional narrative. Furthermore, despite apparent moves towards target-like norms in the narrative task where informational context is the primary concern, in role-plays (where the affiliational imperative is involved), learners clearly diverge from native-like norms for reference.

I use the framework of Accessibility Theory (Ariel, 1990, 2001) to conceptualise learners' responses to the informational imperative when choosing referring expressions. Under this theory, the speaker's choice of referring expression signals how accessible they presume the referent to be for the hearer. Ariel (1990) does propose additional social motivations for the raising or lowering of accessibility marking. However, for the present analysis (which is concerned with referent status), politeness theory provides a useful perspective on the notion of using lower accessibility markers (more unambiguous referring expressions) as a means of expressing deference to the referent. Understanding deference as 'the conveying of relative status' (Fraser & Nolen, 1981, p. 98), it is clear that referring expressions can perform this function. Brown and Levinson (1987, pp. 178–187) demonstrate that shifts in accessibility marking, such as the use of a description rather than a null form, can be used to convey deference (p. 185). Brown and Levinson focus on strategically motivated shifts towards more deferential forms, but this is usefully modified by Fukuda and Asato's (2004) stipulation that in Japanese, high values of power and distance are sufficient to trigger deference regardless of the content of a particular utterance. Thus, it is possible in principle to propose that whenever speakers refer to someone of higher status than themselves, increased explicitness could be used to show deference to the referent. Most fundamentally, this may be the choice between an overt referring expression as opposed to a null form, such as in (1) where two utterances with otherwise very similar meaning uttered by the same speaker are distinguished by explicit deference in (a) through use of the description *sensei*, and the absence of such deference in (b).

(1) increased explicitness to index deference

    a. *sensei ga kibishikute*
        '**The teacher** is strict [and].'
    b. Ø *kibishii n desu yo*
        '[**He**] is strict.' (native speaker JA5, extracts from role-play R11)[1]

Methods

The data analysed in this chapter comes from a two-stage longitudinal study of six English-speaking learners of Japanese featuring both role-play and narrative tasks, with comparison data from six native speakers of Japanese. At the beginning of the study period, the learners were at what could be considered a pre-intermediate L2 level. At that point, all had completed two years' classroom study of Japanese in the same British university. The same learners completed the tasks again after a further period of between nine and eleven months of study abroad in Japan. This period captures development in learners' vocabulary, grammatical competence and communicative ability in Japanese, as achieved through extended contact with the target language and culture through study abroad. Further information on the participants is given in Appendix A, Table 2.A1.

18 Jo Lumley

Table 2.1 Summary of role-play tasks

Task	Hearer	Specified third person and status relative to the speaker	Topic
RI1	Student advisor	Speaker's teacher: higher status	Complaint about problems caused by speaker's Japanese teacher
RI2	Teacher	Speaker's classmate, same age: same status	Complaint about problems caused by a fellow student
RI3	Classmate (same age)	Speaker and hearer's teacher: higher status	Planning a teacher's retirement party

The main analysis in this chapter is of performance on three role-play tasks. The tasks were designed to elicit reference to specified third persons in the course of a conversation between the participant and a native Japanese-speaking facilitator. The task descriptions defined a communicative goal and specified the nature of the relationship with the third person as well as that person's name, age and gender. This made it possible for participants to imagine a social context for the conversation and gave them access to a full range of referring expressions from names to null forms. The role-plays are summarised in Table 2.1, with full task descriptions in Appendix B.

The role-plays are also analysed in comparison with participants' performance in a narrative retelling task. In this task they recounted, using the third person, the actions of several characters from a short section of a silent film to a Japanese-speaking facilitator. To maintain comparability with the role-plays, in the narrative task only reference to any of the three named characters is analysed (see Appendix B for the full task description). Since the narrative task only includes referents who are explicitly fictional, it shows how participants use a similar set of referential devices to that available in the role-plays, but in a case where the affiliational imperative is minimised. This contrasts with the role-plays, where both affiliational and informational imperatives are consistently in play.

In both types of task, only third-person reference is used for this analysis, in quantities summarised in Table 2.2.

Analyses in this chapter depend on the features of referring expressions summarised in (2):

(2) features of referring expressions analysed

    a. the referent's status relative to the speaker: same or higher
    b. two aspects of the referent's accessibility: competition for the role of antecedent and distance from antecedent (see Table 2.3)
    c. the type of expression used on a simplified accessibility marking scale: null form > pronoun > description (single- or multi-word) > name

Table 2.2 The number of referring expressions produced (specified third-person referents only)

Group	Task type	
	Role-play	Narrative
Pre-study abroad learners	107	117
Post-study abroad learners	127	94
Japanese native speakers	237	120

Table 2.3 Coding for discourse pragmatic variables of distance and competition (each from highest to lowest referent accessibility)

Distance from antecedent (non-initial reference only)	The antecedent is found in a. the same utterance (S) b. the previous utterance (P) c. earlier than the previous utterance (E) d. earlier than the previous utterance with intervening reference to another person (I)
Competition for the role of antecedent	a. low competition: only one suitable antecedent in the preceding three utterances b. high competition: no suitable antecedents, or more than one suitable antecedent in the preceding three utterances

Reference in the narrative task is considered in terms of (2)b and c only. In (2)b, two of Accessibility Theory's four accessibility determining factors (Ariel, 1990, pp. 28–29) are considered. The accessibility marking scale in (2)c simplifies more complex proposals of Accessibility Theory (Ariel, 2001, p. 31) based on Ariel's criteria of rigidity alone: 'how close [an expression] is to pointing to one entity unequivocally in a potentially ambiguous context' (Ariel, 1990, p. 81). For reference to person, this is particularly important as it underpins the claim that names mark lower accessibility than descriptions because they usually point more unambiguously to a particular referent.

Results

Interaction between referent social status and discourse pragmatic variables

To consider how far the referent's social status affects the selection of referential form, it is first necessary to examine whether referent status interacts with discourse pragmatic variables affecting referent accessibility in the data. This makes it possible to establish the likelihood of any apparent responses to referent status being due to the underlying influence of discourse pragmatic variables that raise or lower the accessibility of one type of referent more than the other.

Tests of association were performed between referent status and each of the following two discourse pragmatic variables: distance from antecedent, and competition for the role of antecedent. These variables are defined in Table 2.3 (previous section) and the results of the statistical tests in Table 2.4.

For each participant group, only one of two discourse pragmatic variables has some significant interaction with status. The strongest interaction is that for distance and referent status for pre-study abroad learners (Cramér's V = 0.429, $p < 0.001$). Here, same-status referents tend to have somewhat raised accessibility because they are more often found closer to their antecedents, in particular in the most accessible category of antecedent in the same utterance. At the post-study abroad stage, the only significant interaction is a much more modest one between competition and referent status (Cramér's V = 0.191, $p < 0.05$). Specifically, same-status referents tend (to some extent) to have lower accessibility, and higher-status referents have higher accessibility on this measure. Finally, for native speakers, there is a moderate association between distance and referent status (Cramér's V = 0.212, $p < 0.05$). However, the distribution patterns for native speakers reveal that same- and higher-status referents are distributed quite evenly between higher and lower accessibility categories on this measure.[2]

For learners before study abroad, the increased accessibility of same-status referents due to a tendency to be closer to their antecedents is likely to have some effect on the choice of form types for same- compared to higher-status referents. However, further testing shows that for this group, distance from antecedent does not, on its own, significantly affect the choice of referring expression for third-person referents in role-play tasks (χ^2 (2, $N=90$) = 9.666, $p > 0.05$). Any effect of distance from antecedent is therefore likely to be rather modest despite the large effect size. At the post-study abroad stage, although the significant interaction of

Table 2.4 Interactions between discourse pragmatic variables and referent social status

Group	Variables	Chi-square	df	Cramér's V
Pre-study abroad learners	Referent status, distance	16.598***	3	0.429***
	Referent status, competition	1.430	1	–
Post-study abroad learners	Referent status, distance	1.300	3	–
	Referent status, competition	4.656*	1	0.191*
Native speakers	Referent status, distance	9.890*	3	0.212*
	Referent status, competition	3.141	1	–

* $p < 0.05$, *** $p < 0.001$

competition with referent status appears weaker, competition itself significantly relates to the learners' choice of referring expression (χ^2 (3, $N=127$) = 29.859, $p<0.001$; Cramér's V = 0.433). This means that a tendency for higher-status referents to be more accessible for this group is relevant to the discussion of the relationship between referent status and accessibility marking.

Reference to higher-status persons as deference

Analysis of all overt referring expressions used for higher-status persons confirms that, with very few exceptions, they were deferential. In the role-play tasks used, both specified higher-status third persons are teachers in a university context. The deferential terms used were all descriptions or names, while pronouns were used sparingly and non-deferentially. However, all deferential reference using names and descriptions involved the description *sensei* 'teacher' or the title *-sensei* following a family name, as summarised in (3)a–c.

(3) representative examples of deferential expressions used for higher-status persons[3]

    a. name: family name followed by title *-sensei*
       Haradasensei *wa (.) osake o nomu ga kirai desu kara*
       'Because **Harada-sensei** hates drinking alcohol.' (learner L04, pre-study abroad)
    b. description (complex): multi-word description headed by *sensei* '[the] teacher'
       um **watashi no sensei** *wa kibishisugiru to omoimasu*
       'Um, [I] think **my teacher** is too strict.' (learner L03, post-study abroad)
    c. description (simple): *sensei*
       sensei itsumo nanji ni shigoto o owaru no kana
       '[I] wonder what time **the teacher** usually finishes work.' (native speaker, JA3)

The main source of terms referring to higher-status persons that are not clearly deferential is a single learner who, before study abroad only, used the title *-san* with names several times as illustrated in Example (4)a, which is not normally appropriate for referring to one's own teacher. The other occasional uses of pronouns and non-deferential descriptions by other speakers, such as in examples (4) b and c, are not necessarily inappropriate in context.

(4) representative examples of non-deferential expressions used for higher-status persons

    a. name: family name followed by title *-san*
       watashi wa **Sakaisan** *to hanashimashita*
       'I spoke to **Sakai-san**.' (learner L06, pre-study abroad)

b. description
   mukoo wa chotto iraira
   'The other person [gets] a bit angry.' (learner L01, post-study abroad)
c. pronoun
   kare donna mono suki deshoo
   '[I wonder] what sort of things he likes.' (learner L02, post-study abroad)

It is therefore possible to consider that speakers in this study were expressing deference to higher-status persons when they used overt referring expression rather than null forms, given that examples of type (3) represent the great majority of such reference. It is also clear that *-sensei* as a title and *sensei* as a description are very dominant within this.

The effect of referent social status on the group level

Key results on the group level are given in Table 2.5. Tests of independence for form type and referent status for each group are summarised in Table 2.6, alongside the effect size for all significant interactions, with the key details discussed in the following subsections.

Learners at the pre-study abroad stage as a group

At the pre-study abroad stage, a chi-squared test shows a significant interaction of moderate strength (Cramér's $V = 0.335$, $p < 0.01$) between referent status and the type of referring expression used. The most noticeable effect of third-person referent status for learners before study abroad is on descriptions, which are found much more often for higher- than same-status referents. For instance, Example (5)a shows an extract from the role-play of a pre-study abroad learner who used descriptions and null forms to refer to a higher-status person. With the more frequent use of descriptions for higher-status third persons, there are correspondingly fewer uses of names, null forms and pronouns.

(5) Examples of reference from pre-study abroad learners

a. Higher-status referent (learner L04, extract from role-play R11)

L04:	***watashi no sensei** wa hontoo ni majime da shi*
	'**My teacher** is really serious.'
L04:	*Ø amari shinsetsu janai shi [laughter]*
	'And [**he**]'s not very kind.'
JP1:	*hai*
	'Yes.'
L04:	*Ø machigai ga kirai desu*
	'[**He**] hates mistakes.'
JP1:	*hai*
	'Yes.'

Table 2.5 Referring expressions used by referent social status, use of deferential expressions for higher-status referents and referring expressions used on a narrative task (group level)

Group	Form type	Same-status referent %	Same-status referent no.	Higher-status referent %	Higher-status referent no.	(no. of deferential)	Narrative comparison %	Narrative comparison no.
Pre-study abroad	Null form	40.4	17	33.3	20	–	30.8	36
	Pronoun	8.5	7	0.0	0	–	4.3	5
	Description	14.9	4	40.0	24	(24)	6.8	8
	Name	36.2	19	26.7	16	(13)	58.1	68
Post-study abroad	Null form	35.9	14	48.9	43	–	30.9	29
	Pronoun	12.8	5	1.1	1	(0)	5.3	5
	Description	28.2	11	31.8	28	(27)	16.0	15
	Name	23.1	9	18.2	16	(16)	47.9	45
Native speakers	Null form	61.0	64	40.2	53	–	49.2	59
	Pronoun	8.6	9	0.8	1	(0)	8.3	10
	Description	5.7	6	50.8	67	(67)	15.0	18
	Name	24.8	26	8.3	11	(11)	27.5	33

24 Jo Lumley

Table 2.6 Interactions between referent social status and form choice (group level)

Group	Chi-square	df	Cramér's V
Pre-study abroad	11.976**	3	0.335**
Post-study abroad	9.265*	3	0.270*
Native speakers	62.219***	3	0.512***

* $p<0.05$, ** $p<0.01$, *** $p<0.001$

L04: soshite [///] (.) desukara watashi wa **sensei** ni chotto kowai desu
'And, so I am a bit afraid of **the teacher**.'
JP1: aa soo desu ka hai
'Ah, yes, is that so.'
L04: soshite **sensei** wa (.) haya [///] hanasu no ga totemo hayai desu kara
'And because **the teacher** speaks very quickly'
JP1: hai
'Yes.'
L04: yoku wakarimasen
'[I] don't understand well.'
JP1: mm
'mm'
L04: um dooshitara ii desu ka
'Um, what should [I] do?'
JP1: soo desu ne
'Well'
JP1: ano eeto (.) sensei to hanshimashita ka
'Um have [you] spoken to the teacher.'
L04: mm
'mm'
JP1: soodan shimashita
'Had a conversation [with him].'
L04: mada Ø hanashimasendeshita
'[I] haven't spoken [to **him**] yet.'

b. Same-status referent (learner L05, extract from role-play R12)

L05: **Ishidasan** wa (.) nanimo shinakatta desu [///] shinakatta
'**Ishida-san** hasn't done anything.'
JP1: Ishidasan to issho no
'[You're in] the same [group] as Ishida-san.'
L05: hai Ø to issho guruupu desu
'Yes, in the same group with [**him**].'

JP1:	*hai*
	'Yes.'
JP1:	*aa soo desu ka*
	'Ah, is that so.'
JP1:	*hai*
	'Yes.'
L05:	*hai*
	'Yes.'
L05:	*soshite (.) watashi wa*
	'And I'
L05:	Ø *isogashisugiru to* Ø *iimashita*
	'[**He**] said [**he**] is too busy'
JP1:	[inaudible]
L05:	*hai*
	'Yes.'
L05:	*dakara eeto purojekuto ga*
	'So, um, the project'
JP1:	*hai*
	'Yes.'
L05:	*aa iie (.)* Ø *soodan shimasen desu [///] soodan shimasen*
	'Ah, no [**he**] doesn't discuss [with me].'

Same-status third persons, on the other hand, were more often referred to using names or null forms, which account for around 76% of references between them. This is illustrated by Example (5)b, from a learner who used only names and null forms in this case; the extract begins with his initial reference to this person.

Learners at the post-study abroad stage as a group

In the post-study abroad group, in third-person reference there is a significant interaction between explicitness and the referent's social status, although weaker than that found before study abroad ($V = 0.270$, $p < 0.05$). The nature of the interaction is that greater status-linked differences are found in the use of higher accessibility markers, with higher-status referents attracting a much lower proportion of pronouns and somewhat greater proportion of null forms than same-status ones. Part of the gap in the proportion of null forms may be explained by a tendency in this group's data for higher-status referents to be more accessible, as established above. Differences in the proportion of descriptions used are much smaller than at the earlier stage. For instance, (6)a shows a learner first using a complex description with *sensei*, and later using a mix of null forms and *sensei* as a simple description for a higher-status referent, while (6)b shows a learner first using descriptions involving *paatonaa* 'partner' and later in the same role-play using names for the same referent.

(6) Examples of reference from post-study abroad learners

    a.   Higher-status referent (learner L03, two extracts from role-play R13)

        L03:   *demo watashi no [///]* **watashitachi no sensei** *wa ima um kono [///] kotoshi no ato de um ritaiya o shimasu*
'But my, **our teacher** will retire now, this, after this year.'

        L03:   *nanka mm demo sayoonara o iu ni kompa o suru yotei to xxx*
'Mm, but there is a plan to have a party to say goodbye.'

        JP3:   *aa mm mm mm*
'Ah, mm.'

        L03:   *demo um donna kompa wa ii to omou?*
'But, um, what kind of party do [you] think would be good?'

        […]

        L03:   *mm demo* **sensei** *wa um osake o nomitakunai xxx*
'Mm but **the teacher** doesn't want to drink alcohol.'

        JP3:   *aa osake nomitakunai n da*
'Oh, [he] doesn't want to drink alcohol.'

        L03:   *mm*
'mm'

        JP3:   *moriagaranai ne*
'It won't be much fun, will it.'

        L03:   *mm*
'mm'

        L03:   *demo Ø tabemono ga suki to omou*
'But [I] think [**he**] likes food.'

    b.   Same-status referent (learner L06, two extracts from role-play R12)

        L06:   *anoo* **issho ni no purojekutowaaku no paatonaa** *wa anoo hatarakimasendeshita*
'Um, **the project work partner with [me]** um didn't work.'

        JP3:   *hai*
'Yes.'

        L06:   *eeto chotto mondai to omoimasu*
'Um, [I] think it's a bit of a problem.'

        L06:   *anoo um (.) jumbi o shinakerebanaranai kedo*
'Um [I] have to prepare but'

        JP3:   *hai*
'Yes.'

        L06:   *anoo* **watashi no paatonaa** *ga konakere [///] uh konai*
'Um, **my partner** doesn't come.'

        JP3:   *hai*
'Yes.'

L06:	*anoo maitoki **watashi no paatonaa** wa isogashii n desu*
	'Um, every time **my partner** is busy.'
JP3:	*hai*
	'Yes.'

[...]

L06:	*maitoki anoo **Ishidasan** to hanashi [///] hanasu toki wa*
	'Every time [I] talk to **Ishida-san**'
JP3:	*hai*
	'Yes.'
L06:	*anoo ashita wa daijoobu desu ka*
	'Um, is tomorrow okay?'
JP3:	*hai*
	'Yes.'
L06:	*demo **Ishidasan** wa iron na iie iie isogashii n desu demo*
	'But **Ishida-san** is no, no, busy and things.'

Development between stages and comparison to native speakers

Before study abroad, learners used descriptions somewhat more than other expressions when referring to higher-status referents, while a combination of null forms and names accounted for most reference to same-status referents. Over time, for higher-status referents the proportion of null forms increased and that of descriptions decreased. For same-status referents the proportion of descriptions increased and that of names decreased. The combined effect is a less clear distinction between the two types of referents, as confirmed by the smaller effect size at the later stage.

The native speaker data shows distinctly different patterns of referent marking for same- and higher-status third persons, with a stronger interaction than those observed for learners (V = 0.512, $p < 0.001$). In the light of the native speakers' behaviour, learners do not appear to become more target-like over time. Native speakers of Japanese used descriptions much more than any other type of overt form when referring to higher-status persons (and used a null form or a description over 90% of the time). On the other hand, learners not only produced descriptions less often than before study abroad, but also came to use null forms more than native speakers in this context. For same-status referents, learners used an increased proportion of descriptions after study abroad, in contrast to native speakers who relied more heavily on names for this type of referent than on any other type of overt form.

The effect of referent social status on the individual level

The data discussed so far can be usefully supplemented by a consideration of learners' individual performances and individual paths of development at from the pre- to post-study abroad stage. However, once individual data is split by referent social status – given in full in Appendix C, Table 2.A2 – the number of tokens produced by each learner alone is low, which considerably weakens what can be concluded on the basis of individual performances.

Individual learners at the pre-study abroad stage

Before study abroad, five of the six learners showed status-based distinctions in their distribution of referring expressions, while one (L04) did not. For same-status referents, there was little consensus in preferences but the most common was for names and null forms by three of six learners (L01, L05, L06). Within the sets of terms they used, three learners preferred the lower accessibility marker of their set (L02, L03, L06), of which two did so strongly, while two had the opposite preference (L01, and L05 strongly so). There were two principal patterns for higher-status referents. For two learners (L01, L03), descriptions and null forms were the only form types used. For a further three learners, within overt forms both descriptions and names were used in roughly similar proportions (L02, L05, L06). Learners with both patterns used the lower-accessibility marker(s) of their sets much more than they used null forms.

Individual learners at the post-study abroad stage

After study abroad, all learners showed some response to referent social status, even L04 who had not done so at the earlier stage. Descriptions were the preferred overt referring expression for three learners (L03, L04, L06); the same learners used null forms relatively sparingly. The other three learners used null forms more than half of the time for same-status referents (L01, L02 and L05 at nearly 80%). As for overt forms, two of them (L01, L05) used names exclusively while the third (L02) preferred pronouns.

For higher-status referents too, learners' behaviour at the later stage was not uniform. No pattern of preferences for overt forms was shared by more than two of the six. Within individual systems, there was a mix of tendencies for reliance on the higher or the lower accessibility marker(s). On the group level, reference to higher-status persons was characterised by a lack of overall preference for descriptions and a comparatively high proportion of null forms. Investigation on the individual level shows that the former was driven by much individual variation in which overt forms were preferred, with only two learners preferring descriptions. As for the latter, the individual picture was much more varied. Although three learners used the lower accessibility marker(s) in their systems more often, this was counterbalanced by one learner (L05) who strongly preferred null forms and two more who used null and overt forms in similar proportions (L01, L06).

Individual development between the stages

In individual terms, there tended to be greater change in learners' choices when referring to higher-status persons than to same-status ones. In five of six learners, there was little-to-no change over time in the proportions of form types used for same-status referents. One (L06), however, changed quite considerably in this respect from a system dominated by names to a more varied one involving names, descriptions and null forms. When referring to higher-status persons, half of the learners showed clear differences at the later stage (L01, L02, L06). Despite the centrality for native speakers of descriptions for overt reference to higher-status persons, only two learners (L03 and L06) used descriptions at native-like proportions; both did so from the earlier stage onwards. All other learners, however, used a lower proportion of descriptions after study abroad than before. In three of four cases (L01, L02, L04), this decrease in descriptions was accompanied by an increase in null forms; the final learner, L05, used an increased proportion of names over time.

Comparison of reference to higher- and same-status persons with reference in narratives

A useful point of comparison to the role-play tasks analysed so far is participants' reference to the main characters in a narrative retelling task. This shows how they behave when reference does not have the same social dimension as it does in the role-play tasks (see Table 2.5).

Pre-study abroad learners' usage patterns in the narrative task were broadly similar to those found for same-status referents in the role-plays, in that they used names and null forms more often than the options in between. However, in narratives they used names considerably more often and null forms somewhat less than for same-status referents in role-plays.

Reference to higher-status persons in role-plays was quite different from reference in narratives, chiefly in that descriptions were used much more frequently in the former than the latter. After study abroad, learners' performance in narratives differed from their earlier one mainly in the decreased proportion of names used, in favour of greater use of items in the middle of the scale, mainly descriptions. They relied noticeably less on names in role-plays for both higher- and same-status referents and used null forms more often in role-plays too. Viewed alongside the native speakers' distribution, learners can be understood as approaching a more target-like distribution of form types in narratives by supplying names less often and some higher accessibility markers more often, even though their proportion of null forms increased only slightly.

For all three groups, the distribution of form types when referring to characters in a narrative was much closer to that used for same-status persons in a role-play and quite different from that found for reference to higher-status persons in a role-play. In role-plays, post-study abroad learners behaved in a way that diverges from their own performance before study abroad as well as from native speakers. In contrast, in narratives there were considerable commonalities between all three groups, with learners moving over time to a distribution that looks more similar to native speakers'. The addition of social factors in the role-plays alongside the discourse pragmatic ones common to both task types is therefore likely to be the cause of the characteristics of post-study abroad learners' patterns of reference in role-play tasks.

Concluding discussion

In this chapter, I have presented longitudinal data from before and after an extended stay in a target language environment, showing how the referential systems of learners of Japanese as a second language responded to referent status when referring to people. This complements the wider body of reference studies examining learners' response to discourse pragmatic variables, so I primarily considered the level of referential specification of the expressions used rather than their specific form. In this sense, it is distinct from related studies such as Marriott's (1993, 1995) which considers the selection of referring expressions by learners of Japanese in terms of their appropriateness.

Data from native speakers establishes that distinct patterns in accessibility marking for higher- versus same-status referents can be observed in Japanese, and that this is not attributable to underlying effects of informational context. In the tasks used here, this manifested as a preference for overt deference using descriptions for higher-status referents, while same-status ones attracted greater proportions of null forms and names. Reference to higher-status persons could be considered the 'marked' case of the two because, for both learners and native speakers, the distribution of referring expressions for higher-status persons was more distinctly different from the comparator of reference to characters in a narrative. Examination of overt forms produced when referring to higher-status persons confirms that learners and native speakers alike used overt referring expressions to index deference to the referent. However, in other respects learners' behaviour was different from that of native speakers. A target-like but weaker effect of referent status at the pre-study abroad stage was followed by an even weaker effect after study abroad which is less similar to native speakers' behaviour, particularly in terms of the increased proportion of null forms for higher-status referents. Some of this increase may be due to the contributing effect of a discourse pragmatic variable (competition for the role of antecedent) somewhat raising the accessibility of higher-status referents. On the individual level, in terms of accessibility marking, learners tended not to change when referring to same-status persons while more often changed for higher-status ones, though the nature of this change varied. Despite learners' move away from a target-like distribution in their response to referent status, their performance on a narrative task referring to fictional characters became more target-like over time. This difference in performance in a socially 'neutral' narrative versus a set of socially contextualised role-plays is likely the result of the additional complexity of managing the affiliational alongside the informational imperative when selecting referring expressions in the latter.

Learners' lack of increase in null forms in the narrative data, despite other moves towards target-like reference, is in some respects a departure from what is most commonly reported in studies of English-speaking learners of Japanese and other second languages like Chinese and Korean which make extensive use of null forms. Lee (2018) reports a similar lack of change for null forms in L2 Korean, but with learners supplying a target-like proportion even at lower proficiency. It is more commonly reported that English-speaking learners use null forms less readily than native speakers, such as by Chang and Zheng (2018) for L2 Chinese. Developmentally, however, previous research often finds English-speaking learners using more null forms with increasing proficiency, although often not reaching native-like proportions (Jin, 1994; Polio, 1995; and Li, 2014 for L2 Chinese; Jung, 2004 for L2 Korean; Yanagimachi, 2000; and Nakahama, 2009a, 2009b for L2 Japanese). This is in keeping with Lozano's (2016, 2018) Pragmatic Principles Violation Hypothesis (PPVH) that learners will more readily be overexplicit than underexplicit, because although both are pragmatic violations, underexplicitness presents a more serious risk to successful communication. Viewed in the light of the PPVH, the previous results of comparable studies, and their own performance in a narrative task, it is therefore especially striking that in role-plays, post-study abroad learners in the present study used null forms for higher-status persons more even than native speakers. This is echoed by findings by Nakahama (2003) and Takeuchi (2014) on L2 Japanese, and Kim (2012) on L2 Korean, who also report learners at higher proficiency levels producing null forms in proportions that exceed those of native speakers. These studies, however, involve fictional characters in narratives, and as such do not directly shed light on the influence of referent status in the present data.

Perhaps study abroad in Japan results in increased awareness of the range of options available for person reference and of their socially consequential nature, particularly when higher-status persons are involved. This would represent a move away from a more automatised use of overt expressions before study abroad, leading to increased involvement of relevant pragmatic representations and new challenges for attentional control (Bialystok, 1993, 1994) after study abroad, and thus for some learners motivating increased avoidance of overt referring expressions for higher-status persons. This kind of behaviour is observed in DuFon's (2000) study,[4] which shows that despite increasing awareness about address terms, learners of Indonesian still exhibit a mixture of overgeneralisation and avoidance at times. The two stages examined here may then be the beginning and middle of a path of development which later reaches something more target-like, although the present data alone cannot substantiate this speculation. In the data examined here, learners' and native speakers' overt reference to higher-status persons almost exclusively uses descriptions with *sensei* '[the] teacher' or names followed by the title-*sensei*. Additional investigation would be needed to establish whether something so apparently straightforward could be the target of avoidance. Research literature on second language acquisition of address pronouns in European languages, where the choice is typically binary, suggests that at earlier stages of development, unambiguous identification of the intended referent overrides interpersonal considerations (Dewaele, 2002, 2004). At later stages of acquisition, learners' address systems remain unstable even after some direct exposure to authentic target language input through study abroad (Barron, 2006) or correspondence (Belz & Kinginger, 2002, 2003). Such findings are about appropriateness rather than explicitness but provide support for the notion that contact with the target language does not guarantee that pragmatic development in the use of referring expressions will reach a target-like state even when the choice involves a limited set of possibilities.

Some features of this study limit the strength of its conclusions. Although the longitudinal design strengthens inferences about development over time, the number of tokens produced by each individual learner means that strong conclusions about individual paths of development are not supported. Given the centrality of the term *sensei* for reference to higher-status persons in this data, the wider generalisability of the findings can only be established with the addition of data from scenarios involving higher-status referents who cannot be referred to using this term – that is, who are not teachers, instructors, medical doctors or the like. Finally, the role-plays used here seek to simulate the context of social relationships but can only approximate the complexity of the effects of actual social relationships in discourse.

Appendix A: Participant information, tasks and data coding

Table 2.A1 Participant information for learners of Japanese (L) and Japanese native speakers (JA)

Participant	Age during study	Gender	Japanese study pre-study abroad	Study abroad period in Japan
L01	20–21	Female	2 years	10 months
L02	21–22	Male	2 years	10 months
L03	20–21	Male	2 years	10 months
L04	20–22	Female	2 years	10 months
L05	20–21	Male	2 years	9 months
L06	28–29	Female	2 years	11 months
JA1	27	Female	–	–
JA2	32	Female	–	–
JA3	23	Female	–	–
JA4	25	Female	–	–
JA5	23	Female	–	–
JA6	29	Female	–	–

Appendix B: Tasks Participant instructions for role-play task R11

You are studying in a Japanese university, and today you have come to the International Students' Advice Centre to speak to the international student advisor about a problem in your Japanese class.

- You find that the teacher is strict and unforgiving of mistakes
- The teacher often speaks too fast for you to understand

Please explain the problem to the international student coordinator and ask whether she can help you. You should speak first to initiate the conversation.
People involved in this situation:

- The international student advisor: KATŌ Miyuki, female, 29 years old
- Your teacher: SAKAI Masahiko, male, 40 years old

Participant instructions for role-play task R12

You are a foreign student in Japan, taking a history class with both Japanese and foreign students. You are supposed to do a joint project with a Japanese student in your history class, but you are having a problem. You have come to speak to your history teacher in her office about it.

- Your Japanese partner has not contributed any work to the project so far
- Your Japanese partner says they are too busy to meet you outside of class to discuss the project

Please explain the problem to your teacher. You should speak first to initiate the conversation.
People involved in this situation:

- Your teacher: NAKAMURA Saeko, female, 50 years old
- Your Japanese partner: ISHIDA Kōsuke, male, the same age as you [for male participants]/ISHIDA Emi, female, the same age as you [for female participants]

Participant instructions for role-play task R13

You are studying in a Japanese university, where you are taking a sociology class. Your sociology lecturer is going to retire at the end of the year. You and your classmate are planning a celebration to say goodbye to your lecturer. Discuss what kind of event you think he might like, and share the information and opinions you each have of him. You know or think the following.

- He likes to socialise with a small group of people
- He does not drink much alcohol

You should speak first to initiate the conversation.
    People involved in this situation

- Your classmate: Suzuki Asako (female, the same age as you)
- Your lecturer: Harada Satoru (male, 61 years old)

Participant instructions for narrative retelling task N13

Konomura Hiroshi has recently begun to work as a butler at the house of a rich family, the Saitō family. The daughter of the house, Shimako, and her younger brother Jun often fight with each other. Please watch a short clip and tell [name of Japanese facilitator] what happened.

Appendix C

Table 2.A2 Referent social status and form choice for individual learners at both stages

Learner	Form type	Pre-study abroad stage					Post-study abroad stage				
		Same-status referent		Higher-status referent			Same-status referent		Higher-status referent	
		%	no.	%	no.		%	no.	%	no.
L01	Null form	42.9	6	33.3	3		50.0	2	52.9	9
	Pronoun	0.0	0	0.0	0		0.0	0	0.0	0
	Description	7.1	1	66.7	6		0.0	0	29.4	5
	Name	50.0	7	0.0	0		50.0	2	17.6	3
L02	Null form	50.0	5	50.0	4		50.0	4	81.0	17
	Pronoun	40.0	4	0.0	0		37.5	3	4.8	1
	Description	0.0	0	25.0	2		0.0	0	9.5	2
	Name	10.0	1	25.0	2		12.5	1	4.8	1
L03	Null form	0.0	0	28.6	2		14.3	1	16.7	2
	Pronoun	0.0	0	0.0	0		14.3	1	0.0	0
	Description	80.0	4	71.4	5		57.1	4	83.3	10
	Name	20.0	1	0.0	0		14.3	1	0.0	0
L04	Null form	33.3	2	23.1	3		28.6	2	27.3	3
	Pronoun	0.0	0	0.0	0		14.3	1	0.0	0
	Description	33.3	2	38.5	5		42.9	3	36.4	4
	Name	33.3	2	38.5	5		14.3	1	36.4	4
L05	Null form	83.3	5	50.0	5		75.0	3	42.9	6
	Pronoun	0.0	0	0.0	0		0.0	0	0.0	0
	Description	0.0	0	10.0	1		0.0	0	0.0	0
	Name	16.7	1	40.0	4		25.0	1	57.1	8
L06	Null form	16.7	1	23.1	3		22.2	2	46.2	6
	Pronoun	0.0	0	0.0	0		0.0	0	0.0	0
	Description	0.0	0	38.5	5		44.4	4	53.8	7
	Name	83.3	5	38.5	5		33.3	3	0.0	0

Notes

1 In these and following examples, reference to the specified person by the main speaker is in bold in the transcription and translation. Null forms are only indicated in the transcription when they refer to the specified person.
2 In analysis of a fuller set of data for these Japanese native speakers, I have argued (Lumley, 2013, pp. 120–121) that they make a clear distinction between the three higher accessibility categories (S, P and E distance) versus the lowest one (I distance). In the role-play data analysed here, for native speakers, same-status referents are split 77%–23% between the higher and lower categories and higher-status referents are split 73%–27%.
3 These examples are also representative of reference to higher-status persons in this data in that no referent honorifics are used. Such honorifics occur very rarely in the data for all groups.
4 This is based on brief summaries of DuFon's (2000) findings in DuFon (2010, p. 315, p. 321) and Kasper and Rose (2002, pp. 25–30).

References

Ariel, M. (1990). *Accessing noun-phrase antecedents*. London, UK: Routledge.

Ariel, M. (2001). Accessibility theory: An overview. In T. J. Schilperoord & W. Spooren (Eds.), *Text representation: Linguistic and psycholinguistic aspects* (pp. 29–87). Amsterdam, the Netherlands: John Benjamins. doi:10.1075/hcp.8.04ari

Barron, A. (2006). Learning to say 'you' in German: The acquisition of sociolinguistic competence in a study abroad context. In M. A. DuFon & E. Churchill (Eds.), *Language learners in study abroad contexts* (pp. 59–88). Clevedon, UK: Multilingual Matters. doi:10.21832/9781853598531-007

Belz, J. A., & Kinginger, C. (2002). The cross-linguistic development of address form use in telecollaborative language study: Two case studies. *Canadian Modern Language Review, 59*(2), 189–214. doi:10.3138/cmlr.59.2.189

Belz, J. A., & Kinginger, C. (2003). Discourse options and the development of pragmatic competence by classroom learners of German: The case of address forms. *Language Learning, 53*(4), 591–647. doi:10.1046/j.1467-9922.2003.00238.x

Bialystok, E. (1993). Symbolic representation and attentional control in pragmatic competence. In G. Kasper & S. Blum-Kulka (Eds.), *Interlanguage pragmatics* (pp. 43–59). Oxford, UK: Oxford University Press.

Bialystok, E. (1994). Analysis and control in the development of second language proficiency. *Studies in Second Language Acquisition, 16*(2), 157–168. doi:10.1017/S0272263100012857

Brown, P., & Levinson, S. C. (1987). *Politeness: Some universals in language usage*. Cambridge, UK: Cambridge University Press. doi:10.1017/CBO9780511813085

Chang, H., & Zheng, L. (2018). Asymmetries of null subjects and null objects in L1-English and L1-Japanese learners. *Chinese Linguistics, 56*(5), 1141–1166. doi:10.1515/ling-2018-0021

Dewaele, J.-M. (2002). Variation, chaos et système en interlangue française. *Acquisition et interaction en langue étrangère, 17*, 143–167.

Dewaele, J.-M. (2004). *Vous* or *tu*? Native and non-native speakers of French on a sociolinguistic tightrope. *International Review of Applied Linguistics in Language Teaching, 42*(4), 383–402. doi:10.1515/iral.2004.42.4.383

DuFon, M. A. (2000). *The acquisition of linguistic politeness in Indonesian by sojourners in naturalistic interactions* (Doctoral thesis). University of Hawai'i-Manoa, Honolulu, HI.

DuFon, M. A. (2010). The acquisition of terms of address in a second language. In A. Trosborg (Ed.), *Pragmatics across languages and cultures* (pp. 309–331). Berlin, Germany: Mouton de Gruyter.

Enfield, N. J. (2009). Relationship thinking and human pragmatics. *Journal of Pragmatics, 41*, 60–78. doi:10.1016/j.pragma.2008.09.007

Fraser, B., & Nolen, W. (1981). The association of deference with linguistic form. *International Journal of the Sociology of Language, 27*, 93–109. doi:10.1515/ijsl.1981.27.93

Fukuda, A., & Asato, N. (2004). Universal politeness theory: Application to the use of Japanese honorifics. *Journal of Pragmatics, 36*, 1991–2002. doi:10.1016/j.pragma.2003.11.006

Jin, H. G. (1994). Topic-prominence and subject-prominence in L2 acquisition: Evidence of English-to-Chinese typological transfer. *Language Learning, 44*(1), 101–122. doi:10.1111/j.1467-1770.1994.tb01450.x

Jung, E. H. (2004). Topic and subject prominence in interlanguage development. *Language Learning, 54*(4), 713–738. doi:10.1111/j.1467-9922.2004.00284.x

Kasper, G., & Rose, K. R. (2002). *Pragmatic development in a second language*. Oxford, UK: Blackwell.

Kim, H.-Y. (2012). Development of NP forms and discourse reference in L2 Korean. *The Korean Language in America, 17*, 211–235.

Lee, E. H. (2018). The universal topic prominence stage hypothesis and L1 transfer: A study of L2 Korean written narratives by L1 English and L1 Chinese speakers. *Linguistic Approaches to Bilingualism*. Advance online publication. doi:10.1075/lab.17061.lee

Li, X. (2014). Variation in subject pronominal expression in L2 Chinese. *Studies in Second Language Acquisition, 36*(1), 39–68. doi:10.1017/S0272263113000466

Lozano, C. (2016). Pragmatic principles in anaphora resolution at the syntax-discourse interface: Advanced English learners of Spanish in the CEDEL2 corpus. In M. A. Ramos (Ed.), *Spanish learner corpus research: Current trends and future perspectives* (pp. 235–265). Amsterdam, the Netherlands: John Benjamins. doi:10.1075/scl.78.09loz

Lozano, C. (2018). The development of anaphora resolution at the syntax-discourse interface: Pronominal subjects in Greek learners of Spanish. *Journal of Psycholinguistic Research, 47*(2), 411–430. doi:10.1007/s10936-017-9541-8

Lumley, J. (2013). *Pragmatic perspectives on the second language acquisition of person reference in Japanese: A longitudinal study* (Doctoral thesis). Newcastle University, UK. Retrieved from http://theses.ncl.ac.uk/jspui/handle/10443/1875

Marriott, H. (1993). Acquiring sociolinguistic competence: Australian secondary students in Japan. *Journal of Asian Pacific Communication, 4*(4), 167–192.

Marriott, H. (1995). The acquisition of politeness patterns by exchange students in Japan. In B. F. Freed (Ed.), *Second language acquisition in a study abroad context* (pp. 197–224). Amsterdam, the Netherlands: John Benjamins. doi:10.1075/sibil.9.13mar

Nakahama, Y. (2003). Development of referent management in L2 Japanese: A film retelling task. *Studies in Language and Culture, 25*(1), 127–146.

Nakahama, Y. (2009a). Cross-linguistic influence on referent introduction and tracking in Japanese as a second language. *The Modern Language Journal*, *93*(2), 241–260. doi:10.1111/j.1540-4781.2009.00859.x

Nakahama, Y. (2009b). Tasuku no fukuzatsusei, bogo, nihongo nōryoku ga danwa kōsei ni oyobosu eikyō: shiji hyōgen, ukemi hyōgen no shiyō ni tsuite [Effect of task complexity, L1 and proficiency on the use of referential and passive forms in L2 Japanese discourse]. *JALT Journal*, *31*(1), 101–120.

Polio, C. (1995). Acquiring nothing? The use of zero pronouns by nonnative speakers of Chinese and the implications for the acquisition of nominal reference. *Studies in Second Language Acquisition*, *17*(3), 353–377. doi:10.1017/S0272263100014248

Takeuchi, M. (2014). *Subject referential expressions and encoding of referential status in L2 narrative discourse by L1-English learners of Japanese* (Doctoral thesis). Indiana University, Bloomington, IN.

Yanagimachi, T. (2000). JFL learners' referential-form choice in first- through third-person narratives. *Japanese-Language Education Around the Globe*, *10*, 109–128.

3 Use of demonstratives in oral narratives by Japanese learners of English

Bonnie Swierzbin

Introduction

While much is known about second language (L2) learners' use of English articles as reference devices, few studies have examined the frequency with which L2 English speakers use the demonstratives *this*, *that*, *these* and *those*, or indeed *how* they use them, whether for reference or other uses. An important use of demonstratives is pointing to people and objects in the speech situation. However, research on L2 acquisition of English demonstratives has mainly focused on reference in expository writing of university students (Hinkel, 2001, 2002; Jarvis, Grant, Bikowski, & Ferris, 2003; Zhang, 2015; Benell, 2018), with a smattering of studies on oral narratives (Kim, 2000; Kang, 2004; Swierzbin, 2004). A very limited set of studies (Ionin, Baek, Kim, Ho, & Wexler, 2012; Robertson, 2000) compares L2 demonstrative use to article use as evidence of first language (L1) pragmatic transfer.

Although there are overlapping contexts in which both English demonstratives and articles are felicitous (Gundel, Hedberg, & Zacharski, 1993), demonstratives are a crucial part of the English system of reference, specifically because they often refer concisely and efficiently to propositions (1).

(1) A: Colin was accepted to medical school.
B: *That*'s great![1]

Referring to a proposition or event with a demonstrative is more concise than a full noun phrase (NP) and more precise than a personal pronoun. Using a demonstrative in this way is what Himmelmann (1996) calls *discourse deixis*, one of the four categories in his universal taxonomy of demonstratives in narrative discourse. Discourse deixis is a subset of what Halliday and Hasan (1976) term *text reference* and *extended reference*; their categories cover other forms of reference besides demonstratives and cover genres in addition to narratives. Discourse deixis is often not taught in ESL/EFL classrooms, where textbooks and teachers typically focus on basic *situational use* (Himmelmann, 1996) of demonstratives, also called spatial deixis, to point to and contrast physical objects or people in the speech situation in order to introduce them into the discourse. The usual lack of instruction on demonstrative use also extends to Himmelmann's (1996) two remaining categories: *tracking*, where demonstratives refer to participants already established in the discourse, and *recognitional*, where a demonstrative serves as a reminder to the listener to search long-term memory, as in *Where's that orchid I gave you?* Thus, it is important to ask how English learners come to use demonstratives for categories other than basic pointing in the speech situation. In the current study, we explore English learners' use of demonstratives in oral narratives. Additionally, since Himmelmann (1996) claims that he has created a taxonomy of universal uses for demonstratives in narratives, it should be applicable to L2 narratives, so we investigate its usefulness in that regard.

Demonstratives' role in narrative structure

The functional stages of the Narrative genre typically include an optional Orientation followed by a Complication (or series of them), Evaluation and Resolution plus an optional Coda (Martin & Rose, 2008). Telling a narrative, particularly in the Complication stage, requires the speaker to comprehensibly convey a series of events and indicate how those events are related. As part of structuring a narrative, the speaker organizes the events with causal and temporal relationships. Demonstratives may play a role in constructing this overall structure since they can be used to refer to events as part of an expression that creates a temporal relationship (2a) or a causal relationship (2b–c).

(2) a. And as she's running, of course, Charlie Chaplin is coming at *this same moment* down the street, around a corner (NS1)[2]
b. But uh he moved the wrong, wrong wood wedge, and *because of that*, the big ship went into the sea (NNS7)
c. So *that* made the person even more upset (NS3)

Speakers typically organize the events in their narratives in chronological order, where no linguistic marker is needed, but they may choose to include markers such as *and then* or *after that* to emphasize the chronology. However, occasionally speakers depart from chronological order to go back to an earlier event, to predict a coming event, or to indicate that multiple events are taking place simultaneously. To do so, the speaker needs to signal the listener in some way that the events are being reported non-chronologically. One possible indicator is to change verb tense or aspect; however, learners may not have control of such verbal morphology. Bardovi-Harlig (2014), in a study of L2 English written recounts, showed that more than 90% of events told out of chronological order had an explicit linguistic marker, which was typically a time adverbial when learners did not use verbal morphology as a marker. Using a demonstrative in an adverbial gives speakers a concise way to indicate the order of events, for example, *before that* and *at that same time*.

Like temporal relations referenced in narratives, causal relations that are straightforward may need no linguistic marker; that is, the speaker may assume that the listener can infer cause and effect. Alternatively, the speaker may use one of the various linguistic devices that mark causation together with a reference to an event, such as the complex preposition *because of* in (2b) or the causative verb *made* in (2c). Demonstratives are certainly not required to express either temporal or causal relations, but since they are a succinct way to refer to events, they impart smoothness to the narrative flow.

A successful narrative is also unified by cohesive devices. Demonstratives may play a role in cohesion since they can be used to refer to participants (3a) or events (3b).

(3) They broke a Chinese vase.
    a. *That* was valuable.
    b. *That* was careless.
        (Halliday & Hasan, 1976, p. 66)

As Halliday and Hasan (1976) point out, in both cases the effect is cohesive. They also claim that using a demonstrative to refer to an extended passage of text is one of the major cohesive devices in English. An example of this is (4a), where the speaker refers to a series of events with *that*.

(4) a. He knocked over the table and broke it,
       and there was a plant on it,
       so he got a broom to try to clean up the dirt,
       but the broom was holding up the roof,
       so *that* didn't go so well either. (NS3)
    b. Put the cup on the saucer.
       1. Now put *that* over by the lamp.
       2. Now put *it* over by the lamp.
        (Brown-Schmidt, Byron, & Tanenhaus, 2005)

A series of events such as in (4a) is called a *complex event* by Wolter (2006), who points out that demonstratives are preferred over personal pronouns for complex entities, which can be a series of events as in (4a), a set of propositions, or a composite entity that is created when individual entities are related in an utterance (4b). In this example, the demonstrative pronoun would typically be assumed to refer to the composite (cup on the saucer), while the personal pronoun would be assumed to refer to the theme of the first sentence (the cup), as demonstrated in experimental trials (Brown-Schmidt, Byron, & Tanenhaus, 2005).

Regarding the final stage of a narrative, Labov (1972) specifies that the Coda may contain a signal to indicate the end of the narrative, such as *that's it*, while Hudson and Shapiro (1991), who studied children's development of narrative structure, specifically include a *formal ending device* as the final stage. Native English speakers often seem to use *that* as a pronoun in such a device (5).

(5) And, yes, *that*'s what happened (NS3)

Categories of demonstrative use in oral narratives

In the task of narrating events, some of Himmelmann's (1996) categories (discourse deixis, tracking, relational, situational) will occur more frequently than others. Specifically, such a task provides opportunities for the narrator to refer to events and propositions, thus using discourse deixis as in (6), where the speaker refers to the final events of a film with *that*.

(6) *That*'s just the end when he goes and she does this <gesture> and jumps up and down, just like the woman from the house previously (NS1)

In addition, this type of task provides opportunities for the tracking category, where the speaker refers to a participant that has already been mentioned in the narrative. Tracking is exemplified in (7), where the speaker uses the determiner *that* to refer to a film character's job, which she had talked about earlier.

(7) he's just lost *that little job* that he had (NS1)

The number of occasions for using demonstratives in the recognitional category depends in part on whether the interlocutors have or can assume shared experiences with each other. For example, in (8a) the speaker is referring to a jail cell that both the speaker and listener saw in a movie clip about fifteen minutes earlier but has not been mentioned previously by either of them. The recognitional *that* reminds the listener of their shared experience. A speaker could successfully use (8b) if the listener shares the experience of viewing Star Wars films even if the speaker and listener do not know each other.

(8) a. I would assume it's based on him letting those, the constables and all the jail administrators back out of *that* cell (NS1)
    b. She reminds me of *that* woman who played Rey in *The Force Awakens*

Basic situational use of demonstratives, or spatial deixis, is less likely in narratives since there are typically no physical entities from the narrated events to point to during a retelling. However, speakers may employ an expanded type of situational use with reported speech, where the demonstrative is grounded by the person whose speech is reported, as in (9).

(9) the sheriff then writes him a letter of recommendation, saying that he highly recommends *this* trustworthy man for a job (NS1)

Reported speech creates a shift from the utterance situation to the narrated situation, which is typically temporary, but it is also possible to shift so that the interlocutors imagine that the narrated situation is happening in their view (Himmelmann, 1996). Such a shift is called *deixis am phantasma* (translated as deixis in the imagination) (Bühler, 1934, as cited in Himmelmann, 1996).

Stukenbrock (2014) also points out that *deixis am phantasma* is often accompanied by gestures or eye movements as if the imagined participants and events were nearby. An example of this can be seen in (10), where the speaker mimics a film character's gesture with an imaginary wedge in her hand.

(10) some guy told him to find a wedge just like *this* (NS5)

In Himmelmann's analysis (1996) of native English speaker demonstrative usage in Chafe's orally narrated Pear Stories (1980), he found that tracking usage was most common (31%), followed closely by discourse deictic and situational (29% and 27%, respectively) while recognitional usage was least common (13%). The percentage of situational deixis seems rather large for narrations and may be partly explained by Himmelmann categorizing indefinite *this* as situational deixis, claiming that both indefinite *this* and other situational deixis serve to establish referents in the discourse space. While other researchers have disagreed with this categorization (Wald, 1983, as cited in Himmelmann, 1996), there is general agreement that indefinite *this* has a strong tendency to promote the discourse prominence of the referent it introduces into the discourse (Fillmore, 1997; Gundel, Hedberg, & Zacharski, 1993; Prince, 1981), which agrees with Himmelmann's premise.

From the discussion earlier, we can see that even situational use of demonstratives is not simply a matter of the physical locations of the speaker, listener and tangible objects. Furthermore, the use of demonstratives in narratives is even more abstract than basic situational use and involves the personal history of interactions between the interlocutors. Currently, the very limited research on L2 use of English demonstratives does not provide insight into how English language learners navigate the complexities of the English demonstrative system. The present study is a step in that direction.

The work on demonstratives reported here is driven by the following general research question:

How are third-person singular demonstratives used in oral narratives by L2 English speakers whose L1 is Japanese?

This question has four detailed subquestions:

- What is the frequency of these demonstratives in the categories *situational use*, *discourse deictic*, *tracking* and *recognitional*, as defined by Himmelmann (1996)?
- How do the participants use these demonstratives as discourse deixis to structure their narratives?
- How do the participants use situational deixis in their narratives?
- How does demonstrative usage related to the first three subquestions vary by speaking proficiency?

Finally, since Himmelmann's categories are claimed to provide a taxonomy of universal uses of demonstratives in narratives, we also ask how useful this framework is for categorizing demonstratives in L2 narratives.

Methodology

The participants were 15 native speakers of Japanese (9 female, 6 male) who were enrolled in an intensive English program at the University of Minnesota. Details of the participants' age, gender and English proficiency level are shown in Table 3.1 from highest to lowest proficiency. The speaking proficiency of each participant was rated by two experienced SPEAK® raters (Speaking Proficiency English Assessment Kit, Educational Testing Service, 1996), working independently. Similar to the actual SPEAK test protocol, the raters worked from audio recordings of the participants, but unlike the test, the participants were speaking to an interlocutor, not just a recording device. For each participant, three clips were selected from sections of the data where he or she (not the interlocutor) spoke most extensively. Each rater assigned a score to each clip, then averaged the three scores for the final score. The raters' scores, which never differed by more than ten points (on a scale from 20 to 60 points), were averaged to arrive at the overall scores shown in Table 3.1. The overall scores were arranged into proficiency groups (high [H], intermediate [I], low [L]) by one of the SPEAK raters.

Each participant and a native English-speaking (NS) interlocutor of the same gender watched the first half of a silent film (an abridged version of *Modern Times*) together, then only the non-native English-speaking (NNS) participant watched the second half of the film (the interlocutor left the room). Immediately afterwards, the NNS participant narrated the story of the second half to the interlocutor. The participants were not acquainted with their interlocutors before their participation in this study. The task was video-recorded, and the narratives were transcribed from video by the researcher.[3] All of the third-person singular

Table 3.1 Participant profiles

Participant number	Gender	Age	Overall English proficiency score	Proficiency group
NNS9	F	55	58.3	H
NNS14	F	19	53.3	H
NNS7	M	42	51.7	H
NNS1	F	35	50.0	H
NNS4	M	38	50.0	H
NNS2	F	33	48.3	I
NNS6	F	30	48.3	I
NNS13	F	20	48.3	I
NNS15	F	21	48.3	I
NNS5	M	39	45.0	L
NNS10	M	18	45.0	L
NNS12	F	21	41.7	L
NNS3	M	39	40.0	L
NNS11	F	27	38.8	L
NNS8	M	57	31.7	L

noun phrases that included a demonstrative pronoun or determiner (*this, that*) were tallied and analyzed based on English proficiency level and the categories *situational use, discourse deictic, tracking* and *recognitional*, as defined by Himmelmann (1996). To answer the question regarding how these L2 English speakers use demonstratives as discourse deixis to structure their narratives, several factors were examined. For these demonstratives, the type of referent was categorized as *simple event, complex event, formal ending device*, or *proposition*. Demonstrative pronouns and determiners were analyzed separately to determine if the different forms were used for different types of referents. Next, the discourse deictic demonstratives that were part of expressions creating temporal or causal relations were tallied. To answer the question regarding situational use, each demonstrative in that category was analyzed to determine if it was basic situational use (spatial deixis with a physical entity in the utterance situation), or extended situational use (indefinite *this*), or a shift to the narrated situation via direct speech or *deixis am phantasma*.

Results

First, the frequency of third-person singular demonstratives *this* and *that* in the categories *situational use, discourse deictic, tracking* and *recognitional* is presented. Table 3.2 presents the figures for the number of demonstratives used by category, with the percentages in parenthesis indicating the within-group distribution. The results indicate that the total number of demonstratives used by each group increased with rising proficiency level, as shown in the Total Demonstratives column in Table 3.2. The difference in frequency of demonstrative use across the proficiency groups is significant (Kruskal-Wallis χ^2 = 6.14, p = 0.047[4]). The low proficiency group used significantly fewer demonstratives than the other groups (z = −2.36). As a group, 4.2% of the noun phrases used by the low proficiency speakers were demonstratives, compared to 9.5% and 8.0% of the NPs used by the intermediate and high proficiency groups, respectively, which is an indication that the numbers do not simply reflect longer narratives by higher proficiency speakers.

Table 3.2 Frequency of demonstratives by category and proficiency level

	Situational use (%)	Discourse deictic (%)	Tracking (%)	Recognitional (%)	Total demonstratives (%)
High proficiency	18 (19.6)	51 (55.4)	17 (18.5)	6 (6.5)	92 (100)
Intermediate proficiency	6 (14.3)	24 (57.1)	12 (28.6)	–	42 (100)
Low proficiency	6 (26.1)	13 (56.5)	4 (17.4)	–	23 (100)

Across all proficiency groups, the category with the highest frequency of use was discourse deictic. The next most frequently used category was either situational (high and low proficiency groups) or tracking (intermediate proficiency group). Demonstratives in the recognitional category were only used by the high proficiency learners. Discourse deictic demonstratives were used to refer to both simple (11a) and complex (11b) events as well as propositions (11c), and as formal ending devices (11d).

(11) a. they took two, the younger kids away, and then she saw *that* (NNS9)
   b. he felt very strong so he beat the uh guys who was, who were trying to get away, yes and uh after all, after all those guys were arrested once again by the police and uh and because of *that*, he was recommended to a job (NNS7)
   c. and newspaper written uh "Some shops reopen," so he, he notes about *that* (NNS10)
   d. Maybe *that*'s story (NNS8)

All of these ways of using demonstratives are discussed in more detail later in this section.

Speakers also used demonstratives to track already-mentioned objects and participants. In (12a), there is no obvious reason why the speaker chose *that* over the definite article, but in (12b), the speaker needed a way to distinguish among three characters: Charlie Chaplin, his cellmate (*the other guy*) and a prisoner with drugs, who was introduced in the prior utterance and is now tracked with *this other guy* and stressed *this*.

(12) a. So she was ordered to collect some piece of wood, so but finding, in finding *that wood* he made a mistake (NNS2)
   b. Charlie Chaplin with the other guy was eating and *this other guy* was sitting next to him and *this* is the guilty guy (NNS9)

In the situational use category, speakers used reported speech as in (13a), where the speaker paraphrased the words shown on the screen, "Find a wedge like this." They used *deixis am phantasma* as in (13b), where the speaker is gesturing to show the relationship between an imaginary ship and wedge. They also introduced participants with indefinite *this* (13c). The situational use demonstratives are described in more detail later in this section.

(13) a. coworker asked him to pick up some wood, wood, wood, kind of uh, uh, like, like this, like *this wood* (NNS12)
   b. ship is like go like *this* (NNS14)
   c. she found *this* big bread (NNS9)

Four of the five speakers in the high proficiency group used demonstratives in the recognitional category, both to remind the listener (14a) of a character who had been seen in the film but had not yet been mentioned in the narrative and to cue the listener (14b) to use shared cultural knowledge to identify the intended referent.

(14) a. Do you remember *that girl?* (NNS 1)
   b. he went into the restaurant, you know, one of *those*[5] *cafeteria-style* (NNS 9)

To answer the second research question regarding how these L2 English speakers used demonstratives to structure their narratives, we now focus on the demonstratives in the discourse deixis category, and we consider pronouns and determiners separately. As shown in Table 3.3, speakers across proficiency levels used demonstrative pronouns most often to refer to simple events, followed by formal ending devices, and references to complex events. References to propositions were the least frequent and only used by high and intermediate proficiency speakers. Demonstrative determiners were only used to refer to simple and complex events, as indicated in Table 3.4. When comparing the use of determiners versus pronouns across proficiency groups, we can see that both the high and low groups used a higher proportion of pronouns (>70% for each group) while the intermediate group used almost equal numbers of determiners and pronouns.

Table 3.3 Type of referents of discourse deictic demonstrative pronouns by proficiency level

	Simple event (%)	Complex event (%)	Formal ending device (%)	Proposition (%)	Total
High proficiency	21 (50.0)	7 (16.7)	10 (23.8)	4 (9.5)	42
Intermediate proficiency	6 (54.5)	1 (9.1)	3 (27.3)	1 (9.1)	11
Low proficiency	5 (50.0)	2 (20.0)	3 (30.0)	–	10

Table 3.4 Type of referents of discourse deictic demonstrative determiners by proficiency level

	Simple event (%)	Complex event (%)	Formal ending device	Proposition	Total
High proficiency	5 (50.0)	5 (50.0)	–	–	10
Intermediate proficiency	7 (53.8)	6 (46.2)	–	–	13
Low proficiency	1 (25.0)	3 (75.0)	–	–	4

The higher frequency of demonstrative determiners in the speech of some of the intermediate proficiency learners seemed to add more formality and precision, such as the use of *after that scene* instead of *after that*, and *at that moment* instead of *then*. In contrast, formal ending devices were, in fact, typically quite informal, the most common being *that's all*.

Speakers at all proficiency levels used discourse deixis in expressions that created temporal relations among the narrative's events (Table 3.5). Most expressions were used to emphasize normal chronological order (*after that*), and the next most frequent were expressions to indicate simultaneous events (*at that time, at that moment*). The frequency of the latter may be an effect of the particular film the speakers were narrating, where a pivotal scene depends on Charlie Chaplin and the main female character moving down the same street at the same time and crashing into one another. The three speakers with the highest overall English proficiency score used discourse deixis in expressions that create causal relations (*that's why, because of that*) as did one of the intermediate proficiency speakers.

Next, we turn to how these L2 English speakers used situational deixis in their narratives. First, there was no basic situational use, that is, no demonstratives used to point to actual people and objects in the discourse situation. Table 3.6 shows the frequency across English proficiency levels of expanded situational use plus other, not easily categorized, instances of situational use. The subcategory *shift to narrated situation* includes *deixis am phantasma* and all cases where the speakers used some form of reported speech. However, it should be noted that the speakers were interpreting a silent film, and although they may have used the form of direct speech, they engaged in *constructed dialogue* (Tannen, 1989),

Table 3.5 Temporal and causal relations with discourse deixis by proficiency level

	Temporal			Causal
	Chronological order	*Simultaneous events*	*Reverse order*	
High proficiency	15	5	1	6
Intermediate proficiency	5	8	–	1
Low proficiency	4	1	–	–

Table 3.6 Situational use by proficiency level

	Expanded		Other
	Shift to narrated situation	*Indefinite* **this**	
High proficiency	14	4	–
Intermediate proficiency	3	–	3
Low proficiency	6	–	–

which means that they were creatively constructing what they imagined the film characters said and thought.

All of the high-proficiency speakers used some type of expanded situational use, but only one intermediate proficiency and two low proficiency speakers did so. Usage at all levels included instances of both constructed dialogue (15a) and *deixis am phantasma* (15b); in (15a) the speaker interrupts her description of a shack to report what the main female character said, thus creating a temporary shift from the discourse situation to the narrated situation, signalled by *she said*. In (15b) the same speaker shifts the narrated situation first with reported speech (*coworker asked him*), then shifts the whole perspective of the scene to narrate it as if it were in front of the interlocutors. She points while saying *this wood* as if the wood were there, and she gestures during *the shape is like this* to roughly indicate the shape.

(15) a. she said "*this* is house" (NNS12)
    b. coworker asked him to pick up some wood, wood, wood, kind of uh, uh, like, like this, like *this* wood, the shape is like *this* (NNS12)

Only high proficiency speakers used indefinite *this*, but two uses of *that* in the *other* subcategory could also be attempts by intermediate proficiency speakers to introduce participants previously unknown to their interlocutor (16a & b). Such usage may be an indication that the speakers were working on acquiring this structure. The remaining phrase in the *other* subcategory is shown in (16c); it seems to indicate that the speaker is paraphrasing a newspaper headline shown in the film.

(16) a. he found *that* advertisement (NNS2)
    b. he was released from *that* policeman (NNS6)
    c. it says you can have a chance to find a job, like *this* (NNS15)

It is also interesting to note that (16a & b) are two of only three instances (out of 157) of demonstratives in the data that were infelicitous. The third was from a high proficiency speaker who said, "He went into *that* kind of restaurant," which may have been an attempt at recognitional usage, but no more information was provided to identify the kind of restaurant meant.

To sum up the findings, as English proficiency increased, so did the use of demonstratives and the number of ways in which they were used. High proficiency speakers were the only ones to use indefinite *this* and demonstratives in the recognitional category. Also, they more frequently used demonstratives to create temporal and causal relations in their narratives as well as shifting from the narrated situation to the discourse situation with constructed dialogue.

Discussion

The findings indicate that Himmelmann's (1996) taxonomy of demonstrative usage in narratives serves as a valuable lens for a detailed examination of L2 demonstratives. While it is clear that the L2 speakers at all proficiency levels were able to use demonstratives across the categories (with the exception of recognitional, which only the high proficiency speakers used), the focus of this lens provides a more nuanced image and hints at a possible order of acquisition for demonstratives. Himmelmann's taxonomy, however, does not include emotional deixis (Lakoff, 1974), with which the speaker can create a feeling of closeness. Since emotional deixis is not discussed in Himmelmann (1996), it is not clear if it was considered as a possible universal category of demonstrative usage. It is, nevertheless, clear that both English (Lakoff, 1974) and Japanese (Naruoka, 2014) have emotional deixis; therefore, research is needed to explore its universality and possible place in the taxonomy.

Himmelmann's taxonomy helps us see that none of the demonstrative usage in the data is basic situational use; that is, nobody was pointing to concrete entities in the physical surroundings. All of the instances are extended situational use or recognitional (which depends on the interlocutors' shared history), or they refer to entities in the discourse situation. All of these categories of usage are more abstract than basic pointing (Diessel, 2006), and it is unlikely that these L2 learners were taught the extended and abstract uses of demonstratives. So how did they come to acquire and use them so successfully? Possibilities to consider include positive transfer from Japanese, and exposure to both the frequency of demonstratives in native speaker English and their extended and abstract usage, each of which will be discussed in turn.

Japanese has three demonstrative prefixes *ko-*, *so-* and *a-*, which can be added to a variety of base morphemes to create words in numerous classes including pronouns (17a), determiners (17b) and adverbs (17c), among others.

(17) a. *kore*   *sore*   *are*
        this one   that one   that one over there   (all inanimate)
     b. *kono hito*   *sono hito*   *ano hito*
        this person   that person   that person over there
     c. *koko*   *soko*   *asoko*
        here   there   over there

Historically, Japanese demonstratives have been characterized by their basic situational use as in (18).

(18) a. *ko-*forms are used to refer to something near the speaker.
     b. *so-*forms are used to refer to something near the listener.
     c. *a-*forms are used to refer to something at a distance from both the speaker and listener

(Matsushita, 1930, as cited in Hoji, Kinsui, Takubo & Ueyama, 2003).

As with English, this sort of description has proven inadequate for extended uses of demonstratives, and more recently Japanese demonstratives have been studied from syntactic, semantic and pragmatic viewpoints (e.g., Hoji, Kinsui, Takubo &

Ueyama, 2003; Kaneko, 2014; Naruoka, 2014; Taki, 2010). These studies have provided insights about which of the three forms are felicitous in particular situations, and which of them require linguistic antecedents as well as describing the emotional nuances added to discourse by the use of certain demonstratives. Based on examples in the studies cited earlier and Clancy (1980), it seems that Japanese does have demonstrative usage in the situational, tracking and discourse deixis categories. Also, a recognitional use appears to be discussed by Kuno (1973, as cited in Hoji et al., 2003, p. 117), who states that "an a-NP is used for referring to something (at a distance either in time or space) that the speaker knows both s/he and the hearer know personally or have experience in". However, there does not appear to be any research investigating and categorizing demonstratives functionally as Himmelmann (1996) does for English. Such studies are needed in order to provide evidence of what demonstrative features Japanese learners of English might transfer to their L2, in addition to validating his claim of universality.

Along with transfer, another factor that may have influenced the learners' use of English demonstratives is their frequency in the input the learners heard while living in the U.S. Demonstratives are frequent in spoken English; in fact, demonstrative pronouns were used on average more than four times a minute in Lawson's (2001) native English speaker conversational data. *That* was the seventh most frequent word, and when *that* was used to refer (i.e., not a complementizer or modifier such as *that long*), it commonly referred to the specific information in the immediately prior utterance (82% of referential *that* usage). This indicates that conversational English contains frequent discourse deixis. It is also likely to be quite frequent in classroom discourse, as teachers respond to propositions stated by students or react to classroom events (*that's right; can you say a little more about that?; please don't do that;* etc.). In the current study, most of the discourse deixis referred to events (Table 3.3 and 3.4), and in only five instances, high or intermediate proficiency speakers referred to propositions. The comparatively low number of references to propositions may be a function of the narrative task; future research could examine other types of discourse (e.g., informal or academic conversations) to determine if L2 speakers across proficiency levels use demonstratives to refer to propositions.

The word *this* is the thirty-fourth most frequent word in the 10-million-word Cambridge International Corpus (O'Keefe, McCarthy, & Carter, 2007). Although indefinite *this* is considered colloquial (at best) and seems to be infrequently taught in ESL/EFL classrooms, this extended situational use is common in some native English speaker discourse situations. For example, in the larger study from which data for this study is drawn, NS use indefinite *this* more often than definite *this* (27 vs. 21 tokens). It is thus likely that the current study's participants were exposed to indefinite *this* in casual conversation in the United States. Since only high proficiency learners used indefinite *this*, perhaps they had had enough exposure or were at a point in their acquisition of English where they were able to notice this unusual usage of a demonstrative. It seems this form is not a candidate for transfer since, according to Himmelmann (1996, citing Wald,

1983), forms equivalent to indefinite *this* have not been attested in languages other than English, and the data from Gundel, Hedberg, and Zacharski (1993) shows no indefinite use of any of the Japanese demonstrative forms.

From the universal nature of demonstratives and the results of the current study, we can glean some hints about the order of acquisition of L2 English demonstratives. Demonstratives are universal, according to Diessel (2006), assuming that they are defined as a class in terms of their communicative function, which is to "coordinate the interlocutors' joint focus of attention" (p. 472).[6] Establishing joint attention is a basic function of human communication, thus it seems likely that basic situational use is acquired first, followed by discourse deixis, which involves the same psychological mechanisms as basic situational use in order to focus interlocutors' attention on certain linguistic elements (Diessel, 2006). In the present study, the frequency of demonstratives increased significantly from the low to the intermediate proficiency group, specifically in the discourse deixis and tracking categories, which may indicate that those uses of demonstratives are acquired as speakers move to intermediate proficiency. Additionally, in the discourse deixis category, intermediate proficiency learners used more determiners than pronouns while those in the higher and lower groups did not. The intermediate pattern may indicate that learners are leaning on *that* as a cautious choice because they have not yet established the difference between *the* and determiner *that*, a result that Ionin et al. (2012) also found with Korean intermediate learners of English. Finally, it was noted that only speakers in the high proficiency group used the recognitional category and the expanded situational use of indefinite *this*, a possible indication that such usage is acquired later than the other categories. It is important to keep in mind that the categories are established only for narratives; as Lawson (2001) points out, how demonstratives are used depends heavily on type of discourse, so more research is needed with various types of tasks and genres, both oral and written, to ensure that the results are not due to task effects. Moreover, comparisons of L2 data with NS completing the same task would indicate the extent to which the L2 learners' choices are target-like.

The current study asks a question that necessitates starting with demonstrative forms in narratives and investigating the functions for which the demonstratives are used. It is also fruitful to examine L2 learner language in the opposite direction, that is, starting with functions and asking what forms the learners choose to instantiate those functions.

Conclusion

This chapter provides novel information about the functions of demonstratives used by L2 English speakers in the context of an oral narrative. Although demonstratives in English and Japanese have been well studied in the fields of syntax, semantics and pragmatics, both from the point of view of their referential meaning and of their expressive meaning, less is known about them from a functional perspective and very little is known about the functions that L2 English speakers associate with demonstratives. The current study is a small step towards gaining such knowledge. The results indicate that although the L2 learners' use of demonstratives was almost always felicitous in context, only the high proficiency learners used the full range of functionality across the four categories.

Acknowledgements

Many thanks to Jen Killam, Elaine Tarone and Steve Wicht for reviewing earlier versions of this chapter.

Notes

1. Any examples that are not otherwise attributed were drawn from the author's personal collection of family conversations.
2. Examples marked NNSx are drawn from the non-native English speaker data of the current study. For the larger study, this data is taken from same-gender dyads of native English speakers who also completed the task. Native speaker examples (marked NSx) in this chapter are drawn from those dyads.
3. The transcriptions were spot-checked by a second transcriptionist. The two transcripts matched on 96.4% of the noun phrases, which were the main focus of the study. Differences were resolved by discussion between the two transcriptionists.
4. The intermediate group has four members rather than the recommended five for using the Kruskal-Wallis test (Hatch & Lazaraton, 1991).
5. Since the demonstrative is plural, this example was not included in the current study; however, it was drawn from the data for the larger study that the current study is part of.
6. A definition based simply on demonstratives' use to contrast the distance of objects or people is not sufficient to claim universality since some languages (e.g., German, Turkish) have demonstratives that do not have a distance feature (Diessel, 2006).

References

Bardovi-Harlig, K. (2014). Documenting interlanguage development. In Z. Han & E. Tarone (Eds.), *Interlanguage: Forty years later* (pp. 127–146). Amsterdam, the Netherlands: John Benjamins.

Benell, T. (2018). *Referencing for cohesion in L2 academic writing: A corpus analysis* (Unpublished Master's thesis). İhsan Doğramaci Bilkent University, Ankara, Turkey.

Brown-Schmidt, S., Byron, D., & Tanenhaus, M. (2005). Beyond salience: Interpretation of personal and demonstrative pronouns. *Journal of Memory and Language, 53*, 292–313. doi:10.1016/j.jml.2005.03.003

Chafe, W. (Ed.). (1980). *The pear stories: Cognitive, cultural, and linguistic aspects of narrative production*. Norwood, NJ: Ablex.

Clancy, P. (1980). Referential choice in English and Japanese narrative discourse. In W. Chafe (Ed.). *The pear stories: Cognitive, cultural, and linguistic aspects of narrative production* (pp. 127–202). Norwood, NJ: Ablex.

Diessel, H. (2006). Demonstratives, joint attention, and the emergence of grammar. *Cognitive Linguistics, 17*(4), 463–489. doi:10.1515/COG.2006.015

Educational Testing Service. (1996). *SPEAK rater training guide [Brochure]*. Princeton, NJ: Author.

Fillmore, C. (1997). *Lectures on deixis*. Stanford, CA: CLSI Publications.
Gundel, J., Hedberg, N., & Zacharski, R. (1993). Cognitive status and the form of referring expressions in discourse. *Language, 69*(2), 274–307. doi:10.2307/416535
Halliday, M., & Hasan, R. (1976). *Cohesion in English*. London, UK: Longman.
Hatch, E., & Lazaraton, A. (1991). *The research manual: Design and statistics for applied linguistics*. Boston, MA: Heinle & Heinle.
Himmelmann, N. (1996). Demonstratives in narrative discourse. In B. Fox (Ed.), *Studies in anaphora* (pp. 205–54). Amsterdam, the Netherlands/Philadelphia, PA: John Benjamins.
Hinkel, E. (2001). Matters of cohesion in L2 academic texts. *Applied Language Learning, 12*(2), 111–132.
Hinkel, E. (2002). *Second language writers' text*. Mahwah, NJ: Lawrence Erlbaum.
Hoji, H., Kinsui, S., Takubo, Y., & Ueyama, A. (2003). The demonstratives in modern Japanese. In Y. Li & A. Simpson (Eds.), *Functional structure(s), form, and interpretation: Perspectives from East Asian languages* (pp. 97–128). London/New York, NY: Routledge.
Hudson, J., & Shapiro, L. (1991). From knowing to telling: The development of children's script, stories and personal narrative. In A. McCabe & C. Peterson (Eds.), *Developing narrative structure* (pp. 89–136). Hillsdale, MI: Erlbaum.
Ionin, T., Baek, S., Kim, E., Ko, H., & Wexler, K. (2012). *That's* not so different from *the*: Definite and demonstrative descriptions in second language acquisition. *Second Language Research, 28*(1), 69–101. doi:10.1177/0267658311432200
Jarvis, S., Grant, L., Bikowski, D., & Ferris, D. (2003). Exploring multiple profiles of highly rated learner compositions. *Journal of Second Language Writing, 12*(4), 377–403. doi: 10.1016/j.jslw.2003.09.001
Kaneko, M. (2014). The semantics and syntax of Japanese adnominal demonstratives. In P. Hofherr & A. Zribi-Hertz (Eds.), *Cross-linguistic studies on noun phrase structure and reference* (pp. 239–268). Leiden, the Netherlands: Brill.
Kang, J. (2004). Telling a coherent story in a foreign language: Analysis of Korean EFL learners' referential strategies in oral narrative discourse. *Journal of Pragmatics, 36*(11), 1975–1990. doi:10.1016/j.pragma.2004.03.007
Kim, H. (2000). *Acquisition of English nominal reference by Korean speakers* (Unpublished Ph.D. dissertation). University of Hawai'i, Honolulu, HI.
Labov, W. (1972). *Language in the inner city: Studies in the Black English vernacular*. Philadelphia, PA: University of Pennsylvania Press.
Lakoff, R. (1974). Remarks on *this* and *that*. *Regional Meetings: Chicago Linguistic Society, 10*, 345–356.
Lawson, A. (2001). *Topic management and demonstratives in spoken English and French: A corpus-based approach* (Unpublished Ph.D. dissertation). Cornell University, Ithaca, NY.
Martin, J., & Rose, D. (2008). *Genre relations: Mapping culture*. London, UK: Equinox.
Naruoka, K. (2014). Toward meanings of expressive indexicals: The case of Japanese demonstratives *konna/sonna/anna*. *Journal of Pragmatics, 69*, 4–21. doi: 10.1016/j.pragma.2012.06.016
O'Keefe, A., McCarthy, M., & Carter, R. (2007). *From corpus to classroom: Language use and language teaching*. Cambridge, UK: Cambridge University Press.

Prince, E. (1981). Toward a taxonomy of given-new information. In P. Cole (Ed.), *Radical pragmatics* (pp. 223–255). New York, NY: Academic Press.

Robertson, D. (2000). Variability in the use of the English article system by Chinese learners of English. *Second Language Research*, 16(2), 135–172. doi:10.1191/026765800672262975

Stukenbrock, A. (2014). Pointing to an 'empty' space: *Deixis am Phantasma* in face-to-face interaction. *Journal of Pragmatics*, 74, 70–93. doi:10.1016/j.pragma.2014.08.001

Swierzbin, B. (2004). *The role of cognitive status in second language acquisition of English noun phrase referring expressions* (Unpublished Ph.D. dissertation). University of Minnesota, Minneapolis, MN.

Taki, M. (2010). *Anaphoric demonstratives in spoken and written Japanese discourse* (Unpublished Master's thesis). San Diego State University, San Diego, CA. Retrieved from http://sdsu-dspace.calstate.edu/bitstream/handle/10211.10/615/Taki_Mariko.pdf;sequence=1

Tannen, D. (1989). *Talking voices: Repetition, dialogue, and imagery in conversational discourse.* Cambridge, UK: Cambridge University Press.

Wolter, L. (2006). *That's that: The semantics and pragmatics of demonstrative noun phrases* (Unpublished Ph.D. dissertation). University of California, Santa Cruz, CA.

Zhang, J. (2015). An analysis of the use of demonstratives in argumentative discourse by Chinese EFL learners. *Journal of Language Teaching and Research*, 6(2), 460–465. doi:10.17507/jltr.0602.29

4 Do referential marking styles transfer to L2 story retelling?

Yuko Nakahama

Introduction

Functional approaches consider the relationship between form and function within an extended, beyond-sentence-level discourse. Within this framework, Givón (1983) claims appropriate management of reference contributes considerably to coherent discourse, and his premise has been adopted in various studies of L2 referent management in narratives (e.g., Chaudron & Parker, 1990; Huebner, 1983; Jarvis, 2002, Nakahama, 2009). Cross-linguistic influence (CLI) in L2 reference has been systematically investigated through research designs comparing the performance of speakers whose L1 is typologically close to and different from the L2 (e.g., Crosthwaite, 2014a; Jarvis, 2002; Nakahama, 2003, 2009; Polio, 1995). Nakahama (2003) examined CLI in the L2 Japanese of Korean (similar to Japanese) and English (different from Japanese) learners, finding positive influence of CLI in Korean speakers' successful performance in definite/indefinite markings in L2 Japanese since those languages use similar noun marking systems. Evidence of negative transfer was also found in the omission of postposed particles marking indefiniteness and definiteness by low level English speakers. Jarvis (2002) explored similar issues in the opposite direction, studying how reference is introduced and maintained by adolescent Swedish and Finnish learners of L2 English. The former shares similarity with English in prepositional noun marking, while the latter uses postpositional noun marking like Japanese and Korean. Jarvis found ubiquitous article omission in the Finns' L2 English narratives irrespective of learners' age or discourse contexts but not in the Swedes' L2 English data, attributing the phenomenon as CLI from Finnish. Partially replicating Jarvis (2002), the objective of this chapter is to explore whether CLI can be confirmed in the written L2 English prepositional referent marking system, by learners of another language (i.e., Japanese) with postpositional markings.

Tracking referents in L2 discourse: a functional account to explain SLA

The Functional Approach (FA) is one of a variety of frameworks that have been adopted to account for the processes of second language acquisition (SLA). A central idea of FA is that SLA is a process of form-function mapping, for which

Do referential marking styles transfer? 57

learners rely on language-specific cues (Bates & MacWhinney, 1989). As Tomlin (1990) clarifies, within FA are several schools of thought, including those based on Systemic Functional Linguistics (Halliday, 1985) and the North American School (e.g., Bates & MacWhinney, 1989; Givón, 1979; Klein & Perdue, 1992, 1997). While these might approach learner language somewhat differently, the crux of their interests lies in analysing how language is used in discourse.

Givón (1983) has argued for a unit of analysis above the clause and sentence levels and has thus proposed the 'thematic paragraph'. He contends that this provides a better foundation to uncover the rather complicated process of discourse continuity. Givón further asserts that within the thematic paragraph, coherent discourse reflects how well-referential topics are continued and discontinued. According to Givón's (1983) cross-linguistic *topic continuity subscale*, the most continuous topics should be marked with zero anaphora, followed by unstressed/bound pronouns, then stressed/independent pronouns, while full noun phrases (NPs) denote more discontinuous topics (see also Givón, 1978). Givón (1983, p. 18) further proposes an *iconicity principle*, whereby 'the more disruptive, surprising, discontinuous or hard to process a topic is, the more coding material must be assigned to it'. Givón's framework has been adopted in a number of studies of L2 referent management in narratives (e.g., Chaudron & Parker, 1990; Huebner, 1983; Jarvis, 2002, Nakahama, 2009; Takeuchi, 2014). For English, the means of introducing new referents into discourse and their maintenance as a referential topic is summarised in Table 4.1 (partially adopted from Chaudron & Parker, 1990, p. 46).

As discussed above, appropriate management of reference to person contributes greatly to coherent discourse. In both English (e.g., Chaudron & Parker, 1990; Huebner, 1983; Master, 1997; Ryan, 2015) and Japanese (e.g., Clancy, 1985; Doi & Yoshioka, 1990; Nakahama, 2003; Sakamoto, 1993; Takeuchi, 2014), various studies confirm that definiteness markers that display high topic continuity ('the' in English, '*wa*' in Japanese) precede indefiniteness markers that show low topic continuity ('a, an' in English, '*ga*' in Japanese) during L2 acquisition. In L2 reference, definiteness marking is found in both indefinite contexts and the context of the highest topic continuity, since learners tend to choose lexical NPs (Ryan, 2015; Tomlin, 1990). Specifically, where pronouns (for English) and zero anaphora (for Japanese) would be felicitous, learners often use 'the + N' and '*wa*', respectively. In English, a further complication is the difficulty in using articles, as reported in many studies (e.g., Butler 2002; Liu & Gleason, 2002;

Table 4.1 Referential forms of English within discourse contexts

Refer to current topic	Introduce known referent as topic	Introduce new referent
Pronoun	Definite article or left dislocation + def. article.	Indefinite article or existential + indef. article

Master, 1987), with Master (1987) finding acquisition took longer if the L1 had no equivalent article system (e.g., Japanese, Chinese, and Russian).

While overgeneralisation of definiteness markers occurs in indefinite contexts, appropriate use does increase with proficiency (e.g., Andersen, 1977; Huebner, 1983; Toyama, 2005). This has been attributed to an artefact of CLI (Kang, 2004; Nakahama, 2011), or part of a universal tendency (Ryan, 2015). Further, while attenuated forms such as pronouns and zero anaphora are allegedly difficult to perform even at higher proficiency levels (Muñoz, 1995; Ryan, 2015; Tomlin, 1990), Chaudron and Parker (1990) reported otherwise for Japanese learners of L2 English, who tended to use pronouns in place of 'the + N'. This finding is worthy of further exploration, in order to clarify previous claims regarding the acquisition of attenuated forms.

Among further studies, Huebner (1983) longitudinally examined L2 development of English by Ge, an adult bilingual speaker of Hmong and Laotian. Ge's interlanguage mainly consisted of topic-comment structures, and tended to overgeneralise *da* ('the'), which can be interpreted as a topic prominent feature (Huebner, 1983). Interestingly, Ge differentiated referents in topic and comment positions, omitting the subject in the topic position while using *da* ('the') in comment position. The issues raised by Huebner (1983) were explored further by Jarvis (2002), who distinguished between the discourse contexts of new topic, new comment, known topic, known comment, current topic, and current comment (abbreviated NT, NC, KT, KC, CT, CC, respectively) in L2 English story-retelling. Jarvis found that his Swedish and Finnish learners of L2 English tended to differentiate reference marking in new-known-current contexts, but the topic-comment distinction was not obviously marked. The key finding of Jarvis' study was L1 transfer from Finnish to English L2, the details of which I discuss in the following section.

Cross-linguistic influence in L2 referent introduction and tracking

Cross-linguistic influence (CLI) in L2 reference has been systematically investigated through research designs comparing the performance of speakers whose L1 is typologically close to and different from the L2 (e.g., Crosthwaite, 2014a; Jarvis, 2002; Nakahama, 2003, 2009; Nakahama & Kurihara, 2007; Polio, 1995; Tōyama, 2013). Polio (1995) compared Japanese and English learners of Mandarin Chinese, finding that irrespective of learners' L1 and proficiency levels, use of zero anaphora in the highest topic continuity context was significantly lower than in L1 Chinese. This suggests the shared topic prominent features between Chinese and Japanese (zero anaphora in this case) did not contribute to successful marking of referents in the context of highest topic continuity.

Similarly, Nakahama (2009) examined CLI in the L2 Japanese of Korean- and English-speaking learners at three proficiency levels. Korean and Japanese share analogous encoding systems of definiteness and indefiniteness. Specifically, new referents (the most discontinuous context) are marked with *ga* in Japanese and *ka/i* in Korean, whereas already introduced referents are marked with *wa* and *(n) un*, respectively. Japanese takes suffixal markers to distinguish new and known information, while English uses pre-posed article systems: 'a' or 'an' for a single new referent and 'the' for the known referent. In the context of highest topic continuity, Japanese and Korean use zero anaphora while English uses pronouns. Nakahama (2009) found positive influence of CLI in Korean speakers' use of the particles *ga* (indefiniteness marker) and *wa* (definiteness marker) even at a novice proficiency level. English learners of Japanese, on the other hand, had difficulty with the use of both, although performance increased with proficiency. Further evidence of CLI was found in the omission of postposed particles marking indefiniteness and definiteness by low level English speakers.

In the use of zero anaphora, however, the Korean learners of Japanese did not benefit as greatly from similarities in the two languages, mirroring the findings of Polio (1995). Specifically, the lowest-proficiency learners overused NP + *wa*, with Nakahama (2009) arguing that CLI was hindered by linguistic constraints that arose in the use of zero anaphora in passive structures.

Similar issues were explored in Jarvis' (2002) investigation of prepositional referent marking in writing by young Swedish and Finnish learners of L2 English. While English and Swedish share pre-posed marking of nominal referents, Finnish, like Japanese and Korean, employs postpositional particles to mark nouns. In Jarvis' study, occurrences of bare nouns (omission of article) were ubiquitous in Finnish L1 and English L2 narratives, irrespective of new, known, or current contexts, which suggests CLI of referent marking style. As in L1 English, pronoun use was significantly higher in topic than comment position in the most continuous contexts. However, in examining markings of all the referents in the narratives, Jarvis found that the participants did not seem to differentiate topic and comment positions. A more intriguing result from the Finnish learner narratives was that significantly more bare nouns (omission of article) were found in topic position than comment position in known contexts, mirroring the pattern found in Huebner's (1983) case study. As Jarvis argues, this result could be caused by differing noun marking systems between English and Finnish, as article omission was not found in the Swedes' English L2 data.

The objective of the present study is to partially replicate Jarvis (2002) to explore whether CLI can be confirmed in written L2 English referent tracking by learners of a language with postpositional markings. Thus, the motivated change from Jarvis (2002) is the participant group (Japanese). Maintained from the initial study are both the elicitation task and use of written data. It is worth noting that oral performance is generally assumed to reveal greater limitations in language systems, as there is usually less within-task planning time for monitoring and editing, while the written mode tends to elicit longer words and more varied vocabulary (see Chafe & Danielewics, 1987; Drieman, 1962), and thus richer modification of noun marking might be expected. Furthermore, previous studies have shown task complexity plays a role in the accuracy and complexity of L2 referential marking (e.g., Nakahama, 2011; Robinson, 1995). Both Robinson (1995) and Nakahama (2011) found that a more complex task that involves telling a story in the setting of *there* and *then* (T/T) triggers more complex and accurate NP markings (the definite article in Robinson's L2 English and definite and indefinite particles in Nakahama's L2 Japanese) than in the setting of here and now (H/N). Telling a story while looking at picture prompts would be considered a H/N setting (e.g., Chaudron & Parker, 1990; Nakahama, 2009) and telling a story after watching a film would be considered as T/T setting (e.g., Clancy, 1980; Jarvis, 2002; Ryan, 2015). Thus, I believe examining referent introduction and tracking by Japanese learners of English in the written mode in a T/T setting will verify not only CLI (e.g., Jarvis, 2002) but also mode and complexity factors (i.e., Chaudron & Parker, 1990).

The present study therefore addresses the following research questions:

1. Will there be different ways in which discourse contexts (new, known, current) and positions (topic comment) are marked in the introduction and tracking of a protagonist in L2 English narratives across proficiency levels?
2. Will CLI from L1 Japanese be evident in the markings of the protagonist in L2 English written narratives?

Method

Participants

The participants of the study were 37 low-intermediate level learners, 23 mid-intermediate level, and 23 advanced level Japanese learners of English as well as L1 Japanese data from 21 native speakers. These were students at major universities in Japan, and thus older than Jarvis' adolescent group. The levels of English proficiency were decided based on their TOEFL level: up to 470 for low intermediate, 471–510 as mid-intermediate, and 511–600 as advanced. Since the current study closely followed Jarvis (2002) elicitation methods and coding procedures, Jarvis' NS English findings will be used for comparison.

Procedure

The participants watched the segment of the Charlie Chaplin film *Modern Times* called 'Alone and Hungry'. In this segment, an impoverished young woman attempts to steal a loaf of bread, is arrested, escapes, and is eventually befriended by Chaplin, who had attempted to take the blame for the theft. This segment lasts a little over eight minutes, and following Jarvis' procedure, the participants wrote narratives based on the first five minutes, then took a short break before watching and then writing about the remaining three minutes. They could not refer to a dictionary.

Analysis

The coding protocol also followed Jarvis (2002), with coding applied only to the female protagonist in two discourse positions (Topic/Comment) within three discourse contexts (New, Known, and Current). These are illustrated as follows with examples from Jarvis (2002, p. 388), with referents other than the female protagonist highlighted for illustrative purposes.

1. New referent as/within topic (e.g., *A woman stole a loaf of bread.*);
2. New referent as/within comment (e.g., *A woman stole a loaf of bread.*);
3. Continuous referent as/within topic (e.g., *A woman stole a loaf of bread. Then she accidentally dropped it.*);
4. Continuous referent as/within comment (e.g., *A woman stole a loaf of bread. Then she accidentally dropped it.*);
5. Reintroduced referent as/within topic (e.g., *A man picked up the bread and said that he took it, but an eyewitness came and explained what really happened. Eventually, the woman was arrested and taken to jail.*);
6. Reintroduced referent as/within comment (e.g., *A man picked up the bread and said that he took it, but an eyewitness came and explained what really happened. Eventually, the woman was arrested and taken to jail. The man gave the bread back to the baker, but later he was arrested, too.*)

Underlining in 1 and 2 refers to New Topic (NT) and New Comment (NC), respectively, while 3 and 4 represents the contexts of Current Topic (CT), and Current-Comment (CC), and 5 and 6 Known Topic (KT) and Known Comment (KC), respectively. Known contexts refer to circumstances in which the referent had been previously introduced into discourse, but its central status had then been taken by another referent, before being reestablished in on-going focus. Thus, when the referent is reintroduced into discourse after losing its focal point in discourse, the context is marked either KT or KC, depending on the position of the sentence.

If there was no article or other type of marking, these were coded as bare nouns, meaning preposition omission (shown as Ø in Table 4.2). In addition, following Jarvis' design, I counted marked syntactic structures (MSS) in all six contexts. These were cleft structures, overt nouns, pre- or post-modification, right or left dislocation, fronting, inversion and existential structures. It should be noted

Table 4.2 Low-intermediate level learner results in L2 English

	Ø (bare noun)	a (an)	the	Pronoun	Def. Det.	Quant.	Prop. N	Total	Syn.
NT	6 (2)	74 (27)	17 (6)	–	–	3 (1)	–	100 (35)	8
NC	–	100 (2)	–	–	–	–	–	100 (2)	1
KT	3 (4)	6 (8)	33 (41)	56 (70)	2 (2)	–	–	100 (125)	15
KC	6 (4)	6 (4)	20 (13)	63 (41)	5 (3)	–	–	100 (65)	2
CT	2 (7)	6 (22)	13 (51)	79 (299)	0 (1)	–	–	100 (380)	5
CC	2 (5)	5 (10)	13 (29)	79 (173)	1 (1)	–	–	100 (218)	2

NT = new topic; NC = new comment; KT = known topic; KC = known comment; CT = current topic; CC = current comment. Shown in percentage first, with raw frequencies in brackets that, as in Jarvis (2002), the other protagonist (played by Charlie Chaplin) was not included for analysis as many participants simply refer to him by name.

Results

Results are presented below by proficiency level for how the female protagonist was introduced into the discourse and subsequently maintained, as well as the linguistic forms that modified the referent (syntax). Table 4.2 presents the results of the learners at the lowest proficiency level.

L2 English narratives: low-intermediate level learners of English

As Table 4.2 shows, learners seemed to differentiate between the three contexts, that is, New, Known, and Current contexts. They used indefinite articles to introduce the main female character (74% in the topic position and 100% in the comment position), whereas the majority of marking in the Known context were done with pronouns (topic position = 56%, comment position = 63%). In Jarvis' (2002) L1 English data, in the Known context, much higher use of definiteness marking (*the* + N) was found compared to pronouns. Thus, it can be said that the current L2 speakers at the lowest level diverged from Jarvis' NS narratives by overproducing pronouns where definiteness marking should be expected. In the contexts of highest topic continuity (CT and CC), 79% of references made in both topic and comment positions were marked with pronouns, compared to around 70% in Jarvis' L1 English narratives. This indicates that the use of pronouns seems to have reached a target-like level at the lowest proficiency.

Twenty-two occurrences of article drop were observed irrespective of context or discourse positions, though the overall proportion was not large. This was not found in Jarvis' (2002) L1 English narratives except for on a very few occasions, but was ubiquitous in the Finnish L2 English narratives, where it was attributed to L1 transfer as Finnish lacks a prepositional marking system. Recall that Finnish uses a postpositional marking system similar to Japanese; however, unlike Jarvis' Finnish participants, the present Japanese learners displayed relatively few instances of article drop.

L2 English narratives: high-intermediate level learners of English

Table 4.3 illustrates how the female protagonist is marked in L2 English in each context at the mid-proficiency level.

By the high-intermediate level, the usage of the definite marker 'the' in NT contexts had decreased from 17% to 4%. Introduction of the character was only found in topic position at this proficiency level. The great majority of referent introductions was with an indefinite marker, which appears target-like. Article drop had reduced from 22 occurrences at the lowest proficiency level to only five occurrences here. Also reduced was overuse of pronouns. In particular, in the

Table 4.3 High-intermediate level learner results in L2 English

	Ø (bare noun)	a (an)	the	Pronoun	Def. Det.	Quant.	Prop. N	Total	Syn.
NT	0 (0)	91 (21)	4 (1)	–	–	4 (1)	–	100 (23)	6
NC	–	–	–	–	–	–	–	100 (0)	0
KT	1 (1)	4 (3)	44 (34)	49 (38)	2 (1)	–	1 (1)	100 (77)	9
KC	–	2 (1)	54 (33)	38 (23)	2 (1)	–	5 (3)	100 (61)	12
CT	2 (4)	1 (2)	21 (52)	72 (178)	0 (1)	–	4 (9)	100 (246)	5
CC	–	1 (2)	18 (31)	80 (137)	1 (2)	–	–	100 (172)	3

Shown in percentage first, with raw frequencies in brackets

comment position for Known contexts, definite article use increased from 20% to 54%, while pronoun use decreased from 63% to 38%, while a smaller effect was also detected in topic position for Known contexts. Again, target-like use of pronouns in the highest topic continuity contexts was noted.

L2 English narratives: advanced level learners of English

Table 4.4 presents data for the advanced learners. Notably, article drop disappears at this level with only one occurrence found in the CT context. Marking of referent introductions was achieved with indefinite marking, as expected from previous studies (e.g., Chaudron & Parker, 1990; Jarvis, 2002), and thus appropriate use seemed to have been acquired by this proficiency level.

In the Known context and the Current context, regardless of discourse positions, definite markers and pronouns, respectively, account for the majority of forms used, except for slightly higher use of pronouns than definite articles in KC contexts. In other words, contextual overuse of pronouns had disappeared by the advanced level. These results match the L1 findings from Jarvis (2002) and suggest the present L2 learners demonstrated target-like behaviour of referent

Table 4.4 Advanced level learner results in L2 English

	Ø (bare noun)	a (an)	the	Pronoun	Def. Det.	Quant.	Prop. N	Total	Syn.
NT	–	87 (20)	4 (1)	–	–	9 (2)	–	100 (23)	15
NC	–	–	–	100 (1)	–	–	–	100 (1)	1
KT	–	2 (3)	61 (65)	35 (37)	1 (1)	–	1 (1)	100 (107)	8
KC	–	3 (2)	42 (25)	45 (27)	5 (3)	–	5 (3)	100 (60)	7
CT	0 (1)	0 (1)	24 (75)	74 (234)	0 (1)	–	2 (7)	100 (125)	15
CC	–	–	41 (19)	78 (173)	0 (1)	0 (1)	2 (5)	100 (221)	2

Shown in percentage first, followed with raw frequencies in brackets tracking in all six discourse contexts and positions by the time they had reached an advanced level.

Summarising how learners at all proficiency levels referred to the female protagonist in different contexts, it can be said that appropriate use of markings for introductions and maintenance seemed to develop with proficiency. Specifically, while there was a mixture of indefinite and definite markings in referent introduction, especially in discourse topic position at the lowest level, inappropriate definiteness marking decreased with rising proficiency. Overuse of pronouns in the Known context (in place of 'the') persisted until the mid-proficiency level, with the frequency of definite article use target-like only at the advanced level, mainly in the topic position. This under-explicit marking of referents exhibited as overuse of pronouns at the low proficiency level is similar to the overuse of zero anaphora reported in previous studies (e.g., Klein & Perdue, 1992). However, adequate use of pronouns at higher proficiency levels was not anticipated based on other previous findings (e.g., Crosthwaite, 2014b); Ryan, 2015; Tomlin, 1990), which found that learners tend to rely on the use of lexical noun phrases rather than pronouns.

Another noticeable tendency was the L2 use of quantifiers for marking referent introductions, although the number of occurrences were small (3%, 4%, 9% in Low, Mid, Adv, respectively). Excerpt 1 depicts one such example in the NT context by an advanced level speaker.

(1): Use of quantifier in NT (Advanced level, Sp. 4)
One girl was very starving with walking in the street.

Although it is not ungrammatical to choose a quantifier, the indefinite marker 'a' would suffice, and the use of 'one' makes this sentence pragmatically somewhat eccentric. Quantifier use in the L1 Japanese narratives and possible CLI will be explored in the following section.

Regarding how learners might differentiate referring to the protagonist in the topic and the comment positions, the following propensity is worth noting. Across all proficiency levels, the female protagonist was introduced in the topic position (with the exception of three occurrences shown in the comment position), whereas topic maintenance (referred to in the Known and Current contexts) was done in both positions. In other words, it seems that the L2 learners differentiate topic and comment in referent introductions but not maintenance. This replicates Jarvis' (2002) findings for L1 English, L1 Finnish and their L2 English narratives. We now explore whether the same tendency can be found in Japanese L1 narratives.

L1 Japanese narratives

Table 4.5 shows how the referent was prepositionally marked, such as with a 'bare noun' (without any preposition) and with a quantifier (e.g., one woman). As expected, no article (definite or indefinite) was used in L1 Japanese, as

Table 4.5 Results in L1 Japanese

	Ø (bare noun)	a(an)	the	Pronoun	Def. Det.	Quant.	Prop. N	Total	Syn.
NT	80 (16)	0	0	0	0	20 (4)	0	100 (20)	8
NC	100 (1)	0	0	0	0	0 (0)	0	100 (1)	1
KT	64 (77)	0	0	3 (3)	1 (1)	33 (39)	0	100 (120)	21
KC	31 (67)	0	0	17 (8)	7 (3)	9 (4)	0	100 (46)	4
CT	55 (78)	0	0	3 (5)	0	42 (60)	0	100 (143)	30
CC	70 (60)	0	0	10 (9)	9 (8)	10 (9)	0	100 (86)	10

Shown in percentage first, followed by raw frequencies in brackets

postpositional particles mark noun phrases in Japanese. Bare nouns account for most cases, with quantifiers also being common. Though omitted from Table 4.5, definiteness and indefiniteness were marked with postpositional particles, with the results mostly replicating my previous studies of oral storytelling (e.g., Nakahama, 2003, 2009): referent introductions marked by NP + *ga* and referents in Known and Current contexts were mainly marked with NP + *wa*. While zero anaphora was mainly used in the Current context (i.e., highest topic continuity), it was also observed in the Known context. As expected, zero anaphora was not used when referring to the protagonist for the first time.

A noteworthy finding from L1 Japanese narratives was the use of pronouns, which were only found in not-new-contexts, and with a higher percentage of use in comment positions of both Known and Current contexts (KT 3%, KC 17%, CT 3%, KC 10%). The use of Japanese pronouns was rather surprising, as they are seldom reported. For instance, Clancy (1980) reports no uses of the third-person pronouns *kare* (he), *kanojo* (she), or *karera* (they) in retellings of the Pear Story. The following excerpts will closely examine the use of *kanojo* in both topic and comment positions.

(2): Use of *kanojo* in CT (Sp. 19)
   *Chappurin wa 'ie wa doko desu ka?' to kiku to, **kanojo** wa 'doko ni mo nai to kotaeru'.*
   Chaplin TOP 'house TOP where COP Q?' P ask if she TOP 'where P P NEG P answers'
   When Chaplin asks 'Where is your home?', she answers 'Nowhere.'

(3): Use of *kanojo* in CC (Sp. 15)
   *Namida suru **kanojo** ni Chappurin wa hankachi o sashidashi nagusameta.*
   Tears do woman to Chaplin TOP handkerchief OBJ gave and comforted
   (Lit.) Chaplin gave handkerchief and comforted the woman who cried.

(4): Use of *kanojo* in CC (Sp. 15)
   *Chappurin wa shiawasena seikatu o musooshi sore o **kanojo** ni katatte kikaseru noda ga*

Chaplin TOP happy life OBJ dream that OBJ woman OBJ talk made listen but
Chaplin dreamed a happy life, and talked to the woman about it but

(5): Use of *kanojo* in CC (Sp. 10)

*Keisatu wa Chaplin to **kanojo** o tsukamae ni kita wake dewanaku tanni tootta dake noyoo deatta ga...*
Police TOP Chaplin and her OBJ catch to came for NEG just passed only seemed but...
(Lit.) It was not such that they came to catch her and Chaplin, but rather passed through

Importantly, *kanojo* is not only used as a pronoun in Japanese, but has a more common use denoting 'girlfriend'. In fact, except for one speaker who used *kanojo* throughout the narrative, most of the occurrences in the L1 data were after Chaplin and the female protagonist established caring feelings towards each other. Excerpt 2 depicts the scene where Chaplin and the female protagonist escaped from custody together and sat down to make peaceful conversation. By that scene, they had established their liking for each other, and this delineates when the woman becomes Chaplin's love interest. The same interpretation also seems natural for Excerpts 3 and 4 where *kanojo* was used in the comment position. Prior to Excerpt 3, the writer used 'woman' to reintroduce the protagonist into discourse, then treated her as Chaplin's love interest by using 'kanojo' as seen in Excerpt 3. The same interpretation might not be so compelling in Excerpt 5, and that might be explainable by the subject (topic) of the sentence being the police, and thus the writer delineates the happening somewhat more objectively.

Besides bare nouns, quantifiers were often found especially in the Known and the Current contexts, particularly in topic position (KT 33%, KC 9%, CT 42%, CC 10%). Recall that there were few instances of quantifiers in the L2 English data (3%, 4%, 9% of referent introductions in Low, Mid, and Adv levels, respectively). In terms of Japanese L1 narratives, analysis showed that most were used to describe Chaplin and the female protagonist together, using *futari*, meaning *two* in Japanese. Typical use is illustrated in Excerpts 6 and 7:

(6): Use of quantifier, *futari* (KT context, Sp. 3)
Futari *wa tanoshii seikatsu o soozooshiteita.*
Two people TOP happy life OBJ imagine-ing-past
The two (Chaplin and the female protagonist) were imagining happy life together.

(7): Use of Quantifier, *futari* (CT context, Sp. 12)
Futari *wa tanoshisoo ni hanashiteiru*
Two people TOP happily speak-gerund
The two (Chaplin and the female protagonist) were happily talking

Many instances of *futari* were marked with the Japanese topic marker *wa*, since the reader would know who these two people were and thus its use was in the

Known or the Current context. The majority of quantifiers were in fact in those two contexts (43 times in Known contexts and 69 times in Current contexts).

However, Table 4.5 also shows four instances of quantifiers for NT. These were all uses of '*hitori*' (one) to introduce the woman, as illustrated in Excerpts 7 and 8.

(8): Use of quantifier '*hitori*' in NT in L1 Japanese. (Sp. 11)
   Hitori *no mazushii onna no ko ga pan o nusunde toosoo*
   One POS poor female P child NOM bread OBJ steal and ran
   One poor girl stole a loaf of bread and ran
(9): Use of quantifier '*hitori*' in NT in L1 Japanese. (Sp. 19)
   Hitori *no kireina josei wa monohoshisa ni pan o nusunde toosoosuru mo...*
   One POS beautiful woman TOP wanting for bread OBJ steal and ran but...
   Wanting (to eat) bread, one beautiful woman stole a bread and ran but...

Excerpts 8 and 9 above show how the writers used a quantifier 'one' with descriptions of the woman as 'poor' and 'beautiful'. Japanese does not express plurality with the use of a bound morpheme (with occasional exceptions using '*tachi*' attached to animate nouns). Use of the quantifier, as here, ensures the interpretation of there being only one character. As discussed earlier, once the female protagonist was introduced, she was marked with a bare noun (no article or quantifier) except where referred to with Chaplin as '*futari*' (two people; e.g., Excerpts 6 and 7).

Discussion

The comparison of L2 English and L1 Japanese narratives has revealed some evidence of CLI, but this is not as strikingly obvious as in Jarvis' (2002) CLI from L1 Finnish to L2 English. This section first discusses possible positive and negative transfer from L1 Japanese, and then compares similarities and differences between the results in the two studies. I will then discuss possible explanations in terms of language experiences, cognitive maturity, and classroom instructions.

Cross-linguistic influence from L1 Japanese to L2 English

CLI was revealed through close examination of how the female protagonist was introduced and maintained in the discourse throughout L1 Japanese and L2 English narratives. Firstly, the concept of referent quantification, characteristic of how the story is written in Japanese, might have influenced the writing of the story in L2 English. Jarvis' (2002) Finnish L1 and L2 English narratives did reveal some use of quantifiers mainly in NT contexts, although this was not discussed as possible CLI. However, there is a relevant contrast in that Jarvis' L1 English and L1 Swedish narratives showed no quantifier use and, correspondingly, the Swedes' L2 English narratives contained only three occurrences. This contrasts markedly with Jarvis' findings for the Finnish participants and for the present findings relating to Japanese. In short, the results appear to show evidence of CLI from L1 Finnish and L1 Japanese conceptual marking of number to person reference in L2 English.

A second noticeable tendency was the successful use of pronouns. As discussed in previous literature (e.g., Nakahama, 2009, Polio, 1995, Ryan, 2015), learners tend to overgeneralise the use of full NPs in contexts with the highest topic continuity (e.g., zero anaphora in Japanese and pronoun in English). Researchers explicate such a tendency as CLI (Kang, 2004; Nakahama, 2011) or as a universal developmental tendency (Ryan, 2015). While the use of pronouns was expected to be difficult to perform, the Japanese EFL learners in the current study were able to produce pronouns irrespective of proficiency level. They did overgeneralise the use of pronouns in place of definite articles in the context of KT and KC at the lowest proficiency level, but the use of pronouns reached target-like performance at the high-intermediate level proficiency. This effectual use of pronouns replicates the findings of Chaudron and Parker (1990), in that pronouns were successfully used in the obligatorily appropriate context regardless of proficiency level.

This successful performance of pronouns might be explained by Eckman's (1985) Markedness Differential Hypothesis (MDH), which claims that the areas of the target language that are most difficult to learn are those that are different from the L1, while also being more marked than in the L1. Pronouns in English might be considered unmarked for L1 Japanese speakers, since Japanese also allows pronouns but with a more restrictive distribution than in English. Specifically, the singular female pronoun, *kanojo*, can connote girlfriend, and thus the semantic context is more involved and more marked than the English equivalent. Furthermore, we might take into consideration Stockwell et al.'s (1965) complex prescription in determining difficulty of acquisition when comparing the learners' L1 and L2. They argue that if the learners' L1 has more than one meaning attaching to the word, and the L2 has a single meaning attaching to it, then the acquisition of the item would be almost as easy as where both languages share a single meaning attached to the word.

Last but not least, the current study presented a relative degree of success for L2 learners for most of the prepositional markings, including the articles. Recall that difficulty in acquiring articles partially derives from not having the same prepositional system in the L1 (e.g., Master, 1987) and that learners continue to struggle with article use even at the higher proficiency levels (e.g., Butler, 2002; Liu & Gleason, 2002). Further, since countability is the most persistent problem for accurate article use for L2 speakers whose L1s do not have an article system (Master, 1987), difficulties could be predicted since Japanese does not customarily have plural markings (Butler, 2002). However, the current study only examined how the female protagonist was marked in the narratives, and it would be clear to participants that she is a countable entity. Furthermore, except for the beginning scene, where the female character gets introduced into the movie, there were no other major female characters in the segment. Even in the beginning of the film, although another woman plays some important role in the scene, she was introduced into the act after the main protagonist had been introduced and established. Consequently, no complication was involved as to how to refer to the protagonist, and this might have contributed to the story-retelling being reasonably successful in the current study.

Comparison of the current results with *Chaudron and Parker (1990)* and *Jarvis (2002)*

It was rather unanticipated to see how the L1 postpositional marking system of NPs did not affect the way participants marked the protagonist in L2 English narratives. In contrast, in Jarvis' (2002) findings for Finnish speakers, article omission in L2 English was omnipresent irrespective of discoursal contexts or positions across the age groups. Jarvis attributed this to CLI from L1 Finnish, as Finnish does not take prepositional marking of noun reference. Many instances of article omission were also reported across all contexts in Chaudron and Parker's (1990) L2 picture description task narratives. This included New contexts, where more marking is expected. Using the same principle, we would expect similar results in the current study, as Japanese does not mark the information status of NPs prepositionally either. However, as shown in the results, only lower level learners omitted articles (and did so infrequently), irrespective of contexts or positions in discourse, and such a tendency declined with proficiency level. It appears that the conception of prepositional marking was nearly acquired by even the low proficiency learners and thus not many article omissions were found. In addition, greater exposure to the language over time likely facilitated appropriate referent marking and thus generated fewer occurrences of article omissions in discourse.

Given the results of the current study being incongruent with Jarvis (2002) and Chaudron and Parker (1990), I make the following argument. The divergence from Jarvis could have been caused by the different age of the participants (K-12 level learners in Jarvis' study versus adult learners in the present study) and proficiency level (at least two years of English language study versus at least six years). In addition, it is fair to assume that the present participants would have had stronger analytical abilities due to their greater maturity and because they were recruited from universities with highly competitive entry criteria. Further, different instructions and awareness of the function of articles in discourse might have contributed to the differing results in these studies. Japanese learners of EFL who participated in the present study received grammar instruction at university, and they had explicit instruction on article use in junior high school; the Finnish learners of English in Jarvis' study did not receive such grammar-focused instruction. Therefore, differences in length and instruction type as well as cognitive maturity might have helped the Japanese EFL learners to produce appropriate prepositional marking in referring to the protagonist (Jarvis, Personal Communication, April 2010).

The reason for more successful NP marking in the current study as compared with Chaudron and Parker (1990) could also be explained by task complexity. Robinson (1995) showed that more complex tasks (retelling of a story without looking at the pictures) triggered more accurate NP markings than seen for picture description narratives, and equivalent results were found in Nakahama

Table 4.6 Marked syntactic structures (MSS)

	Cleft	Overt	Pre-mod.	Post-mod.	Existential	Left disloc.	Inversion	Total
Low	4	1		27	1	0	0	33
Mid	9	6		15	1	0	1	32
High	5	2		21	3	3	2	36
JNS	3	0	66		2	1	1	73

(2011) in that her T/T story-retelling setting generated more accurate NP markings than a H/N setting. Since the present study utilised a film retelling task (T/T setting) and Chaudron and Parker (1990) a H/N setting storytelling, the present task could have facilitated more accurate use of definite and indefinite articles. Further, the writing mode in my study may have facilitated correct NP marking, as more within-task planning and reflection is generally involved in writing than speaking.

Although the main purpose of the study was to investigate how L2 learners mark the female protagonist in topic introduction and its maintenance within the written discourse, I examined the data supplementarily with marked syntactic structures (MSS) following Chaudron and Parker (1990) and Jarvis (2002). These are summarised in Table 4.6 across proficiency levels and languages (English and Japanese).

In Jarvis' (2002) study, the forms most frequently produced by Finnish L2 English speakers were existential sentences in new contexts and post-modification in not-new contexts. His Finnish L1 speakers' narratives involved mainly post-modification with a few exceptions in the form of left dislocation. Jarvis' English L1 narratives displayed similar patterns to L2 English narratives in that all of the MSS used in NT contexts were existential constructions and, with the exception of determiners in KT contexts, every other NP that has MSS were done with post-modifications.

In the current study, on the other hand, the majority of MSS was found to be pre-modifications for L1 Japanese and post-modifications for L2 English narratives. Only five occurrences of existential constructions were identified in the L2 narratives across proficiency levels, and only two in Japanese L1 narratives. These results also suggest a strong tendency for CLI from L1 Japanese. Similarly, only a very few instances of existential structure were found in Chaudron and Parker's (1990) L2 English narratives.

Conclusion

This study considered whether there are differing ways in which discourse contexts (New, Known, Current) and discourse positions (topic, comments) are marked when introducing and tracking a protagonist in L2 English narratives across proficiency levels. The study also asked whether CLI from Japanese will be evident in marking of the protagonist in L2 English narratives. The results revealed that the L2 learners were generally able to differentiate which forms were to be used depending on each context, and did not seem to differentiate topic and comment positions, except in the New context. Specifically, while they referred to the female protagonist in both topic and comment positions in the Known and the Current contexts, referent introductions were mainly restricted to the topic position. Developmental patterns were found in the marking of the protagonist in that while the lowest level learners slightly overgeneralised the use of definite articles in incongruous contexts (i.e., New and Current contexts), appropriate form-function mapping increased with proficiency. However, use of pronouns seems already appropriate even at the lowest level of proficiency, which was not expected from previous literature.

I identified two possible reasons for this successful performance. First, the findings resonate with Stockwell et al.'s (1965) difficulty scale of acquisition, since the relevant pronoun in Japanese (*kanojo*) has more than two meanings, in contrast to the single meaning of 'she' in English; thus, 'coalescence' on the difficulty scale applies in this case, suggesting relatively easy acquisition for Japanese speakers. The findings also resonate with Eckman's (1985) MDH: since pronouns have a more restricted distribution in Japanese than English, and are therefore more marked, their use in English should be unproblematic for Japanese speakers.

Regarding CLI, some elements of referent marking in Japanese appeared to transfer to L2 English. Specifically, quantification in L1 Japanese seems to have adversely influenced its use in L2 English narratives, though the occurrences were few. CLI was evidenced in terms of MSS in L1 Japanese and L2 English. Pre-modification was the major type of MSS in the former, whereas post-modification was the typical MSS in the latter. Unlike Jarvis' (2002) L1 English and L2 English narratives by Finns, existential structures were very rare in my L1 Japanese and L2 English data. What was most striking in the current study was infrequent use of bare nouns (article omission). There were some occurrences at the lowest proficiency level, but the frequency was much lower than in other relevant studies such as Chaudron and Parker (1990) and Jarvis (2002). This could be accounted for by (1) the high complexity of the task possibly promoting accurate use of NP markings, (2) the writing mode providing the learners opportunities to scrutinise their writing more carefully, or (3) the result of receiving more effective training in the relevant aspects of grammar.

These conclusions do, however, need to be considered in light of the limitations of the study, which involved baseline comparisons with Jarvis' (2002) L1 English narrative data. Jarvis' study collected data from 5th to 9th graders, while the present study involved young adults, meaning that age is a potential confounding factor in these comparisons. Thus, collecting L2 learner narratives from L1 Japanese speakers at the same grade levels as Jarvis' study is recommended (Nakahama and Okabe, in progress) to locate the cause of the differing results.

References

Andersen, R. (1977). The impoverished state of cross-sectional morpheme acquisition/accuracy methodology. *Proceedings of the Los Angeles second language research forum* (pp. 308–319). Los Angeles, CA: Department of English, UCLA.

Bates, E. A., & MacWhinney, B. (1989). Functionalism and the competition model. In B. MacWhinney & E. A. Bates (Eds.), *The cross-linguistic study of sentence processing* (pp. 3–73). New York, NY: Cambridge University Press.

Butler, G. Y. (2002). Second language learners' theories on the use of English articles. An analysis of the metalinguistic knowledge used by Japanese students in acquiring the English article system. *Studies in Second Language Acquisition*, 24(3), 451–480. doi:10.1017/S0272263102003042

Chafe, W., & Danielewicz, J. (1987). Properties of spoken and written language. In R. Horowitz & S. J. Samuels (Eds.), *Comprehending oral and written language* (pp. 83–113). San Diego, CA: Academic Press.

Chaudron, C., & Parker, K. (1990). Discourse markedness and structural markedness: The acquisition of English noun phrases. *Studies in Second Language Acquisition*, 12(1), 43–64. doi:10.1017/S0272263100008731

Clancy, P. (1980). Referential choice in English and Japanese narrative discourse. In W. L. Chafe (Ed.), *The pear stories: Cognitive, cultural, and linguistic aspects of narrative production* (pp. 127–202). Norwood, NJ: Ablex.

Clancy, P. (1985). The acquisition of Japanese. In D. I. Slobin (Ed.), *The crosslinguistic study of language acquisition*, Vol. 1 (pp. 373–524). Hillsdale, NJ: Lawrence Erlbaum. doi:10.4324/9781315802541-5

Crosthwaite, P. (2014a). Definite discourse-new reference in L1 and L2: A study of bridging in Mandarin, Korean, and English. *Language Learning*, 64(3), 456–492. doi:10.1111/lang.12062

Crosthwaite, P. (2014b). *Differences between the coherence of Mandarin and Korean L2 English learner production and English native speakers: An empirical study* (Doctoral thesis). University of Cambridge, Cambridge, UK.

Doi, T., & Yoshioka, K. (1990). Speech processing constraints on the acquisition of Japanese particles: Applying the Pienemann-Johnson model to Japanese as a second language. *Proceedings of the 1st conference on second language acquisition and teaching*, (pp. 23–33). Niigata, Japan: International University of Japan.

Drieman, G. H. J. (1962). Differences between written and spoken language. *Acta Psychologica*, 20, 36–57. doi:10.1016/0001-6918(62)90009-4

Eckman, F. (1985). Some theoretical and pedagogical implications of the markedness differential hypothesis. *Studies in Second Language Acquisition*, 7(3), 289–307. doi:10.1017/S0272263100005544

Givón, T. (1978). Definiteness and referentiality. In J. Greenberg (Ed.), *Universals of human language: Vol. 4 Syntax*. Stanford, CA: Stanford University Press.

Givón, T. (1979). *On understanding grammar*. New York, NY: Academic Press. doi:10.1016/c2013-0-10728-3

Givón, T. (Ed.). (1983). *Topic continuity in discourse: A quantitative cross-language study*. Amsterdam, the Netherlands: John Benjamins. doi:10.1075/tsl.3.01giv

Halliday, M. A. K. (1985). *An introduction to functional grammar*. London, UK: Edward Arnold. doi:10.4324/9780203783771

Huebner, T. (1983). *A longitudinal analysis of the acquisition of English*. Ann Arbor, MI: Karoma. doi:10.2307/413839

Jarvis, S. (2002). Topic continuity in L2 English article use. *Studies in Second Language Acquisition*, 24(3), 387–418. doi:10.1017/S0272263102003029

Kang, J. Y. (2004). Telling a coherent story in a foreign language: Analysis of Korean EFL learners' referential strategies in oral narrative discourse. *Journal of Pragmatics*, 36, 1975–1990. doi:10.1016/j.pragma.2004.03.007

Klein, W., & Perdue, C. (1992). *Utterance structure: Developing grammars again*. Amsterdam, the Netherlands: John Benjamins. doi:10.1075/sibil.5

Klein, W., & Perdue, C. (1997). The Basic Variety (or: Couldn't natural languages be much simpler?). *Second Language Research*, 13(4), 301–347. doi:https://doi.org/10.1191/026765897666879396

Liu, D., & Gleason, J. L. (2002). Acquisition of the article THE by nonnative speaker of English. An analysis of four nongeneric uses. *Studies in Second Language Acquisition*, 24(1), 1–26. doi:10.1017/S0272263102001018

Master, P. (1987). *A cross-linguistic interlanguage analysis of the acquisition of the English article system*. (Doctoral dissertation, University of California, Los Angeles, CA). Retrieved from http://www.sjsu.edu/faculty/pmaster/Master%20Dissertation.pdf

Master, P. (1997). The English article system. Acquisition, function, and pedagogy. *System*, 25(2), 215–232. doi:10.1016/S0346-251X(97)00010-9

Muñoz, C. (1995). Markedness and the acquisition of referential forms. The case of zero anaphora. *Studies in Second Language Acquisition*, 17(4), 517–527. doi:10.1017/S0272263100014431

Nakahama, Y. (2003). Development of referent management in L2 Japanese: A film retelling task. *Studies in Language and Culture*, 25(1), 127–146.

Nakahama, Y. (2009). Cross-linguistic influence on referent introduction and tracking in Japanese as a second language. *Modern Language Journal*, 93(2), 241–260. doi:10.1111/j.1540-4781.2009.00859.x

Nakahama, Y. (2011). *Referent markings in L2 narratives: Effects of task complexity, learners' L1 and proficiency level*. Tokyo, Japan: Hituzi Shobo.

Nakahama, Y., & Kurihara, Y. (2007). Viewpoint setting in L1 and L2 Japanese narratives. In H. Sirai, et al. (Eds.), *Studies in language sciences*, 6 (pp. 179–194). Tokyo, Japan: Kurosio.

Polio, C. (1995). Acquiring nothing? The use of zero pronouns by nonnative speakers of Chinese and the implications for the acquisition of nominal reference. *Studies in Second Language Acquisition*, 17(3), 353–377. doi:10.1017/S0272263100014248

Robinson, P. (1995). Task complexity and second language narrative discourse. *Language Learning*, 45(1), 99–140. doi:10.1111/j.1467-1770.1995.tb00964.x

Ryan, J. (2015). Overexplicit referent tracking in L2 English: Strategy, avoidance, or myth? *Language Learning*, 65(4), 824–859. doi:10.1111/lang.12139

Sakamoto, T. (1993). On acquisition order: Japanese particles WA and GA. *Proceedings of the 3rd conference on second language acquisition and teaching* (pp. 105–122). Nagata, Japan: International University of Japan.

Stockwell, R., Bowen, J. D., & Martin, J. (1965). *The grammatical structures of English and Spanish*. Chicago, IL: University of Chicago Press.

Takeuchi, M. (2014). *Subject referential expressions and encoding of referential status in L2 narrative discourse by L1 English learners of Japanese* (Unpublished doctoral dissertation). Indiana University, Bloomington, IN.

Tomlin, R. (1990). Functionalism in second language acquisition. *Studies in Second Language Acquisition*, 12(2), 155–157. doi:10.1017/S0272263100009062

Toyama, C. (2005). Acquisition of 'wa', 'ga' and no particle: Pragmatic and syntactic operation. *Kanda Gaigo University Journal, 17*, 211–228.

Tōyama, C. (2013). Nihongo gakushūsha no bogo ga shugo-meishiku no dōnyū ni ataeru eikyō: Sakubun ni okeru WA to GA no shiyō kara [The influence of Japanese leaners' first language for introductions of subjects: Use of *wa* and *ga* in compositions]. *Kotoba to Sono Hirogari, 5*, 213–238.

5 Referential movement in L2 vs. Heritage Korean
A learner corpus study

Peter Crosthwaite and Min Jung Jee

Introduction

So far, the chapters in this volume have involved acquisition of 'second' languages by learners for whom the target language is learned as a 'foreign' language, or at least what could be termed an 'additional' language outside of the one spoken at home. However, a rise in the global movement of people as well as complex societal changes for minority language groups have resulted in an increasingly multicultural – and multilingual – language learning environment in many countries. Notably, *heritage* language learning, where learners acquire a minority language (the language typically spoken at home) together with the majority language (typically English) 'simultaneously since birth or sequentially, as a second language' (Montrul, 2018, p. 530), is a (relatively) new area of research in second-language studies (Brinton, Kagan, & Bauckus, 2017). However, it is a movement that has gained much attention in the past decade, covering diverse topics including heritage learner identity (e.g. Leeman, 2015), bilingual development (e.g. Montrul, 2015), agency and motivation (e.g. Deters, Gao, Miller, & Vitanova, 2015), and learners' anxiety towards learning the heritage language (Jee, 2016).

At the linguistic level, studies featuring the acquisition of heritage languages have focused on the lexicon, inflectional morphology, syntax, and phonetics/phonology (Montrul, 2015). Regarding reference, a number of studies have investigated the distribution of null/overt reference for heritage speakers of Spanish (e.g. Silva-Corvalán, 2014; Montrul, 2018), although fewer studies have looked at acquisition of L2 reference systems in a broader sense. In addition, sample sizes for such studies are typically small, with few attempting a corpus-based approach to heritage language production, although interest in this area is also quickly developing as the availability of principled heritage language corpora increases (e.g. Zhang & Tao, 2018; Xiao-Desai & Wong, 2017). This chapter seeks to bring together the fields of L2 reference, heritage language learning, and corpus linguistics, in a corpus-based investigation of referential movement in the writing of foreign L2 vs. heritage learners of Korean.

Heritage language learning

Heritage language speakers (henceforth HLS) are 'the children of immigrants born in the host country or immigrant children who arrived in the host country some time in childhood (Montrul, 2012, p. 2)'. Based on prior studies, HLS often show limited knowledge of their heritage language compared with monolingual native speakers (e.g. Kondo-Brown, 2006; Montrul, 2015) but often demonstrate better knowledge of the heritage language than foreign or second-language learners within certain linguistic domains (e.g. Lee, Moon, & Long, 2009; Lee & Zaslansky, 2015). For example, regarding morphology and vocabulary, HLS normally outperformed L2 learners in oral production tasks and in tests with minimal or non-metalinguistic knowledge (e.g. Bowles, 2011; Montrul, Foote & Perpiñán, 2008). Phonology or pronunciation is another area where HLS are claimed to have an advantage over L2 learners due to earlier exposure to the language (e.g. Au et al., 2002; Lukyanchenko & Gor, 2011). However, in areas such as syntax and semantics, there is great variability influenced by factors including maturational stage, language structure, and personal experience/ contact with the heritage language (Montrul, 2015). For example, HLS experience similar difficulties with L2 learners regarding syntax/pragmatic/discourse interfaces, e.g. use of null and overt subjects (e.g. Silva-Corvalán, 2014).

Specifically regarding Korean HLS, Lee, Moon, and Long (2009) compared HLS, English-speaking L2 Korean learners and Korean native speakers across various measures of grammatical competence (i.e. phonology, syntax, lexis, morphology, collocation, and accent detection) at similar general oral proficiency ratings. HLS performed better in most areas than L2 learners at the same proficiency level, particularly for past tense, relative clauses, locative verbs, and honorifics. In Lee's (2011) study, the effect of onset age of exposure to English on Korean HLS' knowledge of unaccusative and unergative verbs was examined, with early bilinguals unable to distinguish between the two, while late bilinguals, despite gaining higher scores than early bilinguals, performed less well than Korean native speakers. Regarding word association, beginner Korean HLS performed better than non-heritage L2 learners at meaning-based association for nouns in M. Kim's (2013) study. Furthermore, while the HLS showed greater conceptual associations over a non-heritage L2 learner group, no difference was found in the accuracy of collocation-based associations between these groups. Shin and Joo (2015) identified highly frequent lexical errors among Korean–Australian HLS of Korean, and these errors were influenced by interlingual, intralingual, and sociolinguistic factors. The participants also showed a heavy reliance on vocabulary that they learned or heard in their childhood.

Given the varying degrees of success when acquiring different aspects of the heritage language system in previous research, our chapter seeks to explore how Korean HLS and L2 learners of Korean both manage referential movement in the target language. We first turn to how native Korean speakers manage referential movement, before presenting predictions as to how foreign and heritage language learners might manage this process.

Referential movement in Korean

The approach to referential movement taken in this chapter follows Ariel's Accessibility Theory (Ariel, 1991, 2008), which accounts for the speakers'/writers' choice of referring expressions in terms of their estimation of how 'accessible' a referent is for the listener at any given time in the discourse. This theory has been claimed to constitute a language universal, despite language-specific differences in the mapping of NP forms to different levels of accessibility.

For discourse-new reference (the least accessible referential context) in Korean, specific referents are often introduced with numeral + noun or noun + numeral + classifier constructions (1):

(1) 한 아이가 식당으로 들어갔습니다.
    han aika siktangulo tulekasssupnita.
    one boy-NOM[1] restaurant-into entered-HON
    'A boy walked into a restaurant'

While Korean permits numeral constructions (with or without classifiers) for referent introductions, their use is non-obligatory, with referents also introduced through bare (no determiner) nominals that often denote the referent's honorific social status (in 2 below, a teacher):

(2) 선생님이 식당으로 들어갔습니다.
    sensayngnimi siktangulo tulekasssupnita
    teacher-HON-NOM restaurant-into entered-HON
    '(A) teacher walked into a restaurant'

In Crosthwaite (2014), native Korean speakers typically introduced new referents through bare nominals, with more complex descriptions including numerals or embedded relatives used when a referent is introduced into the discourse that may not be completely disambiguated from a previously introduced referent (e.g. a boy vs. another boy/a boy wearing a green hat).

For generic discourse-new reference, English makes use of bare plural, indefinite or definite article NPs (lions, a lion, the lion). Korean generally makes use of nouns with the plural suffix 들 (dul), while numerals or demonstratives (in comparison with the English indefinite/definite articles) only provide specific new or anaphoric readings, respectively (Ionin & Montrul, 2009).

For given reference, we distinguish accessibility in terms of whether the reference is made *co-referentially* (the highest level of accessibility), where the same referent is referred to across clauses in first position; as part of *switch-role* reference, where a referent in first position in one clause moves to second position in the next clause or vice versa (at a reduced level of accessibility); or as *switch-reference* (the lowest level of accessibility), where a referent is reintroduced into the discourse after being absent from a previous (foregrounded) clause.

Regarding co-reference in English, pronouns are typically used. In Korean, zero anaphora are generally used, and (less frequently) full NPs, with the target referent generally in first position (Kang, 2004; Crosthwaite, 2014). Referents may be marked with the nominative affix '이/가'- 'ee/ga' or '은/는'- 'un/nun' topic marking for less accessible referents, through to no marking (in the form of zero anaphora) for highly accessible referents. This claim is based on Sohn (2001) where 'contextually recoverable nominal constructions are usually not to be [explicitly] expressed [in Korean] unless [they are] to be particularly delimited, focused or topicalised' (Sohn, 2001, p. 267), as with (3):

(3) 한 남자가 왔어요. 남자는 문을 열었어요,
han namcaka wasseyo. namcanun mwunul yelesseyo
A man-NOM came. Man-TOP door-ACC opened.
ø 거울을 봤어요.
ø kewulul pwasseyo.
ø mirror-ACC look-PAST-DEC-POL
'A man came. The man opened the door, (he) looked in the mirror.'

For switch-role reference, Koreans generally employ full NPs, although on occasion zero anaphora can be used as Korean speakers may understand who is performing an action (on whom) from the discourse context alone, as shown in (4) where the 'children' and 'teacher' switch roles:

(4) 애들이 선생님에게 이것 좀 빼 달라 햇는데
aytuli sensayngnimeykey ikes com ppay talla haysnuntey
children-NOM teacher-HON-to this please get did then
the children asked the teacher to please get the ball then
ø 사다리를 통해서 빼 보려고 하셨지만
ø satalilul thonghayse ppay polyeko hasyessciman,...
ø ladder-ACC with get try to did but...
(teacher) brought a ladder to try to get the ball, but...
(Crosthwaite, 2014, p. 164)

For switch-reference, Korean generally employs full NPs either in the form of bare nominals or demonstrative NPs, although as with switch-role reference, zero anaphor can also be used when the referent is accessible from the situational or discourse context (5):

(5) ø공을 가지고 놀다가
ø kongul kaciko noltaka
ø ball-ACC have-and play-DEC
he played with the ball and
여동생이 왔는데
yetongsayngi wassnuntey
sister-NOM came-then

a girl came then
ø 여동생에게 공을 준 다음...
ø yetongsayngeykey kongul cwun taum...
ø sister-to ball-ACC gave then...
(he) gave the ball to the girl then...
                                        (Crosthwaite, 2014, p. 167)

Heritage vs. foreign L2 acquisition of Korean reference?

For both heritage and foreign language speakers, there are apparent language-universal tendencies of linguistic form and referential function (such as those predicted by Accessibility Theory) as well as confirmed language-specific differences between certain forms and structures along functional lines. For foreign language learning, the second language learner, already possessing full knowledge of their native language – including knowledge of language-universal discourse-pragmatic constraints on NP form – is faced with the task of learning a new set of referential forms in the target language, then must be able to re-map L2 form to linguistic function in a manner reflecting the norms required for coherence in the L2, all while overcoming any potential influence or transfer of usage from their native language during narrative production.

Aside from the usual errors present in L2 production (e.g. omission of obligatory articles in article-languages by learners from non-article language backgrounds), foreign L2 learners generally produce reference that is either over-explicit, i.e. using a referential form that marks a lower accessibility than the referential context requires; or under-informative, i.e. using a referential form that marks a higher accessibility than the listener is able to reasonably infer. For example, L1 English-speaking learners of Korean are likely to use fewer zero anaphora than native Korean speakers in high-accessibility contexts, in keeping with both the obligatoriness of grammatical subjects in English as well as the general over-explicitness of L2 learners who may at times be unable (at lower levels of proficiency at least, and in oral discourse) to recreate the conditions for the highest accessibility forms to be used (Hendriks, 2003). Rather, a pronominal-led strategy may prevail (following an L1-like form/function mapping), or learners may use a higher frequency of full NPs in the form of bare nominals or complex NPs than native speakers would. However, the opposite has also been shown to be true, with L2 learners sometimes producing more zero anaphora than native Koreans (H.Y. Kim, 2012; Lee & Zaslansky, 2015).

For low-accessibility reference (i.e. switch-reference), an overreliance on demonstrative NPs has been attested in line with an article-led L1-like approach (at least for L2 Mandarin, see Crosthwaite, Yeung, Bai, Lu & Bae, 2018). Korean L2 English learners have been found to swap a demonstrative-led NP approach from their L1 into the article-L2 (Ionin, Baek, Kim, Ko, & Wexler, 2012), and, correspondingly, one may predict frequent use of demonstrative NPs from English-speaking Korean learners. This is also the case for referent introductions, where numeral + noun NPs are used more frequently by L2 learners from article-language backgrounds than native speakers and L2 learners from non-article L1s, who more frequently employ bare nominals or noun + nominative constructions (Crosthwaite et al., 2018).

However, HLS's ability to conform to the target accessibility form/function mappings of their heritage language is less well known. While the dominant language in question here is that of English – an article-language that also makes heavy use of pronouns (and few zeros) for reference maintenance – a question that remains to be answered is whether HLS, as part of their exposure to the target heritage language at home or within their local communities, have internalised enough of the accessibility norms of reference of their heritage language to have any advantage over their foreign L2 Korean-learning counterparts at equivalent general proficiencies. In addition, while previous research on HLS' use of NPs has tended to focus on zero anaphor, there has been comparatively less research exploring the full reference system of HLS, especially when compared against foreign L2 learners of equivalent proficiencies. A notable exception is Lee and Zaslansky's (2015) study on reference using the Gundel, Hedberg, and Zacharski (1993) framework with Korean HLS, which demonstrated such speakers exhibited incomplete knowledge of the use of nominal reference compared with native speakers. HLS used zero anaphora as the same rate as native Korean speakers, but frequently dropped case markers in narratives, which native speakers rarely do. L2 learners, on the other hand, frequently used topic marking for given reference while native speakers and heritage learners tended to use nominative marking. However, the study contained only a small sample (ten heritage speakers, five L2 speakers, and five native speakers), and both heritage and L2 learners were at an upper-intermediate level of proficiency. Lee and Zaslansky's call for a larger sample across various proficiency levels is now addressed in the present study through the investigation of a learner corpus of 100 heritage and foreign L2 Korean written texts at two proficiency levels (beginner and intermediate).

Method

Corpus

The present study analyses the *Korean Learner Language Analysis* (KoLLA) corpus (Lee, Dickinson & Israel, 2012, 2013), which is publicly available for download[2]. The corpus contains 100 personal essays written by L2 undergraduate learners of Korean from four language institutions, three from the United States and one in South Korea. This data is divided into Foreign (FL) and Heritage (HL) subcorpora, which are further subdivided into beginner/intermediate learner groups, with 25 texts available within each grouping. Israel, Dickinson and Lee (2013) define the HL dataset as comprised of learners 'who had Korean spoken at home' (p. 1421), although further details on the learners' relative heritage status (i.e. both parents vs. one parent using Korean, length of time spent in English-speaking country, early or late acquisition of the Heritage language) is unfortunately lacking. The beginner/intermediate distinction in the data appears to be based on university entrance scores or class groupings at the host institutions. It is assumed that English is the dominant language for each grouping. Details of corpus sizes are shown in Table 5.1.

As the overall corpus size is small and inconsistent across subcorpora, normalised median frequencies (per 1,000 words) were used when comparing reference across the learner groups.

Students in each group wrote 'about various topics related to their everyday life' (Lee et al. 2013, p. 292), including family, happiness, travel, cooking, and their studies. Thus, topics were not all on the same *quaestio* (Klein & von Stutterheim, 1987). The *quaestio* is the implicit question that the speaker/writing is attempting to answer through discourse, which potentially constrains the potential number, type, and form of reference to be produced. While differences in *quaestio* across texts theoretically decrease the overall compatibility of the referential forms and contexts used across the four corpora, an examination of the essay topics selected for texts within each grouping suggested an overall similarity in the range of topics across the four subcorpora, and with no single subcorpus containing too many texts on a single topic. Hence, meaningful comparison may still be conducted across the subcorpora. A number of the texts were written from a first-person perspective, but there were still plentiful third-person reference produced across texts as well.

Procedure

The second author, a native speaker of Korean with a PhD in applied linguistics, manually annotated each text for reference type and form using UAMCorpusTool (version 3.3v, O'Donnell, 2008),[4] a freely available corpus annotation package that allows for corpus construction and annotation according to user-defined annotation schemes. For the purposes of the present study, only reference to animate entities was annotated, as animacy is an important predictor of referents' overall status in the discourse (following the animacy scale Human>Animate>Inanimate; Comrie, 1989), and should allow for the full range of new, given, and generic referential contexts to be produced in the students' texts.

A shortened version of the annotation scheme used is shown in Figure 5.1. At the top level, annotations for reference were divided into *new*, *given*, and *generic* reference. Given reference was further subdivided into co-referential, switch-role, and switch-reference contexts. At the next level, the various referential forms

Table 5.1 Corpus size across subcorpora

	Foreign Beginner	*Foreign Intermediate*	*Heritage Beginner*	*Heritage Intermediate*
Sentences	360	373	376	297
Ecels[5]	1601	3483	2278	2676

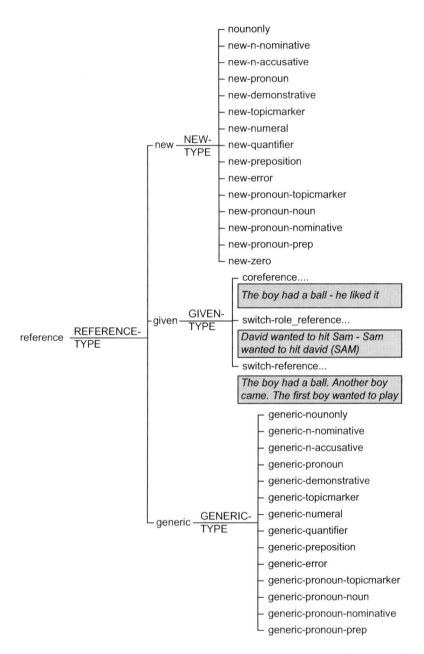

Figure 5.1 Reference annotation scheme (full typology of forms for given reference omitted for space)

found in the dataset were added to the annotation scheme upon encountering them in the data. This included forms that were appropriate syntactically but could potentially be pragmatically infelicitous (i.e. zeros for switch-reference reference), with an 'error' category for forms that were inappropriate syntactically (i.e. nouns with incompatible or missing affix combinations). Upon the first complete annotation of the data, the authors met to discuss any unusual codings and refined the annotation scheme based on any annotation errors, before each individual annotation was re-checked for accuracy and agreement by both authors. There were no disagreements between the authors noted in the final set of annotations of the corpus.

Results

Overview

Table 5.2 describes the distribution (raw, normalised median, median absolute deviation respectively) of new, given, and generic reference across each learner corpus.

A Kruskal-Wallis test was performed on these normalised frequencies for each reference type (new, given, generic) across the five groups, (alpha = 0.016), which showed significant variation across learner groups for *new* (H(3) = 22.58, $p < 0.001$), *given* (H(3) = 14.01, $p = 0.003$), and *generic* reference (H(3) = 21.97, $p = <0.001$). We now discuss each reference type in turn.

Discourse-new reference

Regarding specific (as opposed to generic) discourse-new reference, post-hoc Mann-Whitney test results suggest Foreign Beginners (FB) were significantly more likely to produce discourse-new reference than Foreign Intermediate (FI) learners (U = 35.93, t = 4.46, $p < 0.001$) and Heritage Intermediate (HI) learners (U = 27.02, t = 3.35, $p = 0.005$). Heritage Beginners (HB) were as likely to produce discourse-new reference as HI learners. This suggests frequent use of discourse-new reference within these written essays is a specific feature of FB writing. To explore further, Table 5.3 describes the comparative distribution (raw,

Table 5.2 Distribution of reference across learner corpora

Reference type	Foreign Beginner	Foreign Intermediate	Heritage Beginner	Heritage Intermediate
New	86, 31.09(18.17)	51, 7.27(3.47)	79, 16.60(7.81)	44, 12.84(7.68)
Given	169, 62.83(12.65)	137, 22.53(15.56)	179, 52.18(32.87)	171, 47.39(29.81)
Generic	16, 0(0)	104, 17.54(13.06)	14, 0(0)	45, 8.71(8.71)

Table 5.3 Forms used for specific discourse-new reference

Reference type	Foreign Beginner	Foreign Intermediate	Heritage Beginner	Heritage Intermediate
Noun only	19, 3.67(3.67)	4, 0(0)	20, 0(0)	12, 0(0)
N+Nominative	10, 0(0)	8, 0(0)	12, 0(0)	9, 0(0)
N+Accusative	1, 0(0)	3, 0(0)	2, 0(0)	1, 0(0)
N+Topicmarker	12, 0(0)	2, 0(0)	8, 0(0)	3, 0(0)
N+Preposition	16, 7.14(7.14)	8, 0(0)	16, 5.61(5.61)	8, 0(0)
Pronoun+Nominative	2, 0(0)	6, 0(0)	2, 0(0)	4, 0(0)
Pronoun+Noun	3, 0(0)	0, 0(0)	0, 0(0)	0 (0)
Pronoun+Topicmarker	17, 7.43(2.05)	15, 3.51(3.4)	15, 5.83(2.0)	7, 0(0)
Error	6, 0(0)	5, 0(0)	4, 0(0)	0, 0(0)

median/median absolute deviation) of specific discourse-new referential forms employed across the learner groups.

Despite the prevalence of discourse-new reference in the FB data as compared with the other learner data, there is less apparent statistical variation (following Kruskal–Wallis tests at alpha 0.0055) across learner groups in terms of the normalised frequency of the different forms used for specific discourse-new reference. However, the use of pronouns with accompanying topic markers does appear to be a significant feature of the FB data (H(3)=15.32, $p=0.002$), with FB writers more frequently employing such forms for discourse-new reference than FI (U=22.30, t=1.89, $p=0.022$) and HI writers (U=28.58, t=3.71, $p=0.001$). While HBs also used these forms on occasion, HB use was not statistically significantly different from that of FI or HI writers, suggesting the use of this form for referent introductions is largely specific to FBs. Both FB and HBs frequently introduced themselves in first person (e.g. 저는 나영 인데요, cenun nayeng inteyyo, 'I am Nayoung'); referred to 'we' in the second person (e.g. 우리는 미국사람입니다, wulinun mikwuksalamipnita, 'we are American'); or used possessive pronoun constructions to introduce third-person referents (내 동생은 영국에서 왔습니다, nay tongsayngun yengkwukeyse wasssupnita, 'my younger sibling came from England'), often all within the same text.

The use of N+preposition introductions appears to be a feature of both FB and HB texts (as opposed to intermediate-level writing), but this can be explained through the increased use of specific third-person referent introductions generally, as compared to the preference for generic introductions by FI and HI writers (as discussed in the next section). This is also apparent in the frequent introduction of specific referents through proper names in FB texts.

Regarding the 'error' category, these involve the omission of obligatory nominative (Example 6) or topic marking (7), omission of honorific suffixes (8), conflation of pronouns and topic markers into a single erroneous word (9, 전, cen, which cannot be used in writing but may be used in speech), and misuse of nominative and accusative markers (10 & 11)

(6) 내 [내가] 좋아하는 것과...
nay [nayka] cohahanun keskwa...
I [I-NOM] like-TOP thing-and
I like this and I'm good at it

(7) 저 [저는] '영철' 이에요 [FB]
ce [cenun] 'yengchel' ieyyo
I [I-TOP] 'Yengchel'-am.
I am 'Yengchel'

(8) 아버지 [아버지께서는] 거실에 계세요. [FB]
apeci [apecikkeysenun] kesiley kyeyseyyo.
Father [father-HON-TOP] living at stays
Father is in the living room

(9) 전 [저는] 사년동[안][5] 한국어를 공부했는데도... [FI]
cen [cenun] sanyentong[an] hankwukelul kongpwuhayssnunteyto...
cen [I-TOP] four years-for Korean-ACC studied-although
Even though X [I] studied Korean for four years...

(10) 동생을 [동생이] 초등학교에 가요 [FB]
tongsayngul [tongsayngi] chotunghakkyoey kayo
younger sibling-ACC [younger sibling-NOM] elementary school-at go
My younger brother goes to elementary school

(11) 모두 친구들이 [친구들을] 잘 못 봐요. [HB]
motwu chinkwutuli [chinkwutulul] cal mos pwayo.
Every friends-NOM [friends-ACC] well not see
My friends can't see (this)

There was no apparent regularity in the type of errors across FB/FI/HB groups, although the frequency of errors in the data is small overall. However, no such errors were found in the HI data.

Generic reference

For generic reference, post-hoc Mann–Whitney test results suggest FI learners (normalised median = 17.54) more frequently employed generic referential forms than FB learners (normalised median = 0, U = –24.78, t = –3.26, p = 0.007) and HB learners (normalised median = 0, U = 32.64, t = 4.39, p < 0.001). As the HI learners also frequently used generic referential forms (normalised median = 8.71), there appears to be a general proficiency effect on the use of generic referential forms by intermediate-level writers, although the results for HI learners vs. FB/HB learners were not statistically significant. Table 5.4 shows the generic reference forms used across the learner subcorpora.

Kruskal–Wallis test results (alpha = 0.0083) suggested significant variation in the use of noun forms (H(3) = 15.40, p = 0.001), noun + nominative forms (H(3) = 16.40, p = 0.001) and noun + preposition forms (H(3) = 17.78, p < 0.001). For noun forms, significant variation is found between HB and FI groupings (U = 22.87, t = 3.91, p = 0.001), while for noun + nominative forms, significant variation is found between FB and FI groups (U = –23.48, t = –3.60, p = 0.002) as well as HB and FI (U = 21.50, t = 3.37, p = 0.004). For noun + preposition forms, significant variation is found between FB and FI writing (U = –23.51, t = –3.56, p = 0.002) and HB and FI writing (U = 022.04, t = 3.42, p = 0.004). Overall, there is an increased use of generic reference in intermediate writing as opposed to beginner writing, although this is only statistically significant for the FI group and not the HI group.

An examination of the nominal forms used for generic reference in FB writing strongly indicates overreliance on a narrow range of terms, namely 사람 (salam, people) including 한국 사람 (hankwuk salam, Korean people) or 미국사람 (mikwuksalam, American people), as well as variations of 학생 (haksayng, students) including 독일 학생 (tokil haksayng, German students) or 고등학생 (kotunghaksayng, high school students), each without the (non-obligatory) plural marker 들(tul). FI/HI-level writers demonstrate a much wider range of generic forms as well as exhibit additional complexity within these forms, including reference with

Table 5.4 Forms used for generic reference

Generic reference form	*Foreign Beginner*	*Foreign Intermediate*	*Heritage Beginner*	*Heritage Intermediate*
Noun only	7, 0(0)	25, 1.78(1.78)	0, 0(0)	8, 0(0)
N+Nominative	3, 0(0)	34, 4.86(4.86)	7, 0(0)	10, 0(0)
N+Accusative	0, 0(0)	7, 0(0)	1, 0(0)	4, 0(0)
N+Topicmarker	2, 0(0)	5, 0(0)	1, 0(0)	6, 0(0)
N+Preposition	3, 0(0)	31, 6.06(6.06)	4, 0(0)	17, 0(0)
Error	1, 0(0)	1, 0(0)	1, 0(0)	0, 0(0)

extended dependent clauses such as 기쁜 경험 을 가지고 있는 사람들 (kippun kyenghem ul kaciko issnun salamtul, 'people who have happy experiences') or 나쁜 경험을 많이 당한 사람들 (nappun kyenghemul manhi tanghan salamtul, 'people who have many bad experiences'), while HB writers frequently produce adjective + noun combinations such as 똑똑한 사람 (ttokttokhan salam, clever people), 친절한 사람 (chincelhan salam, kind people) as well as quantifier + noun combinations such as 다른 사람들 (talun salamtul, other people) or 모든 사람 (motun salam, every people/everyone) in their texts. Overall, the findings for generic reference within intermediate-level writing marks a shift from an individual- or character-centred narrative approach as seen in beginner-level writing, as characterised by the very high frequency of new/given specific referential forms in FB/HB texts compared to a more abstract generic referential style in FI/HI texts. This is exemplified in the following extracts from FB (12) and FI texts (13) respectively, where the FB text focuses on two female human referents (Yumi and Yonghee), while the FI text makes numerous generic references to different animal species.

(12) 유미씨도 언니가 하나 있어요.
yumi ssito ennika hana isseyo.
Yumi-HON-also older sister-NOM one there is/have
Yumi has an older sister
이름이 영희예요.
ilumi yenghuyyeyyo.
Name-NOM 'Yenghuy'-is
Her name is 'Yenghuy'
Ø (영희씨는) 모스크바에서 살아요.
Ø (yenghuyssinun) mosukhupaeyse salayo.
Ø (Younghuy-HON-TOP) Moscow at live
Younghuy lives in Moscow
영희 씨 전공이 법학이에요.
Yenghuy-ssi cenkongi pephakieyyo.
Younghuy-HON major law-is
Younghuy's major is law
Ø (영희씨는) 매일 법책을 읽어요.
Ø (yenghuyssinun) mayil pepchaykul ilkeyo.
Ø [Yenghuy-HON-TOP] everyday law book read.
Yenghuy reads law books everyday.
영희씨하고 유미씨 사이가 좋아요!
yenghuyssihako yumissi saika cohayo!
Younghuy-HON-and Yumi-HON relation good-is
Yenghuy and Yunmi have a good relationship
유미 씨는 아주 예뻐요!
yumi ssinun acwu yeyppeyo!
Yumi-HON-TOP very pretty-is!
Yumi is very pretty

Ø (유미씨는) 운동을 참 좋아해요.
Ø (yumissinun) wuntongul cham cohahayyo.
Ø (Yumi-HON-TOP) exercise very like
Yumi likes to exercise
유미씨는 수영장하고 테니스 코트에 자주 가요.
yumissinun swuyengcanghako theynisu khothuey cacwu kayo.
Yumi-HON-TOP swimming pool-and tennis court-at often go
Yumi often goes to the swimming pool and tennis court

(13) 옐로스톤에서 할 것이 많습니다.
Yellowstoneeyse hal kesi manhsupnita.
Yellowstone-at to-do things a lot-is
There are many things to do at Yellowstone
자연에서 사는 동물들이 많아서 재미있습니다.
cayeneyse sanun tongmwultuli manhase caymiisssupnita.
Nature at live animals-NOM many interesting-is
It is fun because there are many wild animals
물소, 사슴, 곰, 늑대와 무스 다 볼 수 있습니다.
mwulso, sasum, kom, nuktaywa mwusu ta pol swu isssupnita.
(water) buffalo, deer, bear, wolf and moose all see can
You can see buffalo, deer, bears, wolves and moose
하지만 늑대들이 아주 드물어서 저는 열심히 찾아봤어도 못 봤습니다.
haciman nuktaytuli acwu tumwulese cenun yelsimhi chacapwasseto mos pwasssupnita.
However wolves-NOM very rare I-TOP hard searched not saw
However I haven't seen any wolves because they are rare
동물 찾는 것외에도 많은 재미있는 것을 경험 할 수 있습니다.
tongmwul chacnun kesoyeyto manhun caymiissnun kesul kyenghem hal swu isssupnita.
Animal search-thing except-also many interesting things experience can-do
You can also have many fun experiences besides seeing wild animals

Given reference by type and form

For given reference, post-hoc Mann-Whitney tests suggest FB writers (normalised median = 62.83) were more likely than FI writers (normalised median = 22.53) to produce given referential forms (U = 29.47, t = 3.66, $p = 0.002$), although there were no significant differences reported among other groupings. Table 5.5 describes the distribution of given referential forms by reference type (co-referential, switch, distal) across subcorpora.

For co-referential reference, significant variation was demonstrated following Kruskal-Wallis comparison (H(3) = 12.75, $p = .005$, alpha = 0.167). However, post-hoc tests revealed significant variation between FB and FI groups only (U = 26.98, t = 3.36, $p = 0.005$), although we note a general non-significant reduction in the median frequency of co-referential reference between HB and

Table 5.5 Forms used for given reference by type

Reference type	Foreign Beginner	Foreign Intermediate	Heritage Beginner	Heritage Intermediate
Co-referential	102, 34.94(16.71)	75, 11.35(11.35)	127, 36.66(30.60)	108, 27.95(19.59)
Switch	14, 0(0)	8, 0(0)	5, 0(0)	11, 0(0)
Distal	53, 19.34(6.86)	54, 8.87(4.75)	47, 11.91(5.85)	50, 11.64(11.64)

HI writers as well. Table 5.6 describes the different forms used for co-reference across the learner corpora.

Overall, and in part due to the need to correct for multiple tests (alpha = 0.0041), Kruskal-Wallis tests performed on the normalised frequencies of co-referential forms found only significant variation in the use of zero for co-reference across learner groups ($H(3) = 17.50$, $p = 0.001$), with FB writers significantly more likely to use this form than FI writers ($U = 25.89$. $t = 3.34$, $p = 0.005$). HB writers were also significantly more likely to use zeros for co-reference than FI writers ($U = -24.67$, $t = -3.26$, $p = 0.007$) but not HI writers ($p = 0.061$). The use of zeros by the beginner learner groups is interesting in that other research on oral data has shown that beginner L2 Korean learners prefer a pronominal or nominal approach to co-reference as they are unable to create the discourse conditions required for zero reference to be used (Hendriks, 2003; Crosthwaite, 2014). However, when given more time in written form, the reverse appears to occur, as shown in this example from an FB text where the referent (Bob Dylan) is mentioned numerous times in co-referential contexts, with each subsequent reference made through zero anaphor for an unbroken chain of individual references (Example 14).

(14) 이 사진은 버브 대이란이 있습니다.
  i sacinun pepu tayilani isssupnita.
  This photo Bob-Dylan-NOM there-is
  In this photo is Bob Dylan
  Ø (버브 대이란은/그는) 민속 음악가 입니다.
  Ø (pepu tayilanun/kunun) minsok umakka ipnita.
  Ø (버브 대이란-TOP/he-TOP) folk musician is
  He is a folk musician
  Ø (버브 대이란은/그는) 많은 고급의 노래를 짓고 많은 음악가를 영감을 줬습니다[6].
  Ø (pepu tayilanun/kunun) manhun kokupuy nolaylul cisko manhun umakkalul yengkamul kwesssupnita.
  Ø (버브 대이란-TOP/he-TOP) many advanced music made many musician inspiration gave

90 *Peter Crosthwaite and Min Jung Jee*

Table 5.6 Forms used for coreferential reference

Coreferential form	Foreign Beginner	Foreign Intermediate	Heritage Beginner	Heritage Intermediate
Zero	60, 17.86(12.80)	24, 0(0)	89, 25.20(21.44)	43, 0(0)
Noun only	0, 0(0)	5, 0(0)	3, 0(0)	4, 0(0)
N+Nominative	4, 0(0)	9, 0(0)	4, 0(0)	10, 0(0)
N+Accusative	0, 0(0)	2, 0(0)	0, 0(0)	5, 0(0)
N+Topicmarker	10, 0(0)	5, 0(0)	8, 0(0)	19, 0(0)
N+Preposition	1, 0(0)	7, 0(0)	4, 0(0)	8, 0(0)
Demonstrative+N	0, 0(0)	7, 0(0)	1, 0(0)	1, 0(0)
Pronoun + Noun	6, 0(0)	1, 0(0)	0, 0(0)	0, 0(0)
Pronoun+ Noun +Topicmarker	15, 0(0)	4, 0(0)	15, 0(0)	6, 0(0)
Pronoun+ Noun + Nominative	1, 0(0)	7, 0(0)	2, 0(0)	5, 0(0)
Pronoun+ Noun Preposition	0, 0(0)	1, 0(0)	1, 0(0)	2, 0(0)
Error	4, 0(0)	2, 0(0)	0, 0(0)	2, 0(0)

He was an inspiration to many advanced musicians and wrote many important songs
Ø (버브 대이란은/그는) 천구백 사십 일 년에서 태어났습니다.
Ø (pepu tayilanun/kunun) chenkwupayk sasip il nyeneyse thayenasssupnita.
Ø (버브 대이란-TOP/he-TOP) 1941 year was born
He was born in 1941
Ø (버브 대이란의/그의) 고향은 Duluth, Minnesota 이었습니다.
Ø (pepu tayilanuy/kuuy) kohyangun Duluth, Minnesota iesssupnita.
Ø (버브 대이란-TOP/he-TOP) hometown Duluth, Minnesota-was
His hometown was Duluth, Minnesota
Ø (버브 대이란은/그는) 오늘 대중의 남습니다.
Ø (pepu tayilanun/kunun) onul taycwunguy namsupnita.
Ø (버브 대이란-TOP/he-TOP) today the public remain
Today he is still recognised by the public
Ø (버브 대이란은/그는) 요사이 로큰롤 명예의 전당 인도 했습니다[7].

Ø (pepu tayilanun/kunun) yosai lokhunlol myengyeyuy centang into haysssupnita.
Ø (버브 대이란-TOP/he-TOP) these days rock and roll hall of fame transferred/handed over
Recently he was inducted into the rock and roll hall of fame.

FB and HB writers also used pronominal constructions with topic marking in co-referential contexts on occasion, which is considered over-explicit if the use is repeated and given the reported preference for zero anaphora to be used according to accessibility norms. These were almost all repeated first-person mentions (Example 15, all from one text):

(15) 저는 음악 감상도 좋아합니다.
      cenun umak kamsangto cohahapnita.
      I-TOP music appreciate/listening to music also like
      I like listening to music
      저는 날마다 음악을 듣습니다
      cenun nalmata umakul tutsupnita
      I-TOP everyday music listen
      I listen to music everyday
      저는 그림 그리기도 좋아해요.
      cenun kulim kulikito cohahayyo.
      I-TOP picture drawing also like
      I also like drawing
      저는 심심할 때 자주 그림 그립니다.
      cenun simsimhal ttay cacwu kulim kulipnita.
      I-TOP bored times often picture draw
      I often draw pictures when bored

FI and HI writers also made use of these forms in co-referential contexts, but their use is marked by a preference for pronoun + nominative constructions over pronoun + topic marker constructions (Example 16).

(16) 제[8]가 한국 사람이기 때문에 한국어를 알아야죠.
      ceyka hankwuk salamiki ttaymwuney hankwukelul alayacyo.
      I-NOM Korean person am because Korean language know should
      I should know Korean because I am Korean
      제가 미국에서 태웠는대도[9] 부모님이 한국에서 오셨어요[10].
      ceyka mikwukeyse thaywessnuntayto pwumonimi hankwukeyse osyesseyo.
      I-NOM US from was born although parents-HON-NOM Korea from came
      I was born in the US although my parents came from Korea

This difference stems from the increase in humility afforded by the 제가 (ceyka) pronoun + nominative marker construction over the equivalent less humble

나는(nanun) pronoun + topic marker commonly employed by lower proficiency Korean learners. In this case, the FB and HB learners in our corpus generally prefer the more humble 저 over 나, but tend to stick to the topic marker variant 저는 (cenun) rather than the nominative 제가 as seen in the higher level texts.

FI writers also used several demonstrative constructions, which are considered over-explicit within co-referential contexts in Korean and appear to represent L1 English definite article-like usage (Example 17).

(17)　…아이를 낳을 수 있으니까 될 수 있는 대로.
　　　… ailul nahul swu issunikka toyl swu issnun taylo.
　　　… children-ACC give birth to because if possible as many as
　　　…because if I give birth I want as much as possible
　　　그 아이 위해서 좋은 환경을 만드세요.
　　　ku ai wihayse cohun hwankyengul mantuseyyo.
　　　That kid for good environment give-please
　　　to give that child a good environment

In terms of the small number of erroneous references produced, FB writers tended to omit required honorific + topic constructions for certain referents (Example 18, although there was one instance of this in a HI text), while FI learners occasionally produced inappropriate suffixes for the context (19).

(18)　부모님은　미국에　살아요[11]. 부모님　[부모님께서는]　플리다에서 자기어까지 와요. [FB]
　　　pwumonimun　mikwukey　saleyo. pwumonim　[pwumonimkkeysenun] phullitaeyse cakiekkaci wayo.
　　　Parents-TOP US at/in live. Parents [parents-HON-TOP] Florida from to come
　　　My parents live in the US. They came up from Florida [to here]

(19)　저는 여행 많이 안했지만 저의 [제가] 가는 데는 참 좋았습니다.
　　　cenun yehayng manhi anhayssciman ceuy [ceyka] kanun teynun cham cohasssupnita.
　　　I-TOP travel many not did my [I-NOM] go place very good-was
　　　Although I haven't travelled much, I was happy with where I have been

Switch-role reference

Overall, little use was made of switch-role reference across corpora, with no significant variation reported following Kruskal-Wallis comparison. Table 5.7 shows the distribution of switch-role reference by form, with only raw frequencies shown (all median/MAD = 0).

As these forms could all be appropriate for switch-role reference given the situational or discourse context, and given none of the attempts at switch-role reference were marked as erroneous, we now move to discuss switch-reference.

Table 5.7 Forms used for switch-role reference

Switch-role reference form	Foreign Beginner	Foreign Intermediate	Heritage Beginner	Heritage Intermediate
Zero	6	1	0	5
Noun only	0	2	0	1
N+Nominative	0	3	2	3
N+Accusative	1	1	0	1
N+Topicmarker	3	1	1	0
N+Preposition	3	0	2	0
Pronoun+Preposition	0	0	0	1

Switch-reference

Despite frequent use of switch-reference reference across each subcorpus, there was no significant variation in the frequency of switch-reference (in general) across subcorpora (H(3)=7.70, p=0.103). Table 5.8 describes the distribution of forms used for switch-reference. With the exception of the zero switch-reference forms used, all other forms have median/MAD=0.

The only individual switch-reference referential form for which significant variation is found is that of zero (H(3)=10.97, p=0.012), with the FB group appearing to make significant use of this form compared with the FI group (U=20.17, t=3.02, p=0.015) and HI group (U=17.65, t=1.56, p=0.048). The use of zero for switch-reference reference may be considered 'unusual' under typical accessibility expectations, as the highest accessibility form is used for lowest accessibility referential context, although this is not uncommon in native Korean discourse (Crosthwaite, 2014). What is surprising is that this form appears to be used felicitously for switch-reference in FB texts but not HB or higher-level texts, as shown in the following lengthy example (19), where the writer switches between discussing themselves, and their friend Jun-Ho. Jun-Ho is referenced in the first and second lines, but is only reintroduced in the final line with a zero anaphor:

(19) 준호에께[12], 안녕하세요?
 cwunhoeykkey, annyenghaseyyo?
 Jun-ho-PRE, how are you?
 Hello Jun-ho, how are you?
 Ø (준호씨는) 잘지냈어요.
 Ø (cwunhossinun) calcinaysseyo.
 Ø (Junho-HON-TOP) well stayed/lived
 How have you been?
 요즘은 날씨가 따뜻해요.
 yocumun nalssika ttattushayyo.

Table 5.8 Forms used for switch-reference

Switch-reference form	Foreign Beginner	Foreign Intermediate	Heritage Beginner	Heritage Intermediate
Zero	24, 3.67(3.67)	6, 0(0)	11, 0(0)	6, 0(0)
Noun only	2	6	4	3
N+Nominative	5	12	3	11
N+Accusative	1	0	2	4
N+Topicmarker	10	8	8	8
N+Preposition	3	5	5	11
Pronoun+Topicmarker	5	8	9	6
Pronoun+Nominative	2	4	0	0
Pronoun+Preposition	0	2	1	0
Error	1	3	4	1

> These days weather warm-is
> These days the weather is warm
> 지렁[13]에 날씨가 어때요?
> cilengey nalssika ettayyo?
> 지렁 at weather how-is?
> How is the weather at [cileng]
> 아마 조금 춥지요.
> ama cokum chwupciyo.
> Probably a bit cold-is
> It is probably cold
> Ø (준호씨는) 열심히 공부하고 있어요?
> Ø (cwunhossinun) yelsimhi kongpwuhako isseyo?
> Ø (Junho-HON-TOP) hard studying is?
> Are you studying hard?

(19) appears to be taken from a personal letter rather than an essay, yet if the FB writer used an L1 English-like approach, the final switch-reference to Jun-ho would likely be pronominal or through a proper name. It is also possible that using zero anaphor for switch-reference may be simpler in the written form than it would be in oral production, where temporal, memory, task-related, and other constraints on accessibility could more seriously impact NP selection.

HB writers produced four errors for switch-reference, FI writers produced three, while FB and HI writers produced only a single error. Specifically, HBs omitted nominative, topic, and prepositional markers where obligatory (one instance per type) and in one instance also used nominative marking where topic marking was required in one instance, while the FI group omitted nominative markers for each of the three errors.

Discussion

The present study conducted a learner corpus analysis of Korean referential movement between heritage speakers and L2 learners at two levels of proficiency. The results indicate that heritage and L2 learners of Korean adopt different linguistic means in writing for both reference introduction and maintenance, at least at lower levels of proficiency.

For referent introductions, FB and HB learners frequently employ specific discourse-new reference as a feature of their written production, while at intermediate levels both foreign and heritage speakers tended towards generic discourse-new reference. While there is a general effect of proficiency on the proportion of specific to generic discourse-new reference among the learner groups, FBs were significantly more likely to produce specific discourse-new reference than their foreign intermediate and intermediate peers, with HBs exhibiting a more balanced use of specific/generic reference. HBs appear to have a wider knowledge of specific/generic forms and also demonstrate the ability to produce more complex NPs, while FBs rely on the use of pronouns or proper names when introducing discourse referents which could either be an indicator of L1-like reference or a relative lack of vocabulary for generic reference in the L2.

For reference maintenance, an effect of proficiency is also apparent in FB and HB's relative preference for zero anaphor and pronominal-led reference. While zero anaphora are common in native Korean production, pronominals are rarely used in oral discourse, although written discourse contains limited pronominal use by natives as such discourse is 'more cohesive in the sense that [there is] more frequent referential linking between adjacent sentences' (Lee, 2018, p. 11). Our findings regarding frequent zero use by beginner learners were also reported in H.Y. Kim (2012) and Lee and Zaslanksy (2015), with the latter suggesting beginner learners of Korean overgeneralise zero for both 'activated' and 'centre of attention' cognitive statuses of the GHZ model, while higher level and native speakers only use zero for the 'centre of attention' status. However, the very frequent use of zero by beginners reduces the potential impact of mode (written vs. oral) on the data as one may expect a *reduction* in zero forms in favour of pronominal forms if written texts indeed require more in the way of explicit cohesion. Rather, the beginners produced more zero *and* more pronominal forms in their texts, in line with the general character-focused narrative style of writing employed by these beginners throughout. In addition, while both foreign and heritage intermediate speakers did use pronominal co-reference on occasion, they tended towards more humble forms with accompanying nominative marking, while the beginners preferred to use plain pronominal forms with accompanying topic marking. This finding was also reported in Lee and Zaslansky (2015), who noted native speakers used topic marking for discourse-specific purposes, such as to mark contrast. However, beginner learners (whether foreign or heritage) are yet to acquire this global form-function mapping, instead marking almost all given reference with a single form-function mapping. We also consider this finding to be a potential effect of instruction for beginner L2 Korean learners, with many Korean textbooks introducing the plain form in earlier units in the form of short dialogues between friends and longer narratives involving young people who are familiar with each other. On the other hand, heritage learners are often limited to speaking the heritage language with siblings and immediate family at lower levels of proficiency, which would also not typically require the extensive use of humble forms.

Our findings regarding the use of zero for switch-reference in foreign (beginner) writing are also similar to Lee and Zaslanky (2015), who found frequent zero use in topic-switch contexts, suggesting that such learners do have knowledge of the syntactic specification for such forms in the target language. However, unlike Lee and Zaslansky (2015), the FI learners in our study used demonstrative NPs on occasion (an English-like usage) as also seen in Crosthwaite et al. (2018), while the heritage learners rarely did so.

Finally, FB, HB, and FI writers occasionally omitted case marking where obligatory, or used inappropriate case marking in certain contexts. Heritage intermediate learners, however, demonstrated considerable mastery of such markings with almost no errors present in the dataset, standing in contrast to the other learner groups with a clear advantage in the ability to produce appropriate case markings across each referential context.

Conclusion

The present study is one of the few corpus-based studies into L2 reference that have attempted to compare the production of heritage vs. foreign language learners of the target language. Significant effects of proficiency as well as heritage vs. foreign language status were found for reference introduction and maintenance within our corpus, with foreign beginner learners in particular standing out as unique in the means used for referential movement as compared with heritage beginners or foreign/heritage intermediate speakers. This suggests heritage learners' knowledge of and ability to produce reference in the written form is different to that of foreign learners at equivalent levels of proficiency. This should be considered when preparing instructional materials, pedagogy, and assessment for these respective groups, who are often taught separately within tertiary institutions, but who are sometimes taught together.

However, before we can make firmer conclusions as to the source of these differences, a more varied cross-sectional heritage dataset is strongly recommended. Information as to the details of the HLS in this study were limited, and we were thus unable to know if they were born in the L2 context or immigrated as children or adults; whether only one or both parents were speakers of the heritage language; or whether the HLS considered their language identity to be fixed or whether they held relatively fluid or transitioning identities. Comparison with equivalent L1 native Korean data is also advisable when considering intermediate foreign vs. heritage learners, as are further studies with better control over the writing topic or comparing oral vs. written forms of production. We aim to explore such variables in future research.

Notes

1 NOM = Nominative marker, HON = honorific form.
2 http://cl.indiana.edu/~kolla/
3 Ecels refers to whitespace delimited 'words' (Lee, Dickinson, & Israel, 2012).
4 http://www.corpustool.com/download.html
5 There is also a spelling mistake here, with the correct form shown in square brackets.
6 This should be spelt 젖습니다.
7 Uncommon usage – should be 인도 되었습니다.
8 Humble form of 내.
9 Should be '태어났는데도'.
10 Honorific expression of '오다'.
11 Should be '살아요'.
12 Should be 게.
13 We are unsure as to what the writer is referring to, although it appears to be a specific place

References

Ariel, M. (1991). The function of accessibility in a theory of grammar. *Journal of Pragmatics*, 16(5), 443–463. doi:10.1016/0378-2166(91)90136-L
Ariel, M. (2008). *Pragmatics and grammar*. Cambridge, UK: Cambridge University Press.
Au, T., Knightly, L., Jun, S.-A., & Oh, J. (2002). Overhearing a language during childhood. *Psychological Science*, 13(3), 238–243. doi:10.1111/1467-9280.00444
Bowles, M. (2011). Measuring implicit and explicit linguistic knowledge: What can heritage language learners contribute? *Studies in Second Language Acquisition*, 33(2), 247–272. doi:10.1017/S0272263110000756
Brinton, D. M., Kagan, O., & Bauckus, S. (Eds.). (2017). *Heritage language education: A new field emerging*. London, UK: Routledge.
Comrie, B. (1989). *Language universals and linguistic typology: Syntax and morphology*. Chicago, IL: University of Chicago Press.
Crosthwaite, P., Yeung, Y., Bai, X., Lu, L., & Bae, Y. (2018). Definite discourse-new reference in L1 and L2: The case of L2 Mandarin. *Studies in Second Language Acquisition*, 40(3), 625–649. doi:10.1017/S0272263117000353
Crosthwaite, P. R. (2014). *Differences between the coherence of Mandarin and Korean L2 English learner production and English native speakers: An empirical study* (Unpublished Doctoral dissertation). University of Cambridge, Cambridge, UK.
Deters, P., Gao, X., Miller, E. R., & Vitanova, G. (Eds.). (2015). *Theorizing and analyzing agency in second language learning: Interdisciplinary approaches*. Bristol, UK: Multilingual Matters.
Gundel, J., Hedeberg, N., & Zacharski, R. (1993). Cognitive status and the form of referring expressions in discourse. *Language*, 69, 274–307. doi:10.2307/416535
Hendriks, H. (2003). Using nouns for reference maintenance: A seeming contradiction in L2 discourse. In G. Ramat (Ed.), *Typology and second language acquisition* (pp. 291–326). Berlin, Germany: De Gruyter.
Ionin, T., Baek, S., Kim, E., Ko, H., & Wexler, K. (2012). *That's* not so different from *the*: Definite and demonstrative descriptions in second language acquisition. *Second Language Research*, 28(1), 69–101. doi:10.1177%2F0267658311432200

Ionin, T., & Montrul, S. (2009). Article use and generic reference: Parallels between L1- and L2-acquisition. In M. García Mayo & R. Hawkins (Eds.), *Second language acquisition of articles: Empirical findings and theoretical implications* (pp. 147–173). Amsterdam, the Netherlands: John Benjamins.

Israel, R., Dickinson, M., & Lee, S. H. (2013). Detecting and correcting learner Korean particle omission errors. *Proceedings of the 6th international conference on natural language processing (IJCNLP-13)*. Nagoya, Japan.

Jee, M. J. (2016). Exploring Korean heritage language learners' anxiety: 'We are not afraid of Korean!' *Journal of Multilingual and Multicultural Development, 37*(1), 56–74. doi:10.1080/01434632.2015.1029933

Kang, J. Y. (2004). Telling a coherent story in a foreign language: Analysis of Korean EFL learners' referential strategies in oral narrative discourse. *Journal of Pragmatics, 36*(11), 1975–1990. doi:10.1016/j.pragma.2004.03.007

Kim, H.-Y. (2012). Development of NP forms and discourse reference in L2 Korean. In H.-M. Sohn (Ed.), *Korean language in America (special issue): Innovations in teaching Korean* (pp. 211–235). The American Association of Teachers of Korean.

Kim, M. (2013). The mental lexicon of low-proficiency Korean heritage learners. *Heritage Language Journal, 10*(1), 17–35.

Klein, W., & Stutterheim, C. v. (1987). Quaestio und referentielle Bewegung in Erzählungen. *Linguistische Berichte, 109*, 163–183.

Kondo-Brown, K. (Ed.). (2006). *Heritage language development: Focus on East Asian immigrants.* Amsterdam, the Netherlands: John Benjamins.

Lee, T. (2011). Grammatical knowledge of Korean heritage speakers: Early vs. late bilinguals. *Linguistic Approaches to Bilingualism, 1*(2), 149–174. doi: 10.1075/lab.1.2.02lee

Lee, E. (2018). The universal topic prominence stage hypothesis and L1 transfer: A study of L2 Korean written narratives by L1 English and L1 Chinese speakers. *Linguistic Approaches to Bilingualism, 9*(3), 2–31. doi:10.1075/lab.17061.lee

Lee, E., & Zaslansky, M. (2015). Nominal reference in Korean heritage language discourse. *Heritage Language Journal, 12*(2), 132–158.

Lee, S., Moon, J., & Long, M. (2009). Linguistic correlates of proficiency in Korean as a second language. *Language Research, 45*(2), 319–348.

Lee, S. H., Dickinson, M., & Israel, R. (2012). Developing learner corpus annotation for Korean learner particle errors. *Proceedings of the 6th linguistic annotation workshop.* Jeju, Republic of Korea.

Lee, S. H., Dickinson, M., & Israel, R. (2013). Corpus-based error analysis of Korean particles. In S. Granger, G. Gilquin, & F. Meunier (Eds.), *Twenty years of learner corpus research: Looking back, moving ahead* (pp. 289–299). Louvain-la-Neuve, Belgium: Presses Universitaires do Louvain.

Leeman, J. (2015). Heritage language education and identity in the United States. *Annual Review of Applied Linguistics, 35,* 100–119. doi:10.1017/S0267190514000245

Lukyanchenko, A., & Gor, K. (2011). Perceptual correlates of phonological representations in heritage speakers and L2 learners. *Proceedings of the 35th annual Boston University conference on language development* (pp. 414–426). Somerville, MA: Cascadilla Press.

Montrul, S. (2012). Is the heritage language like a second language? *EUROSLA Yearbook, 12,* 1–29.

Montrul, S. (2015). *The acquisition of heritage languages.* Cambridge, UK: Cambridge University Press.

Montrul, S. (2018). Heritage language development: Connecting the dots. *International Journal of Bilingualism, 22*(5), 530–546. doi:10.1177%2F1367006916654368

Montrul, S., Foote, R., & Perpiñán, S. (2008). Gender agreement in adult second language learners and Spanish heritage speakers: The effects of age and context of acquisition. *Language Learning, 58*(3), 503–553. doi:10.1111/j.1467-9922.2008.00449.x

O'Donnell, M. (2008). The UAM CorpusTool: Software for corpus annotation and exploration. *Proceedings of the XXVI Congreso de AESLA* (pp. 3–5). Almeria, Spain.

Shin, S., & Joo, A. (2015). Lexical errors in Korean-Australian heritage learners' compositions. *Journal of Korean Language Education, 26,* 129–162. doi:10.18209/iakle.2015.26..129

Silva-Corvalán, C. (2014). *Bilingual language acquisition: Spanish and English in the first six years.* Cambridge, UK: Cambridge University Press.

Sohn, H. M. (2001). *The Korean Language.* Cambridge, UK: Cambridge University Press.

Xiao-Desai, Y., & Wong, K. F. (2017). Epistemic stance in Chinese heritage language writing – A developmental view. *Chinese as a Second Language Research, 6*(1), 73–102. doi:10.1515/caslar-2017-0004

Zhang, J., & Tao, H. (2018). Corpus-based research in Chinese as a second language. In C. Ke (Ed.), *The Routledge handbook of Chinese second language acquisition* (pp. 48–62). London, UK: Routledge.

6 Under-explicit and minimally explicit reference
Evidence from a longitudinal case study

Jonathon Ryan

Introduction

Underpinning a great deal of communication are references to people, in which speakers use a referring expression (RE) to clarify which individuals they mean. In doing so, they must select an expression that is not only grammatically and semantically permissible but is also pragmatically appropriate for various aspects of the discourse context. This dual processing demand, lying as it does at the confluence between pragmatics and grammar, has proved an intriguing site for SLA research. However, despite the substantial body of previous research, to date there have been few longitudinal studies involving post-intermediate learners, and very few based on data elicited in ways other than prompted production tasks; the present study works within this research space, presenting a longitudinal case study of one Korean user of English.

Since definitions of reference can vary considerably, it is worth specifying exactly which phenomena are to be examined here. Following Bach (2008), a rather restrictive definition has been adopted, equating to the Conversation Analysis term *recognitional reference* (Sacks & Schegloff, 2007), in which the speaker intends for the addressee to identify the real-world referent. To be in a position to do so, the addressee must have prior knowledge of the individual; for present purposes, this includes knowledge through prior mention of an otherwise hearer-new individual. Consequently, reference is nearly always achieved through use of a definite noun phrase (NP) (Bach, p. 28). Not included under this definition are mentions of hypothetical individuals (e.g. *the next person you see*), generic NPs (e.g. *the first born in a family*), introductions of hearer-new individuals (e.g. *a friend of mine; my neighbour*) and both specific and non-specific indefinites (e.g. *a doctor*). For present purposes, the focus is further restricted to singular third-person references.

In addition to this definition, the present study adopts Accessibility Theory (AT) (Ariel, 1990, 2001) as its key linguistic framework (see the introduction to this volume for an overview). The key idea behind the AT model is of a hierarchical arrangement of NP types that maps to a hierarchy of accessibility. In this way, zero anaphora (ø) and pronouns specialise as *high-accessibility markers* (HAMs), signalling that the referent is readily recoverable from short-term memory; conversely, *low-accessibility markers* (LAMs) such as proper names and *the* + noun, indicate that the referent must be recovered from long-term memory. Referent accessibility is determined by the sum of various weighted factors, principally the distance between anaphors and antecedents, the presence of other referents (competition), salience (e.g. topicality; physical presence), and unity (e.g. the effect of discourse boundaries) (Ariel, 1990, 2001).

Accessibility marking in L2 reference

A number of studies have reported findings relevant to the developmental trajectory of L2 reference, typically through cross-sectional studies comparing features of reference by learners at different language levels (e.g. Crosthwaite, 2013; Nakahama, 2009; Takeuchi, 2014). Several other studies have included a longitudinal analysis, including Lumley's (2013) study of English-speaking learners of Japanese (two measurements, approximately 18 months apart), Kim's (2000) study of Korean learners of English (two measurements, either 8.5 or 13 months apart), and Broeder (1991) and Klein and Perdue's (1992) studies of developmental patterns in low-level learners (three measurements over two-and-a-half years).

Although there are important and undoubted effects of cross-linguistic influence (see for example Jarvis, 2002; Nakahama, 2009, 2011), the weight of evidence suggests there are certain developmental patterns that occur largely irrespective of the configuration of source and target languages. This trajectory was depicted by Chini (2005) as beginning with an early 'pragmatic and lexical' stage, characterised chiefly by alternations between bare nouns or names, and zero anaphor (ø). The latter is used where the referent is easily identifiable from context and appears to chiefly occur for reference maintenance in topic position (Chini, 2005; Klein & Perdue, 1992). Also acquired early are deictic expressions. Thereafter, further forms are incorporated, beginning with (if they exist) anaphoric pronouns and marking for (in)definiteness. At intermediate levels, an '(over-) explicit lexical' stage is reached, whereby learners overuse full NPs in contexts in which pronouns or ø would be appropriate. This is followed by a more advanced 'syntactic' stage at which learners have greater control over syntactic devices for maintaining reference, such as passive voice (Nakahama, 2011) and (in some languages) clitics (Chini, 2005).

In terms of accessibility marking, this trajectory is from one of *under-explicitness* at beginner levels, to *over-explicitness* at intermediate and low-advanced levels (see also Ahrenholz, 2005; H.-Y. Kim, 2000). These terms relate to mismatches between the accessibility of the referent and the accessibility signalled by the RE. An expression is under-explicit when it indicates higher accessibility than warranted, such as when a pronoun is used where a name would be felicitous; it is over-explicit when it indicates a lower accessibility than warranted, such as the use of a name in place of a pronoun.

Under-explicitness, although most characteristic at lower levels, persists at higher levels mainly in relation to referent introductions (Nakahama, 2003;

Ryan, 2016) and evidence to date from referent tracking relates mainly to the use of ø in place of pronouns (e.g. Lumley, 2013; Nakahama, 2011; Ryan, 2012). However, there are exceptions. In particular, Lozano (2009, 2016, 2018) reports occasional infelicitous use of ø to mark topic shift among advanced English and Greek learners of Spanish, while the author of the present study found one Chinese participant greatly over-using pronouns in place of full NPs (Ryan, 2015).

By contrast, over-explicitness characterises a great deal of reference at intermediate to low-advanced levels. It is illustrated in the following extract, in which *the young lady* is used in place of *her*.

> so the policeman um ran after the lady
> and ø caught the la- the young lady um at last,
> and ø send the young lady to the tr- truck.
>
> (Ryan, 2015, p. 847)

As shown in this example, over-explicitness tends to occur more often in focus position or when the referent shifts between focus and topic position. It is not adequately explained by cross-linguistic influence, since it occurs seemingly irrespective of the L1 and L2 in question, being reported for – among others – Chinese learners of German (Hendriks, 2003), Turkish and Moroccan learners of Dutch (Broeder, 1991), English learners of Japanese (Lumley, 2013), Dutch learners of French (Gullberg, 2006), English learners of French and French learners of English (Leclercq & Lenart, 2013), and Mandarin and Korean learners of English (Crosthwaite, 2014). It is also not accounted for by learners creating fewer opportunities for the use of high-accessibility markers (Ryan, 2015). Among proposed explanations are the possibilities that choosing fuller NPs eases processing load (Chini, 2005; Gullberg, 2006); that it is a means of avoiding pronoun errors (Gullberg, 2006); and that it is a strategy to promote clarity (Leclercq & Lenart, 2013; Lumley, 2013; Ryan, 2015). The latter is in keeping with Lozano's (2016) recently proposed Pragmatic Principles Violation Hypothesis (PPVH), which holds that infelicities resulting in over-explicitness are weak violations of Gricean principles with limited communicative consequence, while under-explicitness represents a strong violation at risk of triggering miscommunication; when in doubt, learners will opt for the weaker violation.

Despite these general tendencies across learner populations, as with other areas of learner language, studies of L2 reference must remain alert to the possibilities of cross-linguistic influence. Such influences are evidenced in the production of errors and in the acquisition of new RE types (e.g. Crosthwaite, 2013; Nakahama, 2011) but to date are less clear in terms of the felicity of accessibility marking. For instance, even where there is an identical referential feature in the L1 and L2, such as use of ø in subject position in Greek and Spanish, learners may routinely use infelicitous forms until advanced levels (Lozano, 2018). More generally, the relationship between L1 endowment and L2 output proves complex and far from simply a matter of language transfer (e.g. Odlin, 2003).

In relation to the present case study, the relevant cross-linguistic comparison is between English and Korean,[1] where one relevant observation is the availability of (but highly infrequent use of) third-person pronouns in Korean. In reference maintenance contexts, where English speakers use pronouns, Korean speakers alternate between the use of ø and either bare NPs (Crosthwaite, 2014; H.-Y. Kim, 2000) or full names (S.-H. Kim, 2013; Song, 2005). An unmediated transfer of this strategy to English would lead to (1) under-explicitness by way of infelicitous use of ø; (2) over-explicitness by way of infelicitous use of names and bare nouns; and (3), under-use of pronouns overall. These predictions are, in fact, generally in keeping with previous findings for L1 Korean L2 English (Crosthwaite, 2014; Kang, 2004; H.-Y. Kim, 2000) but are also generally true for intermediate/advanced L2 reference. However, as will become apparent, they are not borne out in the present findings.

The current study

This study aims to explore the (under-researched) area of development in accessibility marking from a longitudinal perspective. Although the overall developmental trajectory appears well established, it is unclear whether, for example, pragmatic development in an ESL context is best characterised by steady growth, alternating periods of growth and stability, or even periods of backsliding, perhaps as new RE types and strategies are added to the speaker's repertoire. With such issues in mind, the following research questions were posed:

1) What changes are evidenced in the participant's RE system over the period of the study?
2) How does the participant's accessibility marking evolve over this period?

The first question focuses particularly on the RE types that the participant used, including errors of form and the expansion or contraction of this repertoire. The second question focuses on the issue of pragmatic felicity, and in particular longitudinal evidence of over- and under-explicitness.

Methodology

Participant

This longitudinal case study focuses on interview data from one Korean learner of English, Yoona. Yoona was recruited as part of a wider study involving 12 participants and 4 researchers, aiming to track the experiences of international students in mainstream study.

At the time of the first interview, Yoona was 24 years old and on the second day of a bachelor degree program in New Zealand; the final interview was shortly prior to her final examination nearly two-and-a-half years later. She had previously graduated in the same field in Korea, where she also had some work experience. Upon arriving in NZ, Yoona studied academic English programmes in two different institutions for a total of 13 months, successfully completing an English certificate programme with an exit level equivalent to IELTS 6.5, placing her at the threshold between an upper-intermediate and advanced level of English. Despite her writing and reading results being strong, in the first interview she spoke at length about her concerns with her level of spoken English. However, her mainstream studies involved very rich language input, including a large amount of academic reading, essays, and other written assignments, regular lectures, group work, oral presentations, and also several workplace internships. She also virtually always spoke English on campus (though never at home with her Korean-born husband and family). Thus, by the end of her studies, she felt that her communication skills and general confidence in using English were greatly improved, and this accords with the author's general appraisal based on comparisons of the interview recordings.

Data elicitation

Yoona participated in 18 interviews with the researcher between July 2016 and October 2018, with these lasting generally for between 45 minutes and an hour. The interviews were very loosely structured and free flowing, framed around the general question of 'how are your studies going?' As such, although elicited, these are authentic interview data designed to discover aspects of Yoona's experiences rather than intentionally to elicit acts of reference.

For the purposes of the analysis of reference, the first, middle, and final interviews were selected for detailed transcription. As it happened, the middle recording (August, 2017) is the shortest of the 18, being only 22 minutes long due to an interruption. To supplement it, the first 15 minutes of the following interview (September, 2017) were also included. These 15 minutes captured a full retelling of a series of events involving classmates and tutors, and is thus rich in references. Extracts from the three time periods (July, 2016; Aug.–Sept. 2017; Oct. 2018) include roughly similar numbers of referent introductions and acts of referent tracking.

Analysis: Accessibility coding

In the first stage of analysis, third-person singular references to people were coded as either 'introducing' or 'tracking', and further coded by RE type (typically by NP category). For each act of referent tracking, the referents were then coded for accessibility using a system drawing on work by Toole (1996). This coding system provides a measure of referent accessibility that is independent of linguistic form, thereby avoiding the risk of circular reasoning (see discussion in H.-Y. Kim, 2000; Ryan, 2012; Tomlin, 1990). Toole applied the original system to widely varying types of data, with the findings indicating that '[t]he factors which affect referential choice are universal and apply regardless of genre' (1996, pp. 285–286).[2]

For reasons of space, the refined system is only briefly sketched here (see Ryan, 2012, 2015 for detailed explanation). Each referent is scored as the sum total of eight weighted criteria which either enhance or reduce accessibility, producing a single aggregated number between −1 and 8; since both −1 and 8 are rare, these are conflated with the scores at 0 and 7, respectively. These are reported as *degrees of accessibility*, ranging from D0 to D7. The assumption is that the scores roughly correspond to an interactants' sense of referent accessibility, in the sense that the higher the number, the higher the presumed accessibility of the referent.

The first and most heavily weighted criterion combines the concepts of distance (between an anaphor and its antecedent) and unity. Weighting for distance is given to referents mentioned in the current or previous proposition. Weighting for unity is given for referents mentioned in the current or previous 'episode': in film retelling tasks, as reported in Ryan (2015), these are demarcated by the clear temporal boundaries that exist between scenes; for free-flowing interview and conversation data, this concept has been reframed loosely as *narrative or thematic episode*, with episodes identified as starting with the signalling and establishment of major new topics and ending with their closure. In the present data, in many cases these were marked by disjunctive markers (e.g. 'Oh, another thing I wanna tell you'), news announcements, or questions following silences (see Wong & Waring, 2010, for a summary of such practices). Topics in the interviews typically lasted at least two to three pages of transcript data, and sometimes considerably more.

Also requiring some further specification was the concept of discourse topicality (labelled global topicality in Ryan, 2015). Discourse topics were defined as the person most central to the thematic episode. In the majority of cases, each episode involving person reference had an obvious (and single) person who was readily identifiable as the main topic.

Though the system is not without limitations, its application to NS data reveals distributions of high- and low-accessibility markers in general accordance with Accessibility Theory (Ryan, 2015). Drawing on Ryan (2012, 2015), Table 6.1 presents an overview of the RE types associated with each of the accessibility

Table 6.1 Accessibility coding in English (based on Ryan, 2012, 2015)

Accessibility range	Code	Associated REs	Alternative RE options (Ryan, 2015) (%)
High	D7	pn, ø	<1
	D6	pn, ø	7
	D5	pn, ø	12
Intermediate	D4	pn, LAM	pn = 56, LAM = 44
	D3	LAM, pn	LAM = 74, pn = 26
Low	D2	LAM	6
	D1	LAM	4
	D0	LAM	0

ø = zero anaphora, pn = pronoun, LAM = low-accessibility marker (names, determiner + noun) codes in L1 English, alongside the frequency with which other RE types are used. As displayed, accessibility contexts D5 to D7 represent high degrees of accessibility, where NS usually opt for pronouns or ø, while in contexts D0 to D2, they overwhelmingly avoid such forms, opting instead for names and determiner + noun combinations (with or without further modification). The intermediate range contexts of D3 and D4 appear to lie near a juncture allowing greater variation, though with LAMs clearly preferred at D3 and a slight tendency for HAMs at D4.

Findings: Longitudinal data

RE types used

Table 6.2 presents an overview of the RE types that Yoona used for referent tracking across the three interviews.

Most notable in these data is the high proportion of pronouns used in each of the three interviews. Subject pronouns, object pronouns, and zero anaphora (ø) together accounted for more than 80% of all references, with the proportion climbing slightly over the period (2016 = 81.3%; 2017 = 88.7%; 2018 = 88.2%). As explored further below, this suggests there was little if any over-explicitness, but perhaps substantial under-explicitness. In contrast to pronouns, ø was noticeably infrequent across all three interviews, with no cases at all in 2018. This is rather surprising given both their legitimate use in English (mainly in coordinate constructions with co-referential subjects), and their wide distribution in Korean discourse. The differing frequencies in the use of names can be accounted for by the nature of the stories told, and especially the number of referents known to the interviewer by name.

Across all three interviews, there were very few errors of form in the production of REs. There were, for instance, no pronoun errors (e.g. production of *he* instead of *she*) and few referential uses of bare nouns (e.g. *tutor* in place of *the tutor*) with none at all in 2018. In relation to the first research question, then, overall these initial figures offer little indication of changes in Yoona's referring behaviour over the two-and-a-half years.

Table 6.2 RE types used in referent tracking

	ø	*he/she*	*him/her*	*Name*	*the/my/her* + NP	*Bare NP*	*Other*	*Total*
2016	5	121	27	19	5	2	3	181
2017	8	126	23	1	15	3	3	168
2018	0	100	27	7	7	0	3	144

Accessibility marking

It seemed clear from all three interviews that Yoona was skilled in tracking references, with relatively few indications of miscommunication or obvious infelicities. Here, this impression is explored by analysing the distribution of REs by accessibility context (D0–D7). Table 6.3 presents this overall distribution, with percentages provided for high-accessibility markers (HAMs) (subject, object, possessive pronouns, and ø).

These figures lead to five rather striking observations:

(1) Yoona's use of pronouns within the higher accessibility contexts was highly consistent.
(2) Pronoun use dominated in all but the lowest accessibility contexts.
(3) There is effectively no evidence of over-explicitness in the data.
(4) There is substantial evidence of under-explicitness.
(5) There is strong evidence that Yoona's patterns of accessibility marking remained highly stable across the two-and-a-half years of the study.

Elaborating firstly on the first three observations, across the three interviews Yoona made 323 references in contexts D5–D7 and all but one of these was with a high-accessibility marker, nearly always pronoun. The only exception was a single use of a name at D6 in the first interview. In 2017, such consistency was maintained across an even wider distribution of contexts, encompassing all 132 references between D4–D7. This contrasts strikingly with previously reported distributions both in L1 English (see Table 6.1) and L2 English. While intermediate and advanced L2 English is routinely over-explicit, this is clearly not the case with Yoona. Furthermore, Yoona's consistency in selecting pronouns appears markedly greater than has been reported for L1 English; native English speakers are highly consistent in using HAMs only in context D7, with full NPs accounting for about one in ten references at D5–D6 (Ryan, 2015; see also Table 6.1). This can be partly explained by NSs occasionally varying their RE selection for purposes beyond ensuring that referents are identifiable, for instance to achieve

Table 6.3 Distribution of pronouns by accessibility context (Yoona)

	2016 Total	% HAMs	2017 Total	% HAMs	2018 Total	% HAMs
D7	24	100	48	100	9	100
D6	45	98	52	100	38	100
D5	46	100	16	100	45	100
D4	20	95	16	100	8	75
D3	6	83	12	83	9	89
D2	6	17	6	67	5	60
D1	9	44	6	33	3	33
D0	10	0	4	0	3	0

particular stylistic effects,[3] to signal the structuring of discourse (Vonk, Hustinx, & Simons, 1992), or to provide additional information such as stance, as in *poor old Gladys* (Stivers, 2007). In not applying such strategies, Yoona's referring practices at D4–D7 are best characterised as being consistently *minimally explicit*, as they are felicitous but minimally informative.[4]

In the lower-accessibility contexts of D1 to D3, it appears that Yoona was frequently *under-explicit*, selecting pronouns where full NPs are felicitous. At D3, where full NPs might be expected to account for around 75% of references, her selections were dominated by pronouns (23/27; 85%). Under-explicitness is particularly unequivocal at D2 and D1, where almost half of her total references were by pronouns (15/35); by comparison, they are relatively rare in NS speech and attributable to 'occasional misjudgements during unplanned speech' (Ryan, 2015, p. 845).

The consistency in Yoona's RE selections confirm that her minimal-ness and under-explicitness are not the result of random infelicities, but instead result from highly rule-governed behaviour in which she systematically marked less-accessible referents as though they were more highly accessible. Thus, Yoona's system of accessibility marking appears to involve a slightly different mapping of NP-type to degree of accessibility, with pronouns being used for a wider range of accessibility. This appears particularly clear within the intermediate range of D3–D4, which marks a juncture in L1 English between the use of high- and low-accessibility markers, but where Yoona overwhelmingly used pronouns across the three years. More tentatively (due to the small data set) but also more intriguingly, in 2017 and 2018 this is also the case at D2, where pronouns appear more unequivocally infelicitous and are perhaps prone to triggering miscommunication (as will be discussed). The fact that such pronoun use became more frequent after 2016 could suggest a slight shift to even greater under-explicitness over time.

Yoona's system of accessibility marking can, therefore, be described for each of the three data collection points of the study, though more tentatively for the lower-accessibility contexts where there is less data. This is presented in Table 6.4 alongside expected felicitous RE selection based on distributions in NS data (based on Ryan, 2015).

Table 6.4 Yoona's system of accessibility marking

Context	Felicitous REs	Yoona		
		2016	2017	2018
D7	pn, ø	pn	pn	pn
D6	pn, ø	pn	pn	pn
D5	pn, ø	pn	pn	pn
D4	pn, LAM	pn	pn	pn
D3	LAM, pn	pn	pn	pn
D2	LAM	LAM	pn	pn
D1	LAM	LAM	LAM	LAM
D0	LAM	LAM	LAM	LAM

In terms of longitudinal development, there is thus the tentative suggestion that Yoona's system of accessibility marking may have become more under-explicit after 2016. Overall, however, the most notable observation is again the overall stability of the system over the two-and-a-half years.

It is also worth mentioning that, like native speakers in previous studies, referent accessibility was a very strong predictor of Yoona's RE selection, with no additional effect detected within the contexts of topic shift or focus position. By contrast, language learners are elsewhere reported as tending to be particularly over-explicit in both of these contexts (e.g. Ryan, 2015).

From these analyses, a picture emerges in which Yoona's referring behaviour differs markedly from what was anticipated based on the previous literature. Over-explicitness, which is so characteristic within the speech of many SLLs, seems entirely absent from Yoona's talk except perhaps in the limited sense of under-using ø. Instead, her talk is characterised by a notable tendency towards minimal informativity by way of extensive use of pronouns, at times erring on the side of under-explicitness. To confirm this finding, the following subsection provides qualitative analyses of extracts coded as containing under-explicit pronouns.

Qualitative analyses

As will be demonstrated, the qualitative analyses support the evidence for an absence of over-explicitness and relatively frequent under-explicitness. To convincingly illustrate the latter, in most cases somewhat extended extracts of text are required to give a sense of distance, competition, unity, and so on. These analyses also suggest some longitudinal developments that are not captured in the quantitative analyses.

As discussed in the methodology section, plural references, references in reported speech, and references made by the interviewer were not coded for accessibility, but are taken into account when determining the accessibility of subsequent references. For ease of reading, Yoona's references are bolded. The identity of the referents is distinguished in subscript (e.g. $_A$ or $_B$) and the accessibility scores are presented in superscript.

Examples of under-explicitness are readily identifiable across all three interviews. Extract 1 begins 31 minutes into the final interview, and illustrates Yoona's tracking of multiple referents with minimal, and perhaps occasionally under-explicit reference. The extract contains references to four individuals within a short space of time. Included are a pronominal reference to $_{(B)}$Grace coded at D2 (line 10), which was successful despite potential ambiguity from referent $_{(A)}$ in line 08. Similarly, the pronoun in line 11 (coded D3) initially seems ambiguous given the competition from $_{(B)}$ and $_{(D)}$, but soon becomes clear once $_{(B)}$Grace is ruled out by the non-co-referential 'before $_{(B)}$Grace.' The final pronoun in line 17 is also minimally explicit (coded D3) but is clear within the communicative context Yoona describes.

Extract 1

```
01  Y:  actually, um, (B)Grace⁽ⁱⁿᵗʳᵒ⁾ was in semester two with me
02          but I had hadn't talked to (B)her⁵ until semester six,
03  J:  oh
04  Y:  because we were like in different stream, and
05  J:  oh yep, yep
06  Y:  I didn't really catch up with anybody, so
07  J:  yep
08  Y:  except (A)my Filipino friend⁻¹ and yeah,
09          and I yeah, I felt international students are all the same,
10          but but (B)her² (C)friend⁽ⁱⁿᵗʳᵒ⁾ was quite close with (D)Emma⁻¹,
11          so I got close to (C)her³, before (B)Grace³,
12          and (C)she³ told me that – before going to placement we met at the library –
13          and then (C)she⁶ said 'you going to placement with (B)Grace, together like?'
14          'oh, do I?' and then 'How is (B)she? I'm so worried about my English,
15          like I'm gonna met my supervisors
16          and then like I have to become independent,'
17          and then (C)she's³ like 'you're fine',
```

Consideration of such extracts supports the conclusion that Yoona frequently used pronouns in contexts where a fuller form might be expected. However, despite differing from L1 norms, Yoona's management of multiple referents in such an economical and yet communicatively successful way appears skilful.

Extract 2 is from 13 minutes into the interview, and illustrates the ambiguity that occasionally arises from under-explicitness. Immediately prior to this, Yoona had been discussing the impact of her closest friend (A) needing to repeat a semester and therefore being placed in different classes. She then speaks of the consequent need to communicate more with others. In line 14, 'another kiwi girl' (B) is introduced into the discourse. In line 16, she states that 'she's actually like a Filipino kiwi.' Here, *she* seems felicitous for referring to (B), who had accessibility D5; it seems under-explicit for (A), who was coded at D3. This caused some confusion as I knew that (A) was ethnically Filipino, hence the clarification request initiated in line 19 to determine whether they were both Filipino. Further ambiguity arose from another under-explicit (D3) pronoun in line 28.

Extract 2: October 2018

```
01  Y:  but since (Y & A)we split from each other, I had to make a friend?,
02  J:  yeah
03  Y:  and I had to talk to other people, or other girls,
04          other kiwi students, yeah.
05  J:  mm
```

06 Y: yeah y'kn[ow, I think
07 J: [so that, that was the turning point,
08   so[rt of when you were forced to kinda
09 Y: [yeah I think,
10   and, yeah, turning point to become a little bit more independent,
11 J: yeah,
12 Y: yeah,
13   but since, yeah, that semester, yeah, semester five,
14   I was with $_{(B)}$another kiwi girl, and sh- I learned a lot from $_{(B)}$her[5],
15   the- like the attitudes and the communication way, and skill,
16   I learned a lot, and, $_{(A)}$she's a – she's[3] actually like a Filipino kiwi,
17   but $_{(A)}$she's[6] like – they have like different communication way,
18   so, yeah, so
19 J: oh, just to clarify, you mean the- they're[(A & B)] both Filipino kiwi?
20 Y: no no
21 J: nah nah $_{(A)}$your original friend was and $_{(B)}$the other is
22 Y: kiwi,
23 J: just pakeha-kiwi?
24 Y: yeh
25 J: yup
26 Y: yeh,
27 J: mm
28 Y: but $_{(A)}$she[3] has grown up here so, $_{(A)}$she[6] only speak English too, so
29 J: yeah
30 Y: but it was kinda different experience,

Extract 3 illustrates minimal – and perhaps under-explicit – reference in a somewhat different context. At about 11 minutes into the interview, the topic switched to recalling where our discussions had left off in the last interview two months previously, and specifically a dilemma Yoona had described regarding her working schedule: she had wanted to keep working under the same supervisor, but this would have meant changing to a night shift, creating other difficulties. In this extract, the focus of interest is the introduction of this supervisor in line 09. Of interest is that Yoona uses a pronoun to do so, and that – perhaps counterintuitively – this proves communicatively successful. As a referent introduction, no accessibility code is given.

Extract 3: October, 2018

01 J: yeh, you- I remember you changed your time didn't you,
02   because you were (0.6) working nights, and then
03   (1.0)
04   or ev[enings and then changed to
05 A: [oh yeah
06   (0.7)

```
07         ye[ah
08   J:    [or day time, yu[p
09   A:                    [yeh, (0.3) and I text ₍ₐ₎her,
10         (0.6)
11   J:    mm
12   A:    tell ₍ₐ₎her that I preferred PM shift, to do my assignment,
13         and then ₍ₐ₎she #said 'oh that's totally fine,'
14   J:    yeh
```

As suggested above, this reference seems rather curious as such *recognitional* introductions are associated with the use of full NPs and sometimes lengthy introduction sequences (Ryan, 2016; Smith, Noda, Andrews, & Jucker, 2005). In this case, the previous reference to the supervisor was 58 days earlier. Yet, as the interlocutor, there was little-or-no processing strain in interpreting this pronoun. In accounting for this, the most relevant consideration is referent accessibility rather than discourse status (as introduced, maintained or re-introduced). Specifically, mutual ground had been collaboratively established over the situation being discussed, with a demonstration of hearer-understanding through lines 01-04. In the establishment of a suitably specific context, the accessibility of the supervisor was increased. Yoona thus correctly judged that a pronoun would be sufficiently clear.

To briefly summarise, then, the qualitative analysis supports and strengthens the quantitative findings regarding extensive minimal and – at times – underexplicit reference. Such evidence of under-explicitness occurs across all three interviews.[5] However, my overall impression was that cases of under-explicitness from the 2017 and 2018 interviews tended to be more striking and perhaps more obviously infelicitous than those in 2016. This forced a closer inspection of the contexts in which these occurred. The most notable difference appeared to be that all of the anecdotes recounted in the 2016 interview required the concurrent tracking of just one or two referents; these could therefore be readily interpreted with little risk of miscommunication. By contrast, in both the 2017 and 2018 interviews there were a number of stories involving a concurrent focus on three or even more referents (see, for example, Extract 1). Since these engender a greater risk of miscommunication from ambiguous RE selection, instances of under-explicitness often appeared more conspicuous by way of (potential) vagueness and therefore requiring additional processing effort for the hearer. This could simply reflect the nature of the stories that Yoona had to tell in 2016; however, it also seems likely that in the later interviews she *chose* to tell more complex stories, or to tell them in richer and more referentially complex ways. This seems very plausible given her greater communicative experience and growing interactional competence.

There were some other subtle indications of developments over time. For instance, Extract 4 from 2016 illustrates a feature only observed in this first interview, whereby a vague plural *they* becomes the antecedent of a singular reference (*she*); this was observed three times in the first interview but not at all in later

Under-explicit and minimally explicit reference 113

interviews. Prior to this extract, Yoona had vaguely mentioned *everyone*, which was inferable as meaning her classmates; this was shortly followed by a co-referential *they*. Line 01 below occurred ten turns (22 propositions) later, and includes a further plural use of *they*. This then becomes the antecedent of a further *they* in line 02; however, here the plural pronoun evidently relates to a singular referent, a classmate who has a daughter 'crazy about K-pop' and wanting 'to go to Korea.' In line 07, this is followed by *she* (line 7). The interpretation of *she* requires inferring that it is one of the classmates, and specifically the individual (*they*) who spoke of a daughter and K-pop. This transition from a vague plural to a specific singular reference seems curious and is somewhat different to the various subclasses of antecedentless pronouns discussed elsewhere (e.g. Gundel, Hedberg, & Zacharski, 2005; Yule, 1982). Nevertheless, it presented no apparent communicative difficulty, and may in fact represent an effective and economical means of temporarily introducing peripheral hearer-new individuals into discourse.

Extract 4: July 2016

```
01   A:   and (B*) they tried to make me like feel comfortable
02        and (B*) they [said] 'oh (A) my daughter really really crazy about K-pop
03        so (A) she really want to go to Korea or something'
04   J:   oh
05   A:   so I said 'oh really' and ø [we] talked to each other,
06   J:   uh-huh
07   A:   and (B) she⁶ was really nice, and actually they really helped me yesterday,
08        cause I wasn't here Monday so I don't – I have no idea about (C) her¹
          lectures,
09        so I said I wasn't here
```

Discussion and conclusion

In relation to the two research questions, in the nearly two-and-a-half year span of the study there is less evidence than expected of (1) shifts in Yoona's system of RE use and (2) patterns of accessibility marking. The development of Yoona's RE system included the apparent elimination of ø and bare nouns by 2018, and by 2017 dropping the practice of occasionally using singular anaphors (*she*) to specify one from a set of vague plural antecedents (*they*). A more substantial development was that by 2017, Yoona was engaging in more complex concurrent tracking of multiple referents, which may reflect greater overall confidence and experience in speaking English. In terms of accessibility marking, there is tentative evidence of increasing use of pronouns in the low-accessibility context D2.

However, the most striking findings overall were Yoona's strong tendency towards minimal and under-explicitness and that she was very seldom if ever over-explicit. These were stable features of her accessibility marking across the length of the study and are counter to the predictions arising from previous studies.

While previous evidence of under-explicitness has mainly involved infelicitous use of ø (in place of pronouns), here it involved the use of pronouns where names and *the* + noun are felicitous, despite the use of pronouns being very infrequent in Korean.

The stability of Yoona's referent tracking system is of interest given the 2 ½ span of the study, and her extensive use of and exposure to English during this period[6]. Numerous factors have been proposed to account for such long-term stability in SLL language systems (see Long, 2003 for an overview), but apparently little specifically in relation to L2 pragmatics. In this case, it seems helpful to consider the competing interactional demands of achieving referential clarity (or *recognition*) and being economical (Levinson, 2007; Sacks & Schegloff, 2007). Achieving clarity can require providing substantial descriptive information, while economy promotes brevity. From this perspective, Chini's (2005) early pragmatic and lexical stage is characterised by lapses in clarity through overuse of ø and omission of determiners. Among factors driving further development will be clarification requests and interactional repairs, as well as positive and negative evidence from language exposure. At the following (over-) explicit lexical stage, clarity is emphasised but at a cost to economy, with over-explicit references and other redundant information slowing communication. This may eventually be a source of frustration as it exasperates the pre-existing communicative 'bottleneck' in which the mind processes language considerably faster than the ability to verbalise it (Levinson, 2000). Subsequent development may therefore be largely driven by internal and external pressures for economical communication, alongside positive evidence from language exposure.

In Yoona's case, her strategy of being highly economical appears to have been largely successful, despite at times being infelicitous by NS standards. There is no contradiction here: as argued by Kasper (1997, pp. 355–356), it is simply flawed reasoning to assume L2 speech acts are communicatively problematic simply because they differ from L1 norms. Here, it appears that Yoona successfully monitored her RE selections for clarity and was well attuned to the interlocutor's ability to recover the referent. Even notably under-explicit REs (e.g. those at D1 and D2) seldom proved communicatively problematic, though some may have required more processing effort from the interlocutor. Indeed, among the 493 references examined, there were only five clarification requests (1.0%). Since these also occur relatively frequently in NS interactions, this can be presumed to be fairly target-like and likely too few to prompt a behavioural change. Conversely, the 488 references that passed unremarked (99.0%) provide Yoona with evidence of success, while also facilitating the economical flow of discourse. In short, then, the stability of Yoona's accessibility marking is likely a reflection of its overall success in terms of both relative clarity and economy.

In further accounting for the differences between these and previous findings, the limitations of the study need to be acknowledged along with reflections on how the data were generated. The most important limitations relate to the limited number of references examined. While the interviews probably provide a sufficient number overall (just under 500), as with previous studies, these are concentrated particularly among the higher accessibility contexts (D5–D7), with references to less-accessible individuals remaining greatly under-researched.

Particularly relevant features of the interview data include the familiarity between the interactants, the relaxed setting, the participant's control over the stories she chose to tell, extensive opportunities to rehearse her ideas prior to the interview, the more naturalistic setting, and the communicative focus being co-constructed by the interactants rather than predetermined by the task. Each of these features likely serves to reduce communicative pressure. Such unpressured performance allows participants 'the opportunity to conceptualise, formulate and articulate their messages with some care' (Ellis, 2005, p. 165), potentially allowing greater precision in RE selection.

By contrast, the vast majority of related studies have made use of elicitation tasks, such as retellings of silent films and picture sequences conducted in classroom or laboratory-type settings (e.g. Ahrenholz, 2005; Chini, 2005; Gullberg, 2006; Hendriks, 2003; Ryan, 2015). Such tasks lend themselves to having predetermined and comparatively inflexible criteria for accuracy in meaning, against which participants feel they are measured. Thus, they involve pressured performance, which has been shown to have a negative impact on language complexity and accuracy (e.g. Ellis & Yuan, 2005). Since this arises from the additional demands required at the level of planning and organising information, it would not be surprising if this also had a negative effect on felicitous RE selection. It could be, then, that over-explicitness is more common in traditional elicitation tasks than in naturally occurring L2 speech. Indeed, even without the challenge of second language use, both planning load and memory load are also associated with greater explicitness in L1 English (Arnold, 2010). With this in mind, further studies of L2 reference are recommended using data generated in unpressured performance, such as through informal interviews, discussions, and conversation.

Notes

1 For greater detail on aspects of Korean reference, the interested reader is directed to H.-Y. Kim (2000) and S.-H. Kim (2013).
2 Parallel systems are found for anaphora resolution, originating within the fields of computational linguistics and natural language processing (see for example Mitkov, 2002). Such systems are designed for automated interpretation rather than accounting for speaker behaviour.
3 This is illustrated in the following media interview with a sports coach: 'Isaac knows clearly what he has got to do. I think everyone that has watched Isaac play knows what Isaac has got to do. And Isaac really needs to understand that the only person that can fix Isaac's problems is Isaac' (Knowler, 2010, July 29).
4 Except in the sense that pronouns are used where ø would be appropriate.
5 Note for instance below in Extract 4 (2016) the use of 'her' in line 08.
6 Although there is insufficient space for details here, as expected there is clear evidence in other domains of her gradually increasing linguistic and pragmatic competence over this period, including her fluency, vocabulary range, grammatical range, and morphological accuracy.

References

Ahrenholz, B. (2005). Reference to persons and objects in the function of subject in learner varieties. In H. Hendriks (Ed.), *The structure of learner varieties* (pp. 19–64). Berlin, Germany: Mouton de Gruyter.

Ariel, M. (1990). *Accessing noun phrase antecedents*. London, UK: Routledge.

Ariel, M. (2001). Accessibility theory: An overview. In T. Sanders, J. Schiperoord, & W. Spooren (Eds.), *Text representation: Linguistic and psycholinguistic aspects* (pp. 29–87). Amsterdam, the Netherlands: John Benjamins.

Arnold, J. E. (2010). How speakers refer: The role of accessibility. *Language and Linguistics Compass, 4*(4), 187–203. doi:10.1111/j.1749-818X.2010.00193.x

Bach, K. (2008). On referring and not referring. In J. K. Gundel & N. Hedberg (Eds.), *Reference: Interdisciplinary perspectives* (pp. 13–58). Oxford, UK: Oxford University Press.

Broeder, P. (1991). *Talking about people: A multiple case study on adult language acquisition*. Amsterdam, the Netherlands: Swets & Zeitlinger.

Chini, M. (2005). Reference to person in learner discourse. In H. Hendriks (Ed.), *The structure of learner varieties* (pp. 65–110). Berlin, Germany: Walter de Gruyter.

Crosthwaite, P. (2013). An error analysis of L2 English discourse reference through learner corpora analysis. *Linguistic Research, 30*(2), 163–193.

Crosthwaite, P. (2014). *Differences between the coherence of Mandarin and Korean L2 English learner production and English native speakers: An empirical study* (Doctoral thesis). University of Cambridge, Cambridge, UK.

Ellis, R. (2005). Planning and task-based performance: Theory and research. In R. Ellis (Ed.), *Planning and task performance in a second language* (pp. 3–34). Amsterdam, the Netherlands: John Benjamins.

Ellis, R., & Yuan, F. (2005). The effects of careful within-task planning on oral and written task performance. In R. Ellis (Ed.), *Planning and task performance in a second language* (pp. 167–192). Amsterdam, the Netherlands: John Benjamins.

Gullberg, M. (2006). Handling discourse: Gestures, reference tracking, and communication strategies in early L2. *Language Learning, 56*(1), 155–196. doi:10.1111/j.0023-8333.2006.00344.x

Gundel, J. K., Hedberg, N., & Zacharski, R. (2005). Pronouns without NP antecedents: How do we know when a pronoun is referential? In A. Branco, T. McEnery, & R. Mitkov (Eds.), *Anaphora processing: Linguistic, cognitive and computational modelling* (pp. 351–364). Amsterdam, the Netherlands: John Benjamins.

Hendriks, H. (2003). Using nouns for reference maintenance: A seeming contradiction in L2 discourse. In A. G. Ramat (Ed.), *Typology and second language acquisition* (pp. 291–326). Berlin, Germany: Mouton de Gruyter.

Jarvis, S. (2002). Topic continuity in L2 English article use. *Studies in Second Language Acquisition, 24*(3), 387–418. doi:10.1017/S0272263102003029

Kang, J. Y. (2004). Telling a coherent story in a foreign language: Analysis of Korean EFL learners' referential strategies in oral narrative discourse. *Journal of Pragmatics, 36*(11), 1975–1990. doi:10.1016/j.pragma.2004.03.007

Kasper, G. (1997). Beyond reference. In G. Kasper & E. Kellerman (Eds.), *Communication strategies: Psycholinguistic and sociolinguistic perspectives* (pp. 345–360). London, UK: Longman.

Kim, H.-Y. (2000). *Acquisition of English nominal reference by Korean speakers* (Doctoral dissertation). University of Hawai'i at Manoa, Honolulu, HI.

Kim, S.-H. (2013). *A corpus-based analysis of discourse anaphora in English and Korean: A neo-Gricean pragmatic approach* (PhD dissertation). The University of Texas at Arlington, Arlington, TX.

Klein, W., & Perdue, C. (1992). *Utterance structure: Developing grammars again.* Amsterdam, the Netherlands: John Benjamins.

Knowler, R. (2010, July 29). All Blacks staff spell it out for Isaac Ross. *The Press.* Retrieved from http://www.stuff.co.nz/sport/rugby/provincial/3967950/All-Blacks-staff-spell-it-out-for-Isaac-Ross

Leclercq, P., & Lenart, E. (2013). Discourse cohesion and accessibility of referents in oral narratives: A comparison of L1 and L2 acquisition of French and English. *Discours: Revue de Linguistique, Psycholinguistique et Informatique, 12,* 3–31. doi:10.4000/discours.8801

Levinson, S. C. (2000). *Presumptive meanings: The theory of generalized conversational implicature.* Cambridge, MA: MIT Press.

Levinson, S. C. (2007). Optimizing person reference – Perspectives from usage on Rossel Island. In N. J. Enfield & T. Stivers (Eds.), *Person reference in interaction: Linguistic, cultural, and social perspectives* (pp. 29–72). Cambridge, UK: Cambridge University Press.

Long, M. H. (2003). Stabilization and fossilization in interlanguage development. In C. J. Doughty & M. H. Long (Eds.), *The handbook of second language acquisition* (pp. 487–535). Malden, MA: Blackwell.

Lozano, C. (2009). Selective deficits at the syntax-discourse interface: Evidence from the CEDEL2 corpus. In N. Snape, Y.-k. I. Leung, & M. Sharwood Smith (Eds.), *Representational deficits in SLA: Studies in honor of Roger Hawkins* (pp. 127–166). Amsterdam, the Netherlands: John Benjamins.

Lozano, C. (2016). Pragmatic principles in anaphora resolution at the syntax-discourse interface: Advanced English learners of Spanish in the CEDEL2 corpus. In M. Alonso-Ramos (Ed.), *Spanish learner corpus research: Current trends and future perspectives* (pp. 235–265). Amsterdam, the Netherlands: John Benjamins.

Lozano, C. (2018). The development of anaphora resolution at the syntax-discourse interface: Pronominal subjects in Greek learners of Spanish. *Journal of Psycholinguistic Research, 47*(2), 411–430. doi:10.1007/s10936-017-9541-8

Lumley, J. R. (2013). *Pragmatic perspectives on the second language acquisition of person reference in Japanese: A longitudinal study* (PhD doctoral thesis). Newcastle University, Newcastle, UK.

Mitkov, R. (2002). *Anaphora resolution.* London, UK: Longman.

Nakahama, Y. (2003). Development of referent management in L2 Japanese: A film retelling task. *Studies in Language and Culture, 25*(1), 127–146. Retrieved from http://www.lang.nagoya-u.ac.jp/proj/genbunronshu/25-1/nakahama.pdf

Nakahama, Y. (2009). Cross-linguistic influence on referent introduction and tracking in Japanese as a second language. *The Modern Language Journal, 93*(2), 241–260. doi:10.1111/j.1540-4781.2009.00859.x

Nakahama, Y. (2011). *Referent markings in L2 narratives: Effects of task complexity, learners' L1 and proficiency level.* Tokyo, Japan: Hituzi Syobo.

Odlin, T. (2003). Cross-linguistic influence. In C. J. Doughty & M. H. Long (Eds.), *The handbook of second language acquisition* (pp. 436–486). Oxford, UK: Blackwell.

Ryan, J. (2012). *Acts of reference and the miscommunication of referents by first and second language speakers of English* (PhD doctoral thesis). University of Waikato, Hamilton, New Zealand.

Ryan, J. (2015). Overexplicit referent tracking in L2 English: Strategy, avoidance, or myth? *Language Learning*, 65(4), 824–859. doi:10.1111/lang.12139

Ryan, J. (2016). Introducing referents for recognition: L2 pragmatic competence and miscommunication. *Journal of Pragmatics*, 97, 55–73. doi:10.1016/j.pragma.2016.04.005

Sacks, H., & Schegloff, E. A. (2007). Two preferences in the organization of reference to persons in conversation and their interaction. In N. J. Enfield & T. Stivers (Eds.), *Person reference in interaction: Linguistic, cultural, and social perspectives* (pp. 23–28). Cambridge, UK: Cambridge University Press.

Smith, S. W., Noda, H. P., Andrews, S., & Jucker, A. H. (2005). Setting the stage: How speakers prepare listeners for the introduction of referents in dialogues and monologues. *Journal of Pragmatics*, 37(11), 1865–1895. doi:10.1016/j.pragma.2005.02.016

Song, J. J. (2005). *The Korean language: Structure, use and context*. Abingdon, UK: Routledge.

Stivers, T. (2007). Alternative recognitionals in person reference. In N. J. Enfield & T. Stivers (Eds.), *Person reference in interaction: Linguistic, cultural, and social perspectives* (pp. 73–96). Cambridge, UK: Cambridge University Press.

Takeuchi, M. (2014). *Subject referential expressions and encoding of referential status in l2 narrative discourse by L1-English learners of Japanese* (PhD dissertation). Indiana University, Bloomington, IN.

Tomlin, R. S. (1990). Functionalism in second language acquisition. *Studies in Second Language Acquisition*, 12(2), 155–177. doi:10.1017/S0272263100009062

Toole, J. (1996). The effect of genre on referential choice. In J. K. Gundel & T. Fretheim (Eds.), *Reference and referent accessibility* (pp. 263–290). Amsterdam, the Netherlands: John Benjamins.

Vonk, W., Hustinx, L., & Simons, W. H. G. (1992). The use of referential expressions in structuring discourse. In J. Oakhill & A. Garnham (Eds.), *Discourse representation and text processing: Special issue of 'Language and Cognitive Processes'* (pp. 301–333). Hove, UK: Lawrence Erlbaum.

Wong, J., & Waring, H. Z. (2010). *Conversation analysis and second language pedagogy: A guide for ESL/EFL teachers*. New York, NY: Routledge.

Yule, G. (1982). Interpreting anaphora without identifying reference. *Journal of Semantics*, 1(4), 315–322. doi:10.1093/jos/1.3-4.315

7 Anaphora resolution in topic continuity

Evidence from L1 English–L2 Spanish data in the CEDEL2 corpus

Fernando Martín-Villena and Cristóbal Lozano

Introduction

Variability in subject expression has been a widely studied phenomenon over the last few decades and is still the focus of a considerable body of research in both native (L1) and second language (L2) grammars. Crucially, the production of L2 Spanish learners, both written and oral, has been investigated in depth with a view to understand how they use referential expressions (REs) like null and overt pronominals (i.e. what has been traditionally called anaphora resolution) and other REs such as lexical noun phrases (NPs), as well as which factors constrain their use in real discourse (e.g. Blackwell & Quesada, 2012; Lozano, 2009b, 2016). Even though L2 learners acquire the morphosyntactic features that license null subjects in L2 Spanish from very early stages (Liceras, 1989; Phinney, 1987), results from both experimental and corpus-based developmental studies (e.g. Lozano, 2009b, 2018; Montrul & Rodríguez-Louro, 2006) have shown that certain features are particularly difficult for non-native speakers even at end-states of acquisition. L2 learners show persistent deficits in selecting felicitous null/overt pronouns when constrained at the interfaces (e.g. syntax–discourse interface), following Sorace's Interface Hypothesis (2011, 2012), which holds that such features are more difficult to acquire than merely syntactic ones. However, Lozano (2009b, 2016) used a near-native corpus of L2 Spanish learners to show that these deficits are rather *selective* and do not necessarily affect the whole pronominal paradigm: most of these deficits were (i) attributed to third person human singular subject REs (whereas the rest of the pronominal paradigm was unproblematic), and (ii) were mainly observable in topic continuity scenarios (whereas topic shift and other scenarios were not problematic). These scenarios will be further explored in this chapter using a corpus approach, which will also allow for the investigation of other less-explored factors that constrain the form of subject REs in native and non-native grammars.

Linguistic background

Subject expression is an essential defining property of human languages. Languages can be subdivided into null-subject (e.g. Spanish, Italian, Greek, Arabic), or non-null-subject languages (e.g. English, French, German) (Rizzi, 1982). The first group syntactically licenses the dropping of overt pronouns in subject position, whereas the second group does not. Thus, Spanish syntax allows the alternation of overt and null pronominal subjects (1a), whereas in English null pronominal subjects are ungrammatical (1b).

(1) a. Él/[Ø] siempre se levanta a las siete.
    b. *He/*[Ø] always wakes up at seven.*

The morphologically rich Spanish verbal system, inflecting for both number and person, makes it possible for most subjects to be understood without being overtly expressed (Geeslin & Gudmestad, 2008; Liceras, 1989; Montrul & Rodríguez-Louro, 2006), as (2) illustrates.

(2) Mañana [Ø] $\begin{Bmatrix} \text{vuelvo} & \text{volvemos} \\ \text{vuelves} & \text{veolvéis} \\ \text{vuelve} & \text{vuelven} \end{Bmatrix}$ a la rutina de una vez por todas.

Tomorrow [Ø] $\begin{Bmatrix} \text{return.1SG} & \text{return.1PL} \\ \text{return.2SG} & \text{return.2PL} \\ \text{return.3SG} & \text{return.3PL} \end{Bmatrix}$ *return to the routine of one time for all.*

'*Tomorrow I/you/(s)he/we/you/they return to routine once and for all.*'

This apparently free syntactic alternation is subtly constrained by discursive factors at the syntax–discourse interface, namely topic continuity vs shift (Blackwell & Quesada, 2012; Lozano, 2002, 2009b, 2016; Rothman, 2009).

In topic continuity scenarios, the subject antecedent is maintained from one clause/sentence to the next. L1 Spanish natives tend to opt for null pronouns to maintain the topic, whereas English requires overt REs (Geeslin & Gudmestad, 2008; Lozano, 2009b, 2016). Sentence (3) illustrates how the first sentential subject *Ada* is maintained along the following sentences via a null pronominal subject ($Ø_i$).

(3) **Ada**$_i$ no quiere separarse de él$_j$, y [$Ø_i$] vuelve a la playa todos los días.; [$Ø_i$] se pasa el tiempo tocándolo$_j$ [...]. Un día [$Ø_i$] conoce a George$_k$ [...]. [$Ø_i$] Encuentra en esta relación el cariño que [$Ø_i$] no recibe de su marido$_j$. [ES_WR_28_3_MAAO, CEDEL2 corpus, Spanish native]

'*Ada$_i$ does not want to separate from him$_j$, and [$Ø_i$] goes back to the beach every day, [$Ø_i$] spends all the time touching him$_j$ [...]. One day [$Ø_i$] meets George$_k$ [...]. [$Ø_i$] Finds in this relationship the love that [$Ø_i$] does not receive from her husband$_j$.*'

Interestingly, it is also grammatically possible to drop overt pronominal subject REs in native English in contexts of syntactic coordination (Crosthwaite, 2011;

Harvie, 1998; Ryan, 2012), but only if there is a continuity in topic (Quesada & Lozano, forthcoming), as illustrated in (4). In our study, this superficial similarity between Spanish and English in coordinated structures is taken as the root of transfer (cf. the results section).

(4) **Jesus**$_i$ did everything that was right and [Ø$_i$] even laid down his life for all of mankind. [EN_WR_19_4_AL, COREFL corpus, English native]

Crucially, the difference between a null-subject language like Spanish and a non-null-subject language like English lies in the notion that null-subject languages license null subjects in any syntactic scenario (coordinated sentences, as in the first instance of Ø$_i$ in (3) earlier, main clauses, as in the three subsequent instances of Ø$_i$, and also subordinated clauses, as in the last instance of Ø$_i$), whereas English does not allow null subjects in non-coordinated scenarios.

Topic shift, by contrast, is typically encoded via overt material, not only overt pronominal subjects but also NPs and proper names (Geeslin, Linford, & Fafulas, 2015; Lozano, 2009b, 2016). Even though overt pronouns are employed to mark topic shift in discourse, research has shown that NPs appear significantly more frequently in these contexts to avoid ambiguity (Lozano, 2009b), particularly if two antecedents of the same gender are brought into discourse or when the number of potential antecedents is high (Lozano, 2016). Sentence (5) illustrates the choice of an NP (*Rafa Nadal*) when there are two same-gender antecedents (*Rafa[el] Nadal* and *su tío* 'his uncle').

(5) **Rafael Nadal**$_i$ es un tenista de unos 24 años nacido en Manacor, un pueblo de las Islas Baleares. Ya [Ø$_i$] creció en un ambiente deportivo ya que su tío$_j$, 'Nadal,' fue un famoso jugador del futbol club Barcelona. **Rafa Nadal**$_i$ comenzó su carrera deportiva desde muy pequeño. [ES_WR_26_2_AVS, CEDEL2 corpus, Spanish native]

'*Rafael Nadal*$_i$ *is a 24-year-old tennis player who was born in Manacor, a town in the Balearic Islands.* [Ø$_i$]*was born surrounded by sports since his uncle*$_j$, *"Nadal," was a famous football player in Barcelona F.C. Rafa Nadal*$_i$ *started his career from a very young age.*'

Factors that constrain the choice of RE in L2 Spanish

Following White's (1986) pioneering study investigating the influence of the pro-drop parameter setting in L2 acquisition, many researchers have investigated whether L2 learners are aware of the alternation between overt and null pronominal subjects in null-subject languages like Spanish. Early studies (Liceras, 1989; Phinney, 1987) indicated that L1 English–L2 Spanish learners can acquire the morphosyntactic properties of the pro-drop parameter from early stages of acquisition (i.e. they are sensitive to the fact that Spanish licenses null pronouns). Years later, a series of experimental studies shifted the attention to how such overt/null alternation is constrained by discursive factors like topic continuity, topic shift, and contrastive focus (e.g. Al-Kasey & Pérez-Leroux, 1998; Lozano, 2002; Rothman, 2009). Interestingly, another series of corpus-based studies has investigated the production of the multiple factors that constrain such alternation in native and non-native Spanish. Even though learners are increasingly aware of the use of REs in such discursive contexts as their proficiency increases, highly advanced learners still show some residual deficits: they overproduce overt subject REs to encode topic continuity and also produce null pronouns in topic-shift scenarios, leading to ambiguity (Lozano, 2009b, 2016; Montrul & Rodríguez-Louro, 2006).

Interestingly, results from both online and offline experimental studies addressing the *Position of Antecedent Strategy* (PAS, Carminati, 2002) confirm the overproduction/overexplicitation phenomenon. Spanish natives observe the PAS, as in (6): a null pronominal subject biases towards an antecedent in a syntactically higher position (topic position) that correlates with topic continuity, whereas an overt pronominal subject biases towards an antecedent in a lower syntactic position (non-subject position), which correlates with topic shift (Alonso-Ovalle, Fernández-Solera, Frazier, & Clifton, 2002; Bel, Sagarra, Comínguez, & García-Alcaraz, 2016; Filiaci, Sorace, & Carreiras, 2014; Gelormini-Lezama, & Almor, 2014).

(6) Diego$_i$ saludó a Carlos$_j$ mientras Ø$_i$/él$_j$ abría la puerta.

***Diego**$_i$ greeted Carlos$_j$ while [Ø$_i$]/he$_j$ was opening the door.*

However, L1 English–L2 Spanish learners have been shown to accept a sort of 'free' variation of null and overt pronouns when establishing continuity in discourse in PAS scenarios (Bel & García-Alcaraz, 2015; Keating, VanPatten, & Jegerski, 2011). These results clearly reflect the tendency of L2 Spanish learners to over-accept overt pronominal subjects in topic continuity. The PAS studies, however, explore topic continuity vs shift in rather limited scenarios: only two antecedents (in subject and object positions respectively) are explored in biclausal/sentential syntactic configurations, which says little about the influence of additional antecedents in other syntactic configurations.

Crucially, another factor that has been shown to account for variability in subject REs is the existence of additional potential/activated antecedents (apart from the actual antecedent) in the discourse preceding the anaphor/RE. Corpus data from native and non-native Spanish show that the production of fuller forms (particularly NPs) increases as the number of potential antecedents increases (Blackwell & Quesada, 2012; Lozano, 2009b, 2016). As originally observed by Givón (1983), more recent experimental findings for native English (Arnold & Griffin, 2007; Contemori & Dussias, 2016) similarly show that the accessibility of an antecedent decreases in the presence of additional characters, which forces the use of fuller forms like NPs and proper names instead of more minimal forms like pronouns. The amount of potential antecedents appears to be an important factor that determines the choice of fuller RE forms as an ambiguity-solving strategy.

Apart from the number of activated antecedents, their gender can also influence the choice of REs in subject position. Corpus results for native and non-native

Spanish in Lozano (2009b, 2016) accounted for the high production of NPs reported in previous studies based on the number (i.e., quantity) and differences/similarities in the gender of the potential antecedents. He found that in contexts with two potential antecedents, when their gender was the same, NPs were more frequently used so as to avoid ambiguity. Similarly, overt pronouns were preferred when there were two antecedents with different gender (see also Abreu, 2009).

Finally, following a concept from the psycholinguistic literature, several sociolinguistic studies have focused on priming (also known as perseveration) and how it applies to subject expression (Cameron & Flores-Ferrán, 2004; Flores-Ferrán, 2002; Geeslin & Gudmestad, 2011; Travis, 2007; *inter alia*). Basically, 'the presence of one form or structure at one point in a linear sequence may trigger subsequent strings of similar forms or structures' (Cameron & Flores-Ferrán, 2004, p. 43), thus suggesting that null subjects will trigger subsequent null subjects and overt pronouns will be followed by overt pronouns. Contrary to the prediction in Givón (1983) that fuller, more activated forms would be followed by less explicit subject REs, Flores-Ferrán (2002) found perseveration effects in topic continuity: overt pronouns were typically followed by overt pronouns, and null pronouns by null pronouns.

Research questions and hypotheses

Based on the review of previous L2 findings reported above, a series of research questions (RQs) with their corresponding hypotheses (Hs) were formulated for the acquisition of topic continuity, which is the scenario at the syntax–discourse interface that has been shown to be particularly problematic in L1 English–L2 Spanish more than other related scenarios like topic shift and contrastive focus (Lozano, 2016).

RQ1: How do subject REs develop in beginner, intermediate and advanced learners of L2 Spanish in topic continuity contexts? Are they pragmatically (in)felicitous?
H1: The higher the proficiency of L2 learners, the closer to native-like competence their performance will be.

RQ2: Does the syntactic environment in which the RE appears influence the choice of RE in topic continuity?
H2: L1 English–L2 Spanish learners will produce higher rates of null pronouns in coordinate sentences than in non-coordinate sentences as a result of L1 influence, therefore showing that their apparently correct pragmatic use of null pronouns is not the result of acquisition but rather L1 influence.

RQ3: What kind of referential chains are found in the production of L2 Spanish learners and natives? Will null pronominal REs be preceded by null pronominal antecedents to mark topic continuity?
H3: Spanish natives will mark topic continuity via null pronominal-subject chains whereas learners will be more explicit by resorting to overt-pronominal and NP chains.

RQ4: Does the number (and gender) of potential antecedents determine the form of subject REs in learners and natives?

H4a: The higher the number of potential antecedents in the immediately preceding context, the fuller the RE forms in both learners and natives.

H4b: In clear cases where gender can determine the resolution of the RE (i.e. scenarios with two potential antecedents), NPs will be produced to disambiguate cases with same-gender antecedents whereas minimal forms (overt pronouns) will be used when the gender of the two antecedents is different.

Method

Corpus

We analysed a sample from the *Corpus Escrito del Español como L2* (CEDEL2) (Lozano, 2009a, in prep; Lozano & Mendikoetxea, 2013), which is freely available online (http://cedel2.learnercorpora.com). CEDEL2 is a growing, large, multi-L1 corpus of L2 Spanish. It currently contains written compositions by learners of typologically (un)related L1s (English, German, Dutch, Portuguese, French, Italian, Greek, Japanese, Chinese, and Arabic) at all proficiency levels (beginner, intermediate, advanced), as well as several equally designed native corpora. In its latest version (CEDEL2 v.2.0, January, 2020), the corpus contains data from over 4,100 participants.

For this study, we analysed a sample from CEDEL2 (version 1.0). As shown in Table 7.1, we analysed 77 texts (20 beginner, 15 intermediate, 22 advanced learners,[1] as well as a control corpus of 20 Spanish natives[2]), amounting to a total of 27,386 words. What is relevant for our purposes is not so much the total number of words in the sample, but rather the total number of subjects in topic continuity that were tagged in the form of null pronouns, overt pronouns, and NPs. The word/subject ratio across the texts of the different groups increased from 2.3% for natives (i.e. an average of 2.3 tagged subjects every 100 words) to 8.6% for beginners, which indicates that the higher the competence in Spanish, the fewer subjects are produced every 100 words. What is crucial for our analysis is the total number of terminal tags: given that each subject RE was tagged in turn for a multiple number of factors (cf. the tagset in Figure 7.1 in the following section), the final number of terminal tags on which statistics were performed was 10,214.

Table 7.1 CEDEL2 corpus sample

Corpus	N texts	Total # words	Total # tagged subj.	Word/subj. ratio (%)	Total # tags
Beginner	20	2,565	221	8.6	2,433
Intermediate	15	4,886	222	4.5	2,413
Advanced	22	11,571	306	2.6	3,293
Spanish natives	20	8,364	196	2.3	2,075
TOTAL	77	27,386	945		**10,214**

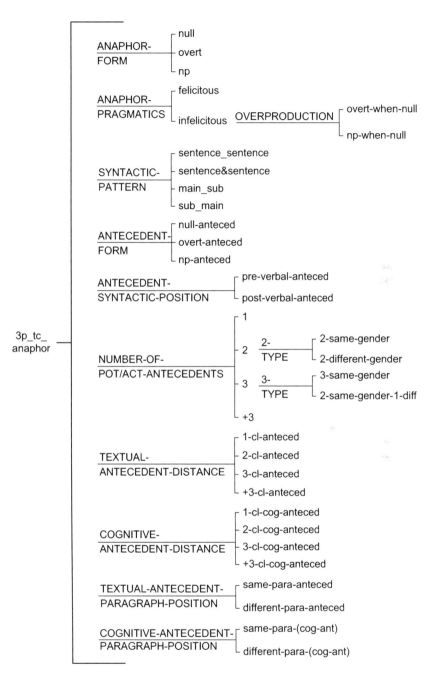

Figure 7.1 Annotation scheme used in the software UAM Corpus Tool

Data annotation and analysis

Essentially, two composition topics from CEDEL2 were analysed (i.e. 'Write about a famous person' and 'Summarise a film you have seen recently') given that they contain numerous scenarios of topic continuity, as illustrated in (7):

(7) Una persona famosa es **Beyonce Knowles**$_i$. **Beyonce**$_i$ esta muy bonita. **Ella**$_i$ canta fantastico. **Ella**$_i$ baila muy bien. [EN_WR_18_18_4_2_LAJ]

*'A famous person is **Beyonce Knowles**$_i$. **Beyonce**$_i$ is very beautiful. **She**$_i$ sings well. **She**$_i$ dances very well'.*

The stand-off XML annotator UAM Corpus Tool (O'Donnell, 2009; http://www.corpustool.com) was used to tag the units (subjects) under analysis and perform χ^2 statistics on the data to test for statistical significance. Each subject was tagged following an annotation scheme or tagset (Figure 7.1), which was designed after Lozano's (2009b, 2016) tagsets. Drawing from the findings in Lozano (2009b, p. 158), whereby the pragmatic deficits of learners in subject expression were described as *selective*, the focus of this study is exclusively on third person animate singular subject REs in topic continuity contexts.

For each of the subjects appearing in finite sentences and marking topic continuity, a number of different properties were coded:

a. *Anaphor form*: RE subjects were classified considering their form, that is, NPs, overt pronouns, or null pronouns. Even though overt and null pronominal subjects have received most of the attention in previous experimental studies (see Alonso-Ovalle et al., 2002; Bel & García-Alcaraz, 2015; *inter alia*), NPs have been shown to be extensively used in both native and learner semi-spontaneous production (e.g. Blackwell & Quesada, 2012; García-Alcaraz & Bel, 2011; Lozano, 2009b, 2016).
b. *Anaphor pragmatics*: drawing from previous findings, topic continuity contexts are typically marked with null pronouns in pro-drop languages such as Spanish. Thus, when the anaphoric form used was a null pronoun, the example was considered pragmatically *felicitous*. By contrast, when a fuller RE expression was used, i.e. an NP (NP-when-null) or an overt pronoun (overt-when-null), the tag assigned was pragmatically *infelicitous*.
c. *Syntactic pattern/environment*: subject REs found in two main syntactic contexts were tagged, i.e. coordinate and non-coordinate sentences/clauses, the latter including juxtaposition and subordination.
d. *Antecedent form*: the form of the antecedent was tagged as NP, overt, or null pronoun, in order to analyse the chains of subject REs created.
e. *Textual and cognitive antecedent paragraph position*: bearing in mind the qualitative observation made by Lozano (2016) that NPs might be used at the beginning of a new paragraph in topic continuity contexts, it was also deemed important to include whether the antecedent (textual and cognitive) appeared in the same or in a different paragraph.

Results and discussion

Results will be presented as per each RQ. The verbal presentation of each result will be closely followed by an interpretation and a discussion.

RQ1: Development of RE forms and pragmatic felicity in topic continuity

Figure 7.2 shows the raw frequencies (and their corresponding percentage) out of the total production of the different REs (null pronoun, overt pronoun, and NP) in subject position as per group (L1 English–L2 Spanish learners [beginners, intermediates, advanced], and Spanish natives). A preliminary analysis of the data according to group reveals that in order to mark topic continuity in Spanish, beginners predominantly produce overt pronouns, intermediates produce mostly null and overt pronouns, and advanced learners and natives produce predominantly null pronouns. In particular, natives produce mostly null pronouns (93.9%) and hardly any overt pronouns (1%, corresponding to two tokens only), as expected. Interestingly, they produce a few NPs (5.1%, ten tokens) to mark topic continuity, an *a priori* unexpected finding to which we will return later. Beginners overuse overt pronouns as a default strategy (56.6%), as illustrated in (8), probably as a consequence of having difficulty when integrating grammatical and discursive information at the syntax–discourse interface (Sorace, 2011; Sorace & Serratrice, 2009) or simply as a reflection of L1 transfer, another issue to which we will return in the following section. Overt pronouns are followed by NPs (24.4%) and some pragmatically felicitous null pronouns (19%). The NPs (24.4%) may be due to the overexplicitation phenomenon reported in the literature (Kang, 2004; Ryan, 2015), also dubbed as the *Repeated Name*

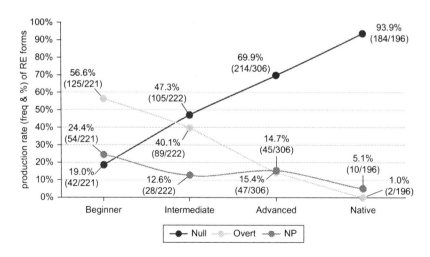

Figure 7.2 Production of RE forms (frequency and %) by group in topic continuity

Penalty (Gelormini-Lezama & Almor, 2011), which mostly corresponds to repetition of proper names, as in *Jennifer* when writing about a famous person like Jennifer López. Intermediates show a null>overt>NP pattern. Their production of pragmatically felicitous null pronouns is noticeable (but still very close to overt pronouns) since they have probably realised that null pronouns are syntactically licensed in Spanish, but they may yet not fully know their real pragmatic function, as illustrated in (9). Advanced learners eventually attain a similar pattern to natives (null>>NP|overt), as illustrated in (10), though we will see later that their attainment differs statistically from natives.

(8) [Beginner] **Tyra Banks**$_i$ es muy bonita. #**Ella**$_i$ es alta. #**Ella**$_i$ es muy simpatico. #**Ella**$_i$ es un cantanté tambien. #**Ella**$_i$ tiene pello rojo. #**Tyra**$_i$ es muy activo. [EN_WR_12_19_3_2_DT]

'*Tyra Banks*$_i$ *is very beautiful. She*$_i$ *is tall. She*$_i$ *is very nice. She*$_i$ *is a singer too. She*$_i$ *has red hair. Tyra*$_i$ *is very active.*'

(9) [Intermediate] En este película, **una mujer**$_i$ tiene un problema con comprando muchas cosas. Muchos veces, #**ella**$_i$ compra todo lo que [Ø$_i$] ve que [Ø$_i$] desea. Porque #**ella**$_i$ gasta tanto dinero, #**ella**$_i$ está en deuda y [Ø$_i$] no puede pagar sus cuentas de tarjeta de crédito. [EN_WR_34_18_10_3_LKF]

'*In this film,* **a woman**$_i$ *has a problem with buying many things. Many times, she*$_i$ *buys everything that* [Ø$_i$] *sees that* [Ø$_i$] *wishes. Because she*$_i$ *spends much money, she*$_i$ *is in debt and* [Ø$_i$] *cannot pay for her credit card accounts.*'

(10) [Advanced] **Pablo Neruda**$_i$ era un poeta y politico chileno. #**El**$_i$ es uno de los mayores poetas del mundo en el siglo XX. [Ø$_i$] Escribió muchas tipas de poesía. [Ø$_i$] Nació en una ciudad se llama Parral. [EN_WR_36_18_6_2_AF]

'*Pablo Neruda*$_i$ *was a Chilean poet and politician.* #*He*$_i$ *was one of the world greatest poets in the 20*th *century.* [Ø$_i$] *Wrote many types of poetry.* [Ø$_i$] *Was born in a city called Parral.*'

Let us explore the results now according to the development of each RE form. Regarding null pronouns, their rate steadily increases across proficiency (19% beginners, 47.3% intermediates, 69.9% advanced, 93.9% natives). For beginners, null pronouns are the least produced form, which probably reflects the non-pro-drop nature of their L1 English, though at each proficiency level they become increasingly and significantly aware that Spanish requires a null pronoun in topic continuity (beginners vs intermediates: $\chi^2=39.984$, $p<0.02$); intermediates vs advanced: $\chi^2=27.569$, $p<0.02$). Crucially, while advanced learners mirror the native trend of mostly producing null pronouns, their behaviour remains significantly different from that of natives ($\chi^2=41.698$, $p<0.02$).

Unlike null pronouns, the production of overt pronouns decreases towards the native norm (56.6%, 40.1%, 14.7%, 1%). In other words, L1 English–L2 Spanish learners start producing mainly overt pronouns to mark topic continuity, probably as a reflection of the non-null-subject setting of their L1. Nevertheless, they become increasingly and significantly aware of the pragmatic infelicity of overt pronouns as their proficiency increases (beginner vs intermediate: $\chi^2 = 12.032$, $p < 0.02$; intermediate vs advanced: $\chi^2 = 43.776$, $p < 0.02$; advanced vs natives: $\chi^2 = 26.369$, $p < 0.02$).

The rates of production of NPs to mark topic continuity decrease across proficiencies towards the native norm. We will explore the factors that constrain NP production when discussing the results of RQ4 below.

As for pragmatic felicity (darkest tones in Figure 7.3), we can observe (i) an increasing and significant trend towards the native norm in the production of pragmatically felicitous null pronouns to mark topic continuity (beginners vs intermediates: $\chi^2 = 39.984$, $p < 0.02$; intermediates vs advanced: $\chi^2 = 27.569$, $p < 0.02$; advanced vs natives: $\chi^2 = 41.698$, $p < 0.02$); and (ii) a corresponding decreasing trend in the use of redundant (and therefore infelicitous) explicit forms (11), which is particularly noticeable for overt pronouns but less so for NPs (overt-when-null and NP-when-null). If we focus exclusively on the frequencies of infelicitous redundant cases, we can observe a trend that is not immediately obvious in the production of NP-when-null, which shows an increasing trend across levels towards the native norm (54/179 = 30.2%, 28/117 = 23.9%, 47/92 = 51.1% and 10/12 = 83.3%) and, as a result, the overt-when-null shows an equivalent decreasing trend. In short, we conclude that the pragmatics of topic continuity at the syntax–discourse interface are acquired gradually in L2 Spanish, as reported in previous research (Lozano, 2009b, 2018; Montrul & Rodríguez-Louro, 2006; *inter alia*), although learners are increasingly sensitive to the most permissible infelicitous option (NP-when-null).

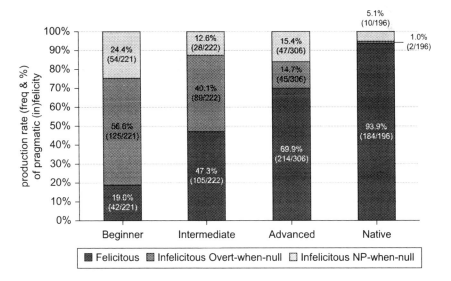

Figure 7.3 Production of pragmatically (in)felicitous forms by group

(11) **Oprah**$_i$ está una persona famosa. #**Oprah**$_i$ está en la telé en la noché. #**Ella**$_i$ es bonita y trabajadora. #**Ella**$_i$ no tiene un esposo. (EN_WR_15_18_3_2_ELP)

'*Oprah*$_i$ *is a famous person.* #*Oprah*$_i$ *is on TV at night.* #*She*$_i$ *is beautiful and hard-working.* #*She*$_i$ *doesn't have a husband.*'

RQ2: Syntactic factors and L1 transfer

The syntactic environment of the sentence/clause containing the subject RE can also have an effect on its form. In our tagging, we discriminated between coordinate and non-coordinate sentences/clauses. It is well known from native English corpus data that zero anaphors are possible with finite verbs only in coordination with coreferential subjects (Crosthwaite, 2011) but, crucially, there must be topic continuity in such coordinate sentences (Quesada & Lozano, forthcoming). If L1 transfer is at stake, a reasonable assumption is to expect L1 English–L2 Spanish learners (particularly beginners) to produce more null pronominal subjects in coordination. Recall that in null-subject languages like Spanish, null pronominal subjects are possible in any syntactic configuration with a finite verb (coordination and non-coordination).

Figure 7.4 shows that when marking topic continuity in native Spanish, null pronouns are obligatory in coordination (100%) as in (12) and are the norm in non-coordination (90.7%). Learners show a clear contrast: null pronouns are clearly the most produced option in coordination. Their rates are rather stable from the outset, with a slight increase towards the native norm as proficiency increases (82.6% beginners, 86% intermediates, 91.1% advanced). By contrast, null pronouns are the least preferred option in non-coordinate contexts, with a

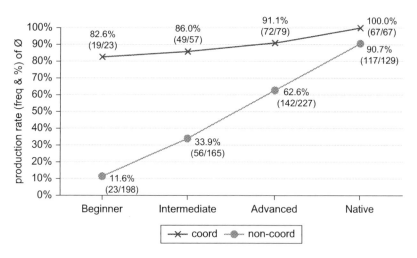

Figure 7.4 Production of null pronominal subjects (Ø) in topic continuity by group according to the syntactic environment of the RE (coordination vs non-coordination)

sharp increasing trend towards the native norm (11.6%, 33.9%, 62.6%). It is clear from the data that the syntactic environment where the null pronominal subject appears is a relevant factor for L1 English–L2 Spanish learners, particularly at low levels (beginners: 82.6% vs 11.6%). Importantly, learners are increasingly aware that null pronouns are allowed in native Spanish in coordinate scenarios, though this mild increase is non-significant amongst them (beginner vs intermediates: $\chi^2 = 0.145$, $p > 0.05$; intermediates vs advanced: $\chi^2 = 0.903$, $p > 0.05$). In fact, advanced learners never attain native-like levels (advanced vs natives: $\chi^2 = 6.236$, $p < 0.02$). Crucially, in non-coordinate scenarios their use of null pronouns increases drastically and significantly across proficiency levels (beginner vs intermediates: $\chi^2 = 26.341$, $p < 0.02$; intermediates vs advanced: $\chi^2 = 31.299$, $p < 0.02$), but once again they cannot eventually attain a native-like behaviour (advanced vs natives: $\chi^2 = 32.864$, $p < 0.02$). These results clearly indicate that from the very outset, L1 English–L2 Spanish learners transfer the structure found in their L1 coordinate contexts (i.e. dropping of overt REs with coreferential subjects), resulting in high rates of null pronouns in their L2 Spanish coordination, but significantly lower rates in non-coordination, where the dropping of overt subject REs is not allowed in their L1. Additionally, these results confirm again that the pragmatics of the syntax–discourse interface in topic continuity are acquired gradually.

(12)   **Ella**$_i$ ha aparecido en muchas películas y [**Ø**$_i$] ha registrado cuatro álbumes. [EN_WR_15_30_1_2_TT]

   '*She$_i$ has appeared in many films and [Ø$_i$] has registered four albums.*'

(13)   Porque **ella**$_i$ gasta tanto dinero, **ella**$_i$ está en deuda y [**Ø**$_i$] no puede pagar sus cuentas de tarjeta de crédito (…) [EN_WR_34_18_10_3_LKF]

   '*Because she$_i$ spends much money, she$_i$ is in debt and [Ø$_i$] cannot pay for her credit card accounts.*'

This finding is relevant for at least two reasons. First, since the pioneering studies by Phinney (1987) and Liceras (1989), numerous studies have confirmed that L2 Spanish learners can acquire the licensing of null pronominal subjects from early stages of development, and that even beginners are aware that null pronouns are possible (see Quesada, 2014 and 2015 for overviews). However, pragmatic nuances are acquired later with increasing proficiency. Our research goes one step further and shows that low-level learners *appear* to have acquired the formal syntactic licensing of null pronominal subjects (cf. 19% in Figure 7.2) but, on closer inspection, what they are doing is simply transferring the structure from their L1 English in topic continuity coordinate structures (82.6% in Figure 7.4), as they are not fully aware yet that null pronouns are possible in non-coordinate structures as well (11.6% in Figure 7.4). Second, our finding has methodological implications for SLA as it shows that the use of learner corpus methods such as a fine-grained, linguistically motivated annotation (coupled with the power of sophisticated tagging and statistical software like UAM Corpus Tool) reveals a differential behaviour in coordination vs. non-coordination with topic continuity that had gone unnoticed in previous research.

RQ3: Referential chains

Our third RQ related to the type of referential chains, potentially influenced by perseveration (e.g. Flores-Ferrán, 2002; Travis, 2007), which are created with null subject REs. As shown in Figure 7.5, when natives produce a null pronominal subject in topic continuity scenarios, its antecedent typically takes the form of (i) a null pronoun most of the time (65.2%), (ii) an NP often (31%), and (iii) an overt pronoun occasionally (3.8%). In other words, two-thirds of the antecedents of a null pronominal subject are null pronouns, showing a perseveration or priming effect, and about one-third is an NP. This entails that $[Ø_i...Ø_i]$ chains are the most common way of marking topic continuity in native Spanish, as expected. This is illustrated in (14), where the native is writing about *Bruce Lee*. The remaining one-third of the native chains are of the type $[NP_i...Ø_i]$, which typically correspond to cases where the antecedent represents a character that has been introduced in discourse for the first time (and hence requires an NP), as in (15). In these contexts, an overt and highly active antecedent is followed by a null RE, which is the most minimal form (Givón, 1983). As for learners, we can observe two trends towards the native norm: they are increasingly sensitive to $[Ø_i...Ø_i]$ chains (26.2% beginners, 49.5% intermediates, 56.5% advanced, 65.2% for natives) but decreasingly sensitive to $[overt_i...Ø_i]$ chains (33.3%, 29.5%, 9.8%, 3.8%). Once again, this confirms the gradual acquisition of the pragmatic properties of topic continuity at the syntax–discourse interface. Notice that beginners do not show a clear pattern in the form of the antecedent, with data ranging from 40.5% to 26.2%, whereas advanced learners show a native-like pattern by not differing significantly from natives except for the overt-null chain (advanced

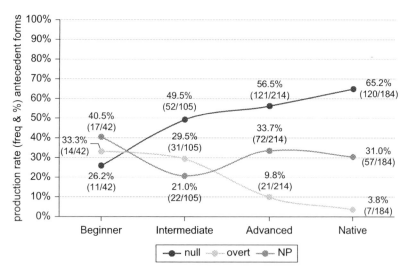

Figure 7.5 Form of the antecedent for null pronominal subjects in topic continuity by group

vs natives on: null-null chain: $\chi^2 = 3.117$, $p > 0.05$; NP-null chain: $\chi^2 = 0.321$, $p > 0.05$; overt-null chain $\chi^2 = 5.462$, $p > 0.02$).

(14) [Ø$_i$] Conocío y [Ø$_i$] llegó a practicar múltiples estilos de lucha, tanto orientales como occidentales. [Ø$_i$] Sometía a su cuerpo a una dura rutina de entrenamientos, destinada a crear la máquina perfecta. [Ø$_i$] Era consciente del movimiento [ES_WR_19_2_NNR]

'[Ø$_i$] *Knew and* [Ø$_i$] *ended up practising multiple fighting styles, Eastern as well as Western.* [Ø$_i$] *Submitted his body to a tough training routine, destined to create the perfect machine.* [Ø$_i$] *Had an awareness of [bodily] movement.*'

(15) **Jacob**$_i$ también se distancia de ella por algo que [Ø$_j$] no le$_i$ quiere explicar. [ES_WR_21_3_ICH]

'*Jacob*$_i$ *also distances from her due to something that* [Ø$_j$] *doesn't want to explain to her.*'

RQ4: The number (and gender) of potential antecedents

In H4a, we predicted that the higher the number of potential (i.e. activated) antecedents in the immediately preceding discourse (which, in turn, decreases the activation of a given antecedent), the fuller the RE forms to be found in both learners and natives. As shown in Figure 7.6, Spanish natives, who predominantly produced null pronouns (93.9%) in topic continuity (cf. Figure 7.2), logically show very low rates of overt REs (overt pronouns and NPs). Such a low rate of overt material is not greatly affected by the number of potential antecedents

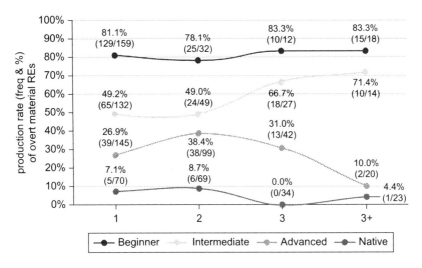

Figure 7.6 Overt material REs (overt pronouns and NPs) produced in topic continuity according to number of potential antecedents (1, 2, 3, 3+) by group

(7.1% for 1 antecedent, 8.7% for 2 antecedents, 0% for 3 antecedents, and 4.4% for 3+ antecedents). In short, an increase in the number of potential antecedents in the preceding discourse does not necessarily trigger the use of fuller forms in topic continuity in native Spanish. Crucially, the effect previously reported (Arnold & Griffin, 2007; Contemori & Dussias, 2016; Lozano, 2016; Quesada & Lozano, forthcoming) has not been found exclusively in topic continuity. As for our non-natives, the effect of potential antecedents is observable in intermediates and advanced learners, but not in beginners, whose high production rates of overt material remain stable across the number of potential antecedents (81.1%, 78.1%, 83.3%, and 83.3%). Intermediates show an increase in the use of overt material as the number of potential antecedents increases (49.2%, 49%, 66.7%, 71.4%), with a remarkable increase in the transition between two to three potential antecedents. The findings for intermediates are in line with previous research, but advanced learners show the opposite pattern: overt material decreases as the number of potential antecedents increases (26.9%, 38.4%, 31%, 10%), except for in contexts with two potential antecedents, which appear to be the most challenging for advanced learners (38.4%). This higher rate of overt forms with two potential antecedents might be better explained by resorting to the gender of such activated antecedents.

An indirect finding that can be observed in the raw frequencies in Figure 7.6 is that, for all groups (learners and natives), the frequency of potential antecedents decreases as its number increases. Overall, there is an overwhelming majority of scenarios where there is only one potential antecedent, followed by scenarios with two potential antecedents, then three, and finally more than three. This is expected since many of the written compositions were related to the description of a famous person (where one potential antecedent is expected), whereas the rest were about the description of a film, where many potential antecedents are expected to appear throughout the narration.

As for H4b, we predicted that, in scenarios where gender can determine the resolution of the RE (i.e. scenarios with two potential antecedents), (i) NPs are predicted to be produced more than overt pronouns to disambiguate cases of antecedents with the same gender (since a null pronoun or even an overt pronoun would result in ambiguity), and (ii) overt pronouns will be produced more when the gender of the two antecedents is different (since an overt pronoun is the most minimal form that can disambiguate such cases, an NP would be rather redundant and a null pronoun could cause ambiguity). Regarding the contexts with two potential antecedents with different gender, we can observe that all groups typically produce more overt pronouns (cf. first half of Figure 7.7) than NPs (first half of Figure 7.8), since an overt pronoun is good enough to disambiguate in topic continuity scenarios like $John_i...Mary_j...[he_i...]$, as predicted. As for cases of two potential antecedents with the same gender, all groups (except for beginners) show slightly higher rates for NPs (second half of Figure 7.8) than overt pronouns (second half of Figure 7.7) since NPs are required so as to avoid ambiguity in scenarios like $John_i...Peter_j...[John_i...]$. Given the low frequencies of production, inferential statistics could not be performed. However, notice also that a visual inspection of each

Anaphora resolution in topic continuity 135

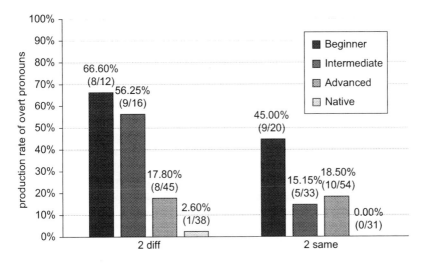

Figure 7.7 Production of overt pronouns in topic continuity with two potential antecedents according to gender (same vs different gender) by group

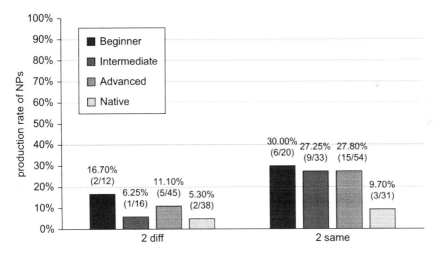

Figure 7.8 Production of NPs in topic continuity with two potential antecedents according to gender (same vs different gender) by group

figure individually confirms our observations: overall, overt pronouns (Figure 7.7) are more frequently used with two different gender antecedents than with two same-gender antecedents, whereas NPs (Figure 7.8) are more frequently used with two same-gender antecedents. These results indicate that the gender of the antecedents constrains the form of the RE, as previously reported for native Spanish and advanced L2 Spanish (Lozano, 2016).

Other relevant results: paragraphs and RE choice

In this section, we briefly report on additional factors that constrain the form of REs in topic continuity. An interesting finding is that to mark topic continuity, even Spanish natives tolerate highly explicit forms like full NPs and proper names to refer to an antecedent that is highly accessible in the preceding sentence(s) (10/196 = 5.1% from Figure 7.2), as illustrated in (16). This can be partially attributed to the number and gender of potential antecedents, as reported in the previous section, but it is noteworthy to highlight the fact that some of this NP production occurs at the beginning of a new paragraph. This may be related to a factor that has been reported in the previous L2 literature: the degree of *unity* between the RE and the antecedent. Corpus-based L2 studies have found that fuller forms are triggered by the transition between scenes when narrating a film (Collewaert, 2019), the transition between pictures when narrating a picture-based story (Quesada & Lozano, forthcoming), and the transition between paragraphs (Lozano, 2016). Descriptive studies also report on the effect of new paragraphs on REs (e.g. Givón, 1983). Our data thus confirm that a new paragraph (16) can break the continuity of topic and therefore trigger the use of fuller forms than expected.

(16) **Rafa Nadal**$_i$ es uno de los mejores tenistas del momento y quizás en un futuro, de la historia. ¶
Rafael Nadal$_i$ es un tenista de unos 24 años nacido en Manacor [ES_WR_26_2_AVS]

'***Rafa Nadal*** *is currently one of the best tennis players and perhaps of the history.* ¶
Rafael Nadal *is a 24-year-old tennis player who was born in Manacor.*'

Our observations in this final subsection of the results are tentative but suggestive. We encourage future researchers to explore these issues in more detail.

Final conclusion

In this study, the use of learner corpus data coupled with a fine-grained, linguistically motivated tagset implemented through relevant tagging software has provided new insights into the nature of the interlanguage of L2 learners. The results show that L1 English–L2 Spanish learners are initially overexplicit in topic continuity contexts since they produce fuller forms than expected (overt instead of null pronominal subjects) to maintain continuity in discourse. This 'overt pronoun strategy' has been previously reported in both the experimental and corpus-based L2 literature. Importantly, learners can gradually acquire the properties that constrain the use of REs in topic continuity at the syntax–discourse interface by reducing their production of explicit forms, while increasing null pronouns towards the native norm. Pragmatic felicity is therefore acquired gradually with increasing proficiency. Additionally, our data for advanced learners reveal that, while their patterns are similar to those of Spanish natives, their production is significantly different, which implies that they cannot attain full native-like pragmatic competence. Future research will need to determine whether the subtleties of topic continuity are eventually acquirable at very advanced and near-native levels of development and whether learners can show the same range of sensitivity to pragmatic felicity as natives do in topic continuity.

By teasing apart the different factors that constrain the use of RE forms in topic continuity in subject position, we have also refined the classic observation that learners of L2 Spanish are aware of the mechanisms that syntactically license null pronouns: learners are less aware of such mechanisms than previously assumed, since their production of null pronouns at beginning levels corresponds to mere transfer of their L1 English coordinate structure only. They are not sensitive to the fact that null pronouns are possible in all syntactic conditions (not only coordinate but also non-coordinate environments) in Spanish. Therefore, it is not entirely correct to assume that when it comes to null pronominal subjects in L2 Spanish, the properties that involve only syntax are acquired rapidly from the outset.

The production of NPs to mark topic continuity is under-researched in the experimental L2 literature on AR. It has been explored in previous L2 corpus-based studies, though such studies are scarce (Bel & García-Alcaraz, 2015; Bel, García-Alcaraz, & Rosado, 2016; Blackwell & Quesada, 2012; Lozano, 2009b, 2016). The present study contributes to our understanding of the factors that constrain the choice of NPs in topic continuity in terms of the number of activated antecedents and their gender differences.

L2 Spanish research on the acquisition of overt and null pronominal subjects has typically focused on the anaphor itself (i.e. on the pronoun), but recent research has shown that the number of activated antecedents (Contemori & Dussias, 2016; Lozano, 2016) as well as gender differences between antecedents (Lozano, 2016) constrain the form of the RE in subject position (null/overt pronoun, NP). Our study shows that, at least in topic continuity, the gender differences of antecedents (and not the number of potential antecedents) can account for the overproduction of not only overt pronouns but also NPs in topic continuity. In particular, our study replicates previous L2 Spanish findings (Lozano, 2016) in that the gender of the two immediately activated antecedents is a factor that constrains the form of the RE: when the last two activated antecedents differ in gender, overt pronouns are more common (as they can resolve the anaphora alone), but when they share the same gender, full NPs are produced for disambiguation purposes. Learners are sensitive to this in general, particularly at advanced levels. The lack of effect of the number of potential antecedents could be either (i) a consequence of the focus of the study in that only topic continuity scenarios were investigated (thus excluding other relevant syntax–discourse scenarios like topic shift and contrastive focus where the number of competing antecedents has been previously shown to be a relevant factor), or (ii) a task-dependent effect (narratives of different types were used: those conducive to more frequent topic continuity scenarios like the narration of a famous person vs. those conducive to topic-shift scenarios, like the film retelling task). Future research will need to investigate these possibilities.

Acknowledgement

Funding agencies: MINECO (Spain), research project grant no. FFI-2016-75106-P & FPU Grant no. FPU17/04684

Appendix

Table A7.1 Learners' biodata

	Mean age	Proficiency* Raw	Proficiency* %	Self-prof.	Age of onset	Length of instr. (yrs)	Length of REs. (months)
Beginner (N=20)	20.2	15.8	36.8	2.4	14.7	3.3	0
Intermediate (N=15)	27.2	27.7	64.2	3.5	19.2	6.3	5.8
Advanced (N=22)	30	39.5	91.8	4.5	15.7	8.2	10.8

* The learners were classified according to the score obtained in the *University of Wisconsin Placement Test – Form 96M.*

Notes

1 See Appendix for Learners' biodata.
2 All participants are native speakers of peninsular Spanish in order to avoid the systematic overuse of overt pronominal subjects found in other Spanish varieties such as Caribbean dialects, as reported in previous studies (Lozano, 2016; Rothman, 2009).

References

Abreu, L. (2009). *Spanish subject personal pronoun use by monolinguals, bilinguals and second language learners* (PhD thesis). University of Florida, Gainesville, FL.
Al-Kasey, T., & Pérez-Leroux, A.-T. (1998). Second language acquisition of Spanish null subjects. In S. Flynn, G. Matohardjono, & W. O'Neil (Eds.), *The generative study of second language acquisition* (pp. 161–185). Hillsdale, NJ: Lawrence Erlbaum.
Alonso-Ovalle, L., Fernandez-Solera, S., Frazier, L., & Clifton, C. (2002). Null vs. overt pronouns and the topic-focus articulation in Spanish. *Journal of Italian Linguistics, 14*(2), 151–169.
Arnold, J. E., & Griffin, Z. M. (2007). The effect of additional characters on choice of referring expression: Everyone counts. *Journal of Memory and Language, 56*, 521–536. doi:10.1016/j.jml.2006.09.007
Bel, A., & García-Alcaraz, E. (2015). Subject pronouns in the L2 Spanish of Moroccan Arabic speakers. In T. Judy & S. Perpiñán (Eds.), *The acquisition of Spanish in understudied language pairings* (pp. 201–232). Amsterdam, the Netherlands: John Benjamins. doi:10.1075/ihll.3.08bel

Bel, A., García-Alcaraz, E., & Rosado, E. (2016). Reference comprehension and production in bilingual Spanish: The view from null subject languages. In A. A. de la Fuente, E. Valenzuela, & C. Martínez Sanz (Eds.), *Language acquisition beyond parameters* (pp. 37–70). Amsterdam, the Netherlands: John Benjamins. doi:10.1075/sibil.51.03bel

Bel, A., Sagarra, N., Comínguez, J. P., & García-Alcaraz, E. (2016). Transfer and proficiency effects in L2 processing of subject anaphora. *Lingua, 184,* 134–159. doi:10.1016/j.lingua.2016.07.001

Blackwell, S. E., & Quesada, M. L. (2012). Third-person subjects in native speakers' and L2 learners' narratives: Testing (and revising) the Givenness Hierarchy for Spanish. In K. L. Geeslin & M. Díaz-Campos (Eds.), *Selected proceedings of the 14th Hispanic Linguistics Symposium* (pp. 142–164). Somerville MA: Cascadilla Press. Retrieved from http://www.lingref.com/cpp/hls/14/paper2662.pdf

Cameron, R., & Flores-Ferrán, N. (2004). Perseveration of subject expression across regional dialects of Spanish. *Spanish in Context, 1*(1), 41–65. doi:10.1075/sic.1.1.05cam

Carminati, M. N. (2002). *The processing of Italian subject pronouns* (Unpublished PhD thesis). University of Massachusetts, Amherst, MA.

Collewaert, K. (2019). *Los mecanismos referenciales en el discurso oral del español como lengua extranjera (ELE): un estudio de corpus basado en neerlandófonos aprendices de ELE* (PhD dissertation). Vrije Universiteit Brussel, Brussels, Belgium & Universidad de Granada, Granada, Spain.

Contemori, C., & Dussias, P. E. (2016). Referential choice in a second language: Evidence for a listener-oriented approach. *Language, Cognition and Neuroscience, 31*(10), 1257–1272. doi:10.1080/23273798.2016.1220604

Crosthwaite, P. (2011). The effect of collaboration on the cohesion and coherence of L2 narrative discourse between English NS and Korean L2 English users. *Asian EFL Journal, 13*(4), 135–166.

Filiaci, F., Sorace, A., & Carreiras, M. (2014). Anaphoric biases of null and overt subjects in Italian and Spanish: A cross-linguistic comparison. *Language, Cognition and Neuroscience, 29*(7), 825–843. doi:10.1080/01690965.2013.801502

Flores-Ferrán, N. (2002). *Subject personal pronouns in Spanish narratives of Puerto Ricans in New York City: A sociolinguistic perspective.* Munich, Germany: Lincom Europa. Retrieved from http://lincom-shop.eu/epages/57709feb-b889-4707-b2cec666fc88085d.sf/de_DE/?ObjectPath=/Shops/57709feb-b889-4707-b2ce-c666fc88085d/Products/%22ISBN%209783895863028%22

García-Alcaraz, E., & Bel, A. (2011). Selección y distribución de los pronombres en el español L2 de los hablantes de árabe. *Revista de Lingüística y Lenguas Aplicadas, 6,* 165–179. doi:10.4995/rlyla.2011.901

Geeslin, K., & Gudmestad, A. (2008). Variable subject expression in second-language Spanish: A comparison of native and non-native speakers. In M. Bowles, R. Foote, S. Perpiñán, & R. Bhatt (Eds.), *Selected proceedings of the 2007 second language research forum* (pp. 69–85). Somerville, MA: Cascadilla Proceedings Project.

Geeslin, K., & Gudmestad, A. (2011). Using sociolinguistic analyses of discourse-level features to expand research on L2 variation in forms of Spanish subject expression. In L. Plonsky & M. Schierloh (Eds.), *Selected proceedings of the 2009 second language research forum* (pp. 16–30). Somerville, MA: Cascadilla Proceedings Project.

Geeslin, K., Linford, B., & Fafulas, S. (2015). Variable subject expression in second language Spanish: Uncovering the developmental sequence and predictive linguistic factors. In A. Carvalho, R. Orozco, & N. L. Shin (Eds.), *Subject pronoun expression in Spanish: A cross-dialectal perspective* (pp. 191–209). Washington, DC: Georgetown University Press.

Gelormini-Lezama, C., & Almor, A. (2011). Repeated names, overt pronouns, and null pronouns in Spanish. *Language and Cognitive Processes, 26*(3), 437–454. doi: 10.1080/01690965.2010.495234

Gelormini-Lezama, C., & Almor, A. (2014). Singular and plural pronominal reference in Spanish. *Journal of Psycholinguistic Research, 43*(3), 299–313. https://doi.org/10.1007/s10936-013-9254-6

Givón, T. (1983). *Topic continuity in discourse: A quantitative crosslanguage study*. Philadelphia, PA: John Benjamins.

Harvie, D. (1998). Null subject in English: Wonder if it exists? *Cahiers Linguistique d'Ottawa, 26,* 15–25.

Kang, J. Y. (2004). Telling a coherent story in a foreign language: Analysis of Korean EFL learners' referential strategies in oral narrative discourse. *Journal of Pragmatics, 36*(11), 1975–1990. doi:10.1016/j.pragma.2004.03.007

Keating, G. D., VanPatten, B., & Jegerski, J. (2011). Who was walking on the beach? Anaphora resolution in Spanish heritage speakers and adult second language learners. *Studies in Second Language Acquisition, 33*(2), 193–221. doi:10.1017/S0272263110000732

Liceras, J. M. (1989). On some properties of the 'pro-drop' parameter: Looking for missing subjects in non-native Spanish. In S. M. Gass & J. Schachter (Eds.), *Linguistic perspectives on second language acquisition* (pp. 109–133). Cambridge, UK: Cambridge University Press.

Lozano, C. (2002). The interpretation of overt and null pronouns in non-native Spanish. *Durham Working Papers in Linguistics, 8,* 53–66.

Lozano, C. (2009a). CEDEL2: Corpus Escrito del Español como L2. In C. M. Bretones & et al (Eds.), *Applied linguistics now: Understanding language and mind/La lingüística aplicada actual: Comprendiendo el lenguaje y la mente* (pp. 197–212). Almería, Spain: Universidad de Almería. Retrieved from https://dialnet.unirioja.es/servlet/libro?codigo=520015

Lozano, C. (2009b). Pronominal deficits at the interface: New data from the CEDEL2 corpus. In C. M. Bretones & et al (Eds.), *Applied linguistics now: Understanding language and mind/La lingüística aplicada actual: Comprendiendo el lenguaje y la mente* (pp. 213–227). Almería, Spain: Universidad de Almería. Retrieved from https://dialnet.unirioja.es/servlet/libro?codigo=520015

Lozano, C. (2016). Pragmatic principles in anaphora resolution at the syntax-discourse interface: Advanced English learners of Spanish in the CEDEL2 corpus. In M. A. Ramos (Ed.), *Spanish learner corpus research: Current trends and future perspectives* (pp. 235–265). Amsterdam, the Netherlands: John Benjamins. doi:10.1075/scl.78.09loz

Lozano, C. (2018). The development of anaphora resolution at the syntax-discourse interface: Pronominal subjects in Greek learners of Spanish. *Journal of Psycholinguistic Research, 47*(2), 411–430. doi:10.1007/s10936-017-9541-8

Lozano, C. (in prep.). *CEDEL2 (version 1.0): The design and creation of an online corpus for L2 Spanish acquisition research.*

Lozano, C., & Mendikoetxea, A. (2013). Learner corpora and second language acquisition: The design and collection of CEDEL2. In A. Díaz-Negrillo, N.

Ballier, & P. Thompson (Eds.), *Automatic treatment and analysis of learner corpus data* (pp. 65–100). Amsterdam, the Netherlands: John Benjamins. doi:10.1075/scl.59.06loz

Montrul, S., & Rodríguez-Louro, C. (2006). Beyond the syntax of the Null Subject Parameter: A look at the discourse-pragmatic distribution of null and overt subjects by L2 learners of Spanish. In V. Torrens & L. Escobar (Eds.), *The acquisition of syntax in romance languages* (pp. 401–418). Amsterdam, the Netherlands: John Benjamins. doi:10.1075/lald.41.19mon

O'Donnell, M. (2009). The UAM Corpus Tool: Software for corpus annotation and exploration. In C. M. Bretones & et al (eds), *Applied linguistics now: Understanding language and mind/La lingüística aplicada actual: Comprendiendo el lenguaje y la mente* (pp. 1433–1447). Almería, Spain: Universidad de Almería.

Phinney, M. (1987). The pro-drop parameter in second language acquisition. In T. Roeper & E. Williams (Eds.), *Parameter setting* (pp. 221–238). Dordrecht, the Netherlands: Reidel.

Quesada, M. L. (2014). Subject pronouns in second language Spanish. In K. L. Geeslin (Ed.), *The handbook of Spanish second language acquisition* (pp. 253–269). Oxford, UK: Wiley-Blackwell. doi:10.1002/9781118584347.ch15

Quesada, M. L. (2015). *The L2 acquisition of Spanish subjects: Multiple perspectives.* Berlin, Germany: De Gruyter.

Quesada, T., & Lozano, C. (forthcoming). Which factors determine the choice of referential expressions in L2 English discourse? New evidence from the COREFL corpus.

Rizzi, L. (1982). *Issues in Italian syntax.* Dordrecht, the Netherlands: Foris.

Rothman, J. (2009). Pragmatic deficits with syntactic consequences? L2 pronominal subjects and the syntax-pragmatics interface. *Journal of Pragmatics, 41,* 951–973. doi:10.1016/j.pragma.2008.07.007

Ryan, J. (2012). *Acts of reference and the miscommunication of referents by first and second language speakers of English* (Unpublished doctoral thesis). University of Waikato, Hamilton, New Zealand.

Ryan, J. (2015). Overexplicit referent tracking in L2 English: Strategy, avoidance, or myth? *Language Learning, 65*(4), 824–859. doi:10.1111/lang.12139

Sorace, A. (2011). Pinning down the concept of 'interface' in bilingualism. *Linguistic Approaches to Bilingualism, 1*(1), 1–33. doi:10.1075/lab.1.1.01sor

Sorace, A. (2012). Pinning down the concept of "interface" in bilingualism: A reply to peer commentaries. *Linguistic Approaches to Bilingualism, 2*(2), 209–216. doi:10.1075/lab.2.2.04sor

Sorace, A., & Serratrice, L. (2009). Internal and external interfaces in bilingual language development: Beyond structural overlap. *International Journal of Bilingualism, 13*(2), 195–210. doi:10.1177/1367006909339810

Travis, C. (2007). Genre effects on subject expression in Spanish: Priming in narrative and conversation. *Language Variation and Change, 19,* 101–135.

White, L. (1986). Implications of parametric variation for adult second language acquisition: An investigation of the pro-drop parameter. In V. J. Cook (Ed.), *Experimental approaches to second language acquisition* (pp. 55–72). Oxford, UK: Pergamon Press.

8 Using the Givenness Hierarchy to examine article use in academic writing

A case study of adult Spanish-speaking learners of English

Jennifer Killam

Introduction

Previous article studies have largely supported what many English instructors have themselves witnessed in the second language (L2) classroom: articles are among the last-acquired language forms (Butler, 2002; Huebner, 1983; Thomas, 1989) and present a particular challenge to learners whose first languages (L1s) lack articles (Amuzie & Spinner, 2013; Chrabaszcz & Jiang, 2014; Crosthwaite, 2016; Ionin, Zubizarreta, & Maldonado, 2008). Much of the existing research has focused on L2 learners' acquisition of *a/an* and *the*, with far fewer studies taking into account the zero article in some form (Díez-Bedmar & Papp, 2008; Ekiert, 2004; Liu & Gleason, 2002; Parrish, 1987). As a result, our present understanding of the ways in which L2 English learners use (or omit) articles across the range of noun phrase (NP) contexts is still surprisingly limited.

The English article system is situated at an intersection of syntax, semantics, and pragmatics (Chesterman, 1991; Hawkins, 1978; Lyons, 1999), confounding clear form-function mapping. While constraints on article use range from relatively straightforward syntactic restrictions to conventional uses that are seemingly idiosyncratic, article selection also communicates discourse-pragmatic information associated with the attentional state of referents and speakers' assumptions about listeners' ability to select intended referents. These complex aspects of NP reference have been captured by Gundel, Hedberg, and Zacharski (1993) in the Givenness Hierarchy, which suggests that referring forms, including articles, are used by speakers to limit the set of potential referents being referred to by signalling the current cognitive status of the intended referent in discourse. Because higher cognitive statuses within the framework entail all lower statuses, the Givenness Hierarchy allows for some variation in the use of referring expressions when signalling cognitive statuses, rather than prescribing the use of one form over another. This feature makes the Givenness Hierarchy ideal for describing unexpected instances of article reference by L2 English learners, and it has since been used to examine learners' use of a range of referring expressions (Kim, 2000; Swierzbin, 2004).

This small-scale exploratory case study utilizes the Givenness Hierarchy to describe Spanish-speaking L2 English learners' patterns of definite, indefinite, and zero article use across three academic writing tasks. Following Chesterman (1991), this study views the zero article as the most indefinite of articles and considers zero article contexts to precede plural or non-count nouns. Consequently, the zero article is expected to be associated with referents that have lower attentional states in discourse, unlike zero anaphora, which are associated with high levels of discourse saliency and accessibility. Although the Givenness Hierarchy does not make explicit predictions regarding the distribution of the zero article in English, the framework's emphasis on the cognitive status of referents rather than referring forms is expected to permit an analysis of zero. In order to explore the Givenness Hierarchy's potential to account for the zero article along with the overt articles, this study is motivated by the following research questions:

1) Do Spanish-speaking learners of L2 English use the definite and indefinite articles in ways that follow the predictions of the Givenness Hierarchy?
2) Can the cognitive statuses of the Givenness Hierarchy be used to describe the distribution of the zero article in L2 English writing?

Literature review

The Givenness Hierarchy

The Givenness Hierarchy (Gundel et al., 1993), which accounts for the distribution of a range of NP referring forms in discourse, posits that referring expressions provide signals to listeners that limit the set of possible referents to those that have, at a minimum, the lowest cognitive status typically associated with the use of that form. Cognitive status refers to the overall attentional state of referents during discourse, and relates to referents' relative referential givenness or newness. The six cognitive statuses of the Givenness Hierarchy are considered universal to all languages, though not every language has a unique set of referring forms associated with each status (Gundel et al., 1993). In descending order from highest to lowest, these cognitive statuses are *in focus, activated, familiar, uniquely identifiable, referential,* and *type identifiable* (Figure 8.1).

Each of the cognitive statuses implicationally entails all lower statuses by invoking Grice's (1975) Maxims of Quantity, resulting in a unidirectional relationship between cognitive statuses and associated referring forms. Consequently, an *activated* referent is also *familiar, uniquely identifiable, referential,* and *type identifiable*, while a *uniquely identifiable* referent is also *referential* and *type identifiable*. Although the hierarchy outlines the minimum cognitive status a referent for a

highest					*lowest*
in focus	activated	familiar	uniquely identifiable	referential	type identifiable

Figure 8.1 The six cognitive statuses of the Givenness Hierarchy (adapted from Gundel et al., 1993, p. 275)

given referring form is expected to have, the form may equally point to a referent with a higher cognitive status through interaction with the Maxims of Quantity. Given that the descriptive information encoded in NPs is frequently insufficient to allow listeners to uniquely identify referents (Gundel, 2003), the cognitive statuses associated with specific referring forms are part of the meaning of those forms and create a necessary condition for their use (Gundel, Hedberg, & Zacharski, 2000). As a result, the use of a referring expression signals an assumption concerning the cognitive status of the referent in the listener's mind. If the assumption holds, the referring expression provides adequate descriptive content to enable the listener to correctly identify the intended referent.

English articles and the Givenness Hierarchy

The Givenness Hierarchy accounts for the distribution of the definite and indefinite articles in English, which are associated with referents that have a minimum cognitive status of *uniquely identifiable* and *type identifiable*, respectively (Figure 8.2).

However, definite and indefinite article use with referents that have higher cognitive statuses is both made possible and constrained by interaction with the Maxims of Quantity (Grice, 1975). For example, the indefinite article is associated with a minimum cognitive status of *type identifiable*, which signals the speaker's belief that the listener can identify the kind of entity that the NP describes (1), though the use of the indefinite article for specific *referential* indefinite referents is also possible through entailment (2).

(1) I have been thinking of getting *a cat*.
(2) When my youngest child was 3 or so, we were at *a friend's* house visiting and my friend was babysitting her infant nephew (example from Gundel, Hedberg, & Zacharski, 2006, p. 4).

While entailment of lower cognitive statuses theoretically allows for use of the indefinite article with referents of higher cognitive statuses than *referential*, the relationship between the Givenness Hierarchy and the first of Grice's (1975) Maxims of Quantity (be as informative as required) means that cooperative speakers will avoid such uses since the indefinite article does not assist listeners in

	highest					→	lowest
	in focus	*activated*	*familiar*	*uniquely identifiable*	*referential*		*type identifiable*
English Articles				the			a/an

Figure 8.2 The relationship between cognitive statuses of the Givenness Hierarchy and the English articles (adapted from Gundel et al., 1993, p. 284)

locating unique referents (Gundel et al., 2000). The definite article, on the other hand, is associated with referents with a minimum cognitive status of *uniquely identifiable*, meaning that referents can be assigned by the listener based solely on the content of the NP. However, a referent may also be *uniquely identifiable* through indirect reference to a unique entity if it is closely associated with a salient referent or concept in the linguistic or extralinguistic environment (Gundel et al., 2006) (3).

(3) I overslept again this morning. *The alarm* didn't go off.

Entailment creates conditions for use of the definite article with the three higher cognitive statuses, *in focus*, *activated*, and *familiar*. Again, interaction with Grice's (1975) second Maxim of Quantity (don't provide more information than is necessary) accounts for the frequency of definite article use with referents that have these higher cognitive statuses (Gundel et al., 2000). Since the descriptive content of full NPs with the definite article is alone sufficient for identifiability, there is no resulting implicature that prevents the association of the referent with a higher cognitive status.

The zero article

The zero article is not currently accounted for in the Givenness Hierarchy framework for English, though it does appear in the frameworks for other languages, including Spanish (Gundel et al., 1993). In attempting to extend the Givenness Hierarchy to incorporate the zero article, the present study draws on the work of Chesterman (1991), which posits that zero is the most indefinite of the articles and alternates with *a/an*. As a result, the zero article is expected to appear with referents that have cognitive statuses at least as restrictive as the indefinite article. In other words, use of the zero article is hypothesized here to be associated with referents that have cognitive statuses of *referential* or *type identifiable*. In terms of its distribution, Chesterman (1991) suggests that zero appears only with plural count (4) and indefinite non-count nouns (5).

(4) Ø *Lions* are beautiful animals.
(5) A lion needs Ø *water* to survive.

Although generic NPs (including uses of the zero article as shown in (4) above) were omitted from Gundel et al.'s (1993) original analysis, two factors support the inclusion of generics here. Firstly, zero does not stand alone in creating generic reference in English, since both the definite and indefinite articles are used in singular generic NPs, as illustrated in (6), while the zero article appears only in plural generic NPs (7).

(6) *A/The* tiger is a dangerous animal.
(7) Ø *Tigers* are dangerous animals.

Secondly, Gundel, Hedberg, and Zacharski (2003) indicate that cognitive status can indeed be assigned to generic NPs. They state that 'since generics refer to a class of objects or individuals that the addressee can be expected to identify, in the sense that he can assign a unique representation that distinguishes the class, they would inherently satisfy the unique identifiability condition' (Gundel et al., 2003, p. 11). Consequently, the study described here examines all uses of the definite, indefinite, and zero articles, including generic NPs.

Spanish articles and the Givenness Hierarchy

The definite and indefinite articles in Spanish are inflected for both gender and number to agree with the nouns they determine, as shown in in Table 8.1. However, despite the greater complexity of article forms in Spanish, the Givenness Hierarchy indicates a strikingly similar pattern between Spanish and English in terms of the association of articles with the cognitive statuses of referents (Gundel et al., 1993) (Figure 8.3). Like English, the Spanish definite article is associated with a minimum cognitive status of *uniquely identifiable*. For example, in (8) the NP *los actores* ('the actors') is *uniquely identifiable* via a bridging inference made from the NP *la película* ('the film').

Table 8.1 The Spanish definite and indefinite articles (adapted from Stockwell, Bowen & Martin, 1965)

	Definite		Indefinite	
	Singular	*Plural*	*Singular*	*Plural*
Masculine	el	Los	un/uno	Unos
Feminine	la	Las	una	Unas
Neuter	lo			

	in focus	activated	familiar	uniquely identifiable	referential	type identifiable
English Articles				the		a/an
Spanish Articles				el/la/lo/los/las ('*the*')		un/una/unos/unas ('*a/an*') Ø (*zero*)

highest ⟶ lowest

Figure 8.3 The relationship between the six cognitive statuses of the Givenness Hierarchy and the English and Spanish articles (adapted from Gundel et al., 1993, p. 284)

(8) La película comienza como todas, con algunas letras las cuales explican, me
'*The film begins as all do, with some letters which explain, I*
imagino, la secuencia que tenían ahí los actores
imagine, the sequence the actors had there' (Blackwell & Quesada, 2012, p. 151)

Again, as in English, interaction with the Maxims of Quantity (Grice, 1975) constrains the definite article in Spanish for use with referents that have cognitive statuses *in focus, activated, familiar,* or *uniquely identifiable*, but no lower. The indefinite and zero articles, on the other hand, are both associated with the cognitive statuses *referential* and *type identifiable*. Examples (9) and (10), taken from Blackwell and Quesada (2012, p. 147), illustrate the use of the indefinite article in the *referential* NP *un coche nuevo* ('a new car') and the zero article in the *type identifiable* NP Ø *coche* ('Ø car'), respectively.

(9) Luis conduce un coche nuevo hoy
'*Luis drives/is driving a new car today*'
(10) Luis tiene Ø coche
'*Luis has Ø car (Luis has a car)*'

There are limited studies of the role of zero in Spanish language article reference. Tacoronte (2014) notes that noun number and countability do not appear to restrict the distribution of any of the articles in Spanish, including zero. As can be seen in (10) earlier, zero may be used in Spanish with singular count nouns, unlike English zero which appears only with plural or non-count nouns. However, (11) illustrates a use of zero in Spanish with a plural NP and (12) provides an example of zero use with a mass noun.

(11) Son Ø hermanos.
'*(They) are Ø brothers.*'
(12) Necesito Ø agua.
'*(I) need Ø water.*'

In apparent agreement with Chesterman (1991), Tacoronte (2014) indicates that the use of zero determiners in Spanish is associated with greater indefiniteness than the indefinite article. However, zero is possible in (11) and (12) because the NP is part of the predicate (Tacoronte, 2014), since NPs in subject position take zero only rarely in cases such as titles, proverbs, and a limited set of formal written contexts (Lim, 1999).

To create generic reference, Spanish requires an overt article. Singular generic NPs permit the use of either the definite or indefinite article, while plural generic NPs take only the definite article (Snape, García Mayo & Gürel, 2013). Examples

(13) and (14) illustrate some possible contrasts between Spanish and English article use in generic NPs with singular and plural nouns.

(13) *El/Un* tigre es un animal bello.
 '*The/A* tiger is a beautiful animal.'
(14) *Los* tigres son animales bellos.
 'Ø Tigers are beautiful animals.'

In addition, Snape et al. (2013) note that, unlike English, the definite article is required when non-count or mass nouns are used to make generic reference, as can be seen in (15).

(15) El petróleo es un recurso no renovable.
 '*Ø Oil is a nonrenewable resource.*'

Thus, despite similarities in Spanish and English articles in terms of their associations with the cognitive statuses of the Givenness Hierarchy, there are a number of syntactic rules that represent potential areas of L1 transfer for Spanish-speaking learners of L2 English, particularly as concerns generic reference.

Predictions of the Givenness Hierarchy for Spanish-speaking L2 English learners

Despite the greater complexity of Spanish articles in terms of number and gender, there is a significant overlap between the article systems of English and Spanish in terms of their association with the cognitive statuses of the Givenness Hierarchy, as shown in Figure 8.3. If, as proposed by Chesterman (1991), the zero article in English alternates with the indefinite article, then the distribution of zero in English is expected to be the same as the distribution of the zero article in Spanish with reference to the cognitive statuses of the Givenness Hierarchy. As a result of these similarities, it seems likely that Spanish-speaking learners of L2 English will positively transfer the association of forms and cognitive statuses from L1 Spanish to L2 English. In support of this hypothesis, researchers working in other frameworks have noted a positive transfer of Spanish article use to English, leading to near native-like accuracy (Chrabaszcz & Jiang, 2014; Díez-Bedmar & Papp, 2008; García Mayo, 2009). Moreover, while there is a potential for interference from L1 Spanish syntactic constraints, including the use of the definite article with mass nouns and in plural generic NPs, Snape et al. (2013) found that intermediate and advanced Spanish-speaking learners exhibited native-like or near native-like use of articles even in these English NP contexts. Given the similarity between association of forms across the cognitive statuses of the Givenness Hierarchy in English and Spanish, this study hypothesizes that learners will use the definite, indefinite, and zero articles in L2 English as predicted by the Givenness Hierarchy.

Method

Participants

Participants were three male and four female adult intermediate to advanced learners of English whose native language is Spanish (Table 8.2). All seven participants were enrolled in a private language school in the United States where the researcher served as an instructor at the time of the study. The language school offered five levels of English study based on proficiency levels associated with the Common European Framework of Reference for Languages (CEFR), but for the purposes of the study only students who had reached an intermediate course level (Level 3 or B1) were eligible for participation. Proficiency levels of participants were determined at the time of enrollment based on simulated TOEIC scores, but at the time of the study all had been enrolled in courses for a minimum of one full term. In addition, each of the participants had studied English previously, typically as a requirement during high school, though they all described their prior English studies as insufficient for developing fluency. Only one participant, David, was interested in pursuing a post-secondary degree, while the other participants had chosen to study English for personal reasons or business purposes.

Materials

Materials consisted of three argumentative expository writing prompts adapted from L2 English textbooks, *NorthStar Reading and Writing 5* (Miller & Cohen, 2009) and *NorthStar Reading and Writing 2* (Haugnes & Maher, 2009) (Appendix A). None of the prompts required participants to have specialized knowledge or conduct research of any kind in order to develop a response. Because the prompts each required a thesis or position supported by two or more arguments, they were considered exemplars of the expository genre outlined by Schleppegrell (2004), which is characterized by high rates of 'elaborated noun phrases' (p. 88) and, thus, was considered appropriate for the study of articles.

Table 8.2 Participant demographics and course enrollment

Course level	Participant name	Home country	Prior education	Level at enrollment
5 (C1)	Rosa	Colombia	College	3
5 (C1)	Pedro	Venezuela	College	3
5 (C1)	Maria	Colombia	College	4
5 (C1)	Ana	Cuba	Graduate	4
4 (B2)	David	Argentina	High school	1
3 (B1)	Carmen	Venezuela	College	2
3 (B1)	Juan	Venezuela	College	2

Procedure

Participants completed a set of three writing tasks over the course of approximately one week, for which they received a small incentive. Due to restrictions of the research site, the written tasks were completed independently on participants' own time. The researcher individually emailed participants three editable documents, each of which had one of the three prompts embedded. Participants were asked not to enable spelling or grammar checking features within the documents. No word count requirements were provided, but participants were instructed to complete the tasks without outside assistance. Participants were asked to return the completed writing tasks to the researcher by email within two weeks, and a reminder email was sent after one week had passed. All but one participant returned three tasks to the researcher. Rosa, a Level 5 (C1) participant, failed to submit the third writing task, though her other two tasks were included in the data. As a result, a total of 20 writing tasks were collected for analysis.

Analysis

Before coding and analysis of the data, all participant names were changed and any identifying information included in the data was deleted. Analysis began with the identification of all full NPs so that only pronouns were excluded. For NPs that had no surface article, the zero article was determined by the lack of an article before plural count or mass nouns, following Chesterman (1991). Due to its simplicity, this approach was thought to mitigate any effect of researcher bias in determining indefinite zero article use.

The highest cognitive status associated with each NP was determined by the researcher through application of the Givenness Hierarchy coding protocol developed by Gundel, Hedberg, and Zacharski (2006). Because participants exhibited a tendency to use the same NPs provided in the prompts embedded in each data collection document when responding to the task, the prompts were considered part of the discourse context for coding purposes. As a result, a *uniquely identifiable* NP in the prompt, such as *the company president* in Prompt 1 (Appendix A), was coded as *familiar* following the coding protocol (Gundel et al., 2006) when used by participants, even for first-mention uses. A subset of tasks representing approximately 10% of the total word count was independently coded by both the researcher and an expert coder in order to establish a measure of interrater reliability. The resulting interrater reliability of 81% was calculated based on a simple percentage of agreement.

Descriptive analysis was utilized for this exploratory cross-sectional dataset. The highest cognitive statuses for all NPs across each of the tasks were tabulated and compared with the Givenness Hierarchy's predictions for the distribution of forms associated with each cognitive status. Participants' use of articles were identified, and articles and cognitive statuses were also compared by task prompt in order to reveal any task-related variability. Finally, in order to determine participants' rates of accuracy with the articles, target-like use (TLU) was calculated using the adapted formula from Swierzbin (2004).

$$\text{TLU} = \frac{\text{N correct suppliance in correct contexts}}{(\text{N correct contexts}) + (\text{N suppliance in incorrect contexts})}$$

To determine correct suppliance of articles in correct contexts, the non-TLU of each article was subtracted from the total number of occurrences of each of the articles. Non-TLU includes uses of articles to describe a referent with a higher or lower cognitive status than predicted by the Givenness Hierarchy, uses that violate the Maxims of Quantity (Grice, 1975) by not providing enough information to identify the referent, and uses that do not conform with other syntactic or customary use constraints. In order to calculate the number of correct contexts for each of the articles, non-TLU was subtracted from the total number of uses and the number of omissions of articles in target-like contexts was added to the resulting figure. Finally, suppliance of articles in incorrect contexts was identified simply by counting the number of times that articles were used in contexts not predicted by the Givenness Hierarchy or other constraints. As a result, this calculation treats both ungrammatical and infelicitous uses as inaccurate.

Results

Twenty writing tasks were collected from the seven participants (an advanced participant, Rosa, failed to submit Task 3). Table 8.3 illustrates the rates of frequency for each article in the collected data.

Cognitive status was assigned to 1,223 NPs, but of those only 823, or approximately 67%, included articles. Other NPs, which accounted for 32.71% of total NPs in the data, consist of NPs that were fronted by determiners other than articles, such as possessive adjectives ('our minds'), demonstratives ('this country'), and quantifiers ('many people'), and were, therefore, excluded from the analysis. Definite and zero articles represented the greatest numbers of article uses at approximately 43% and 37%, respectively, while the indefinite article appeared much less frequently across the data, at about 20% of total article uses. The fact that the definite article is the most frequently occurring article in the data is consistent with native speaker corpus findings (Sinclair, 1999, as cited in Master,

Table 8.3 Total article NPs by frequency and percent of total NPs

	Raw frequency	Percentage of NPs
Definite	352	42.77
Indefinite	164	19.93
Zero	307	37.30
TOTAL ARTICLE NPs	823	100
ARTICLE NPs	823	67.29
OTHER NPs	400	32.71
TOTAL NPs	1,223	100

2002, p. 332). Likewise, zero has also been shown to be a high-frequency article, and Master (1997) found that uses of zero occurred more often than the definite article in his corpus data. Similarly, rates for the indefinite article in Master's study are comparable to those found here.

The definite article

The Givenness Hierarchy predicts that the definite article will be used with referents that have cognitive statuses of *in focus, activated, familiar,* or *uniquely identifiable,* but not lower. As demonstrated in Figure 8.4, the majority of uses of the definite article by Spanish speakers in this study were with *uniquely identifiable* referents. Table 8.4 shows raw frequencies of definite article use by cognitive status as well as the percentage of total definite article use these frequencies represent.

In terms of the Givenness Hierarchy predictions, referents with the cognitive statuses *in focus, activated, familiar,* and *uniquely identifiable* represented the majority of instances of the definite article or about 82% of total uses, aligning with Givenness Hierarchy predictions. The remaining uses were associated with referents with a cognitive status of *referential* (5.68%) or *type identifiable* (11.93%). Although the Givenness Hierarchy does not predict use of the definite article with *referential* or *type identifiable* referents, both *referential* and *type identifiable* uses can largely be accounted for as errors in which learners used *the* in place of one of the indefinite articles zero or *a/an*. Specifically, learners tended to use definite articles with abstract non-count nouns in ways that are required in Spanish but are ungrammatical in English. In Task 1, for example, Carmen (Level 3) used the definite article in place of zero before *terms* in a *referential* NP (16),

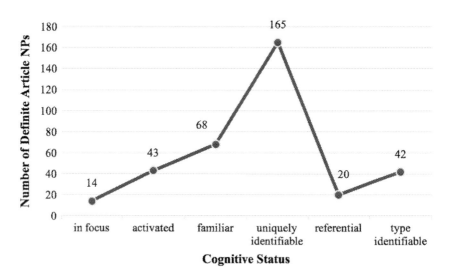

Figure 8.4 Definite article distribution by cognitive status

Table 8.4 Distribution of the definite article across cognitive statuses

Participant name	Course level	Definite NPs (%)	Cognitive status					
			INF (%)	ACT (%)	FAM (%)	UI (%)	REF (%)	TI (%)
Rosa	5	50	2	3	14	22	1	8
Ana	5	38	1	6	3	21	0	7
Maria	5	34	0	8	3	13	3	7
Pedro	5	51	2	7	12	26	2	2
David	4	54	2	10	13	18	5	6
Carmen	3	42	4	4	7	25	2	0
Juan	3	83	3	5	16	40	7	12
TOTAL		352	14	43	68	165	20	42
TOTAL AS PERCENT OF USES		100	3.98	12.22	19.32	46.88	5.68	11.93

while Juan (Level 3) used the definite article in place of zero before *success* in a *type identifiable* NP (17).

(16) Video games offer something rare in *the terms* of education
(17) *The success* come from people who has consistency and focus

This was a common error among the data and all of the L2 English learners in this study used the definite article in this way at least once. One possible reason for the consistency of this error among the data is learners' transfer of Spanish language syntactic constraints for the construction of generic NPs.

Participants' overall TLU for the definite article across each of the academic writing tasks appears in Table 8.5. Task 3 generated some of the lowest TLUs for the definite article for learners. It elicited a high number of non-target-like uses of the definite article with plural generic NPs that had a cognitive status of *type identifiable*. For example, Maria (Level 5), who had the lowest TLU for definite article use in Task 3, repeatedly reproduced the NP Ø *kids* provided in the prompt (Appendix A) as *the kids* (18). Likewise, Juan (Level 3), who had the

Table 8.5 TLU for each of the articles by participant and task

Participant	Task	Definite article (%)	Indefinite article (%)	Zero article (%)
Rosa	1	72	83	90
	2	92	100	100
Ana	1	78	90	70
	2	83	92	67
	3	87	86	79
Maria	1	83	79	57
	2	83	83	75
	3	42	100	72
Pedro	1	100	89	86
	2	83	100	87
	3	77	100	93
David	1	96	91	70
	2	89	100	88
	3	67	91	77
Carmen	1	100	89	92
	2	89	80	73
	3	86	100	91
Juan	1	90	71	56
	2	92	44	50
	3	60	33	53
AVERAGE TLU PER ARTICLE		82	85	76

second lowest TLU for definite article use in Task 3, repeatedly used the definite article with plural generic use of the noun *computers* (19).

(18) I think that *the kids* can learn a lot from computer games
(19) *the computers* is necessary for develop more and more skills

Again, this may be due to L1 interference, since Spanish requires the definite article to create plural generic reference. However, learners who used more fully elaborated NPs associated with *uniquely identifiable* statuses or higher had greater accuracy for Task 3. For example, Carmen (Level 3), who had one of the highest TLU scores for the definite article in Task 3, provided a number of *uniquely identifiable* examples using the definite article, such as (20). Ana (Level 5) had the highest TLU for the definite article for this task and used a number of proper nouns to refer to specific video games or consoles (21).

(20) Myst is one of *the best-selling computer games* of all time
(21) he spend almost all his family-time, and sometimes his study-time, playing *the Xbox*

Using NPs with higher cognitive statuses may have helped Ana to avoid potential negative L1 transfer of Spanish language syntactic constraints associated with generic reference.

The indefinite article

In terms of the distribution of the indefinite article, the Givenness Hierarchy predicts its use with referents that have cognitive statuses of *referential* or *type identifiable*. Although it appeared far less frequently in the data than either the definite or zero article, learners used the indefinite article in ways that closely followed these predictions, as shown in Figure 8.5.

Table 8.6 provides both raw frequencies and percentages of indefinite article use across cognitive statuses, indicating that learners associated the indefinite article with cognitive statuses *type identifiable* 83% of the time and *referential* in 15% of cases, which together accounted for a total of 98% of uses of the indefinite article. As a result, participants in this study exhibited use of the indefinite article as predicted by the Givenness Hierarchy.

TLU calculations for the indefinite article are provided in Table 8.5, which illustrates that the learners in this study were more accurate with the indefinite article (85%) than either the definite (82%) or zero (76%) articles. However, Table 8.5 also demonstrates the variability in accuracy by learner. For example, David (Level 4) had the most accurate uses of the indefinite article across the three writing tasks with an average TLU of 94%. Juan (Level 3), on the other hand, exhibited very low accuracy, with an average TLU of only 49% across the three tasks. Juan made some consistent errors with *a/an* for *type identifiable* referents that have been associated with low-intermediate learners previously in the literature: he sometimes

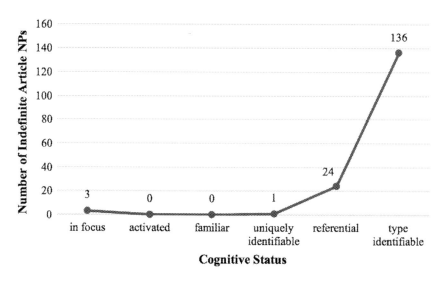

Figure 8.5 Indefinite article use by cognitive status

omitted the indefinite article altogether (22), frequently used it with plural nouns (23), and occasionally used *one* as a replacement for the indefinite article (24).

(22) I don't recommend to choose go out of your country to be *bad person*
(23) Some persons change their way of life being *a news persons*
(24) if you show to any children *one ball* to any sport

In addition, Maria's (Level 5) accuracy with the indefinite article varied across the three tasks. She had the lowest accuracy with Task 1 in which, like Juan, she used the indefinite article with plural NPs, as shown in (25) and (26).

(25) each of them were prepared in their life for *a different things*
(26) if this happen we can become *a partners*

This may likewise be due to L1 transfer, since the Spanish indefinite article can appear in plural NPs.

The zero article

The Givenness Hierarchy does not make explicit predictions for the distribution of zero in English, which appears before plural count and mass nouns. However, based on Chesterman's (1991) suggestion that zero alternates with the indefinite article, it has been hypothesized here that zero should have a distribution across cognitive statuses equal to that of the indefinite article and, therefore, should be associated with referents that have cognitive statuses *referential* and

Table 8.6 Distribution of the indefinite article across cognitive statuses

Participant name	Course level	Indefinite NPs (%)	Cognitive status					
			INF (%)	ACT (%)	FAM (%)	UI (%)	REF (%)	TI (%)
Rosa	5	25	2	0	0	0	2	21
Ana	5	36	0	0	0	0	6	30
Maria	5	20	0	0	0	1	0	19
Pedro	5	22	0	0	0	0	7	15
David	4	24	0	0	0	0	5	19
Carmen	3	27	0	0	0	0	3	24
Juan	3	10	1	0	0	0	1	8
TOTALS		164	3	0	0	1	24	136
TOTAL AS PERCENT OF USES		100	1.83	0	0	0.61	14.63	82.93

type identifiable. As shown in Figure 8.6, participants' use of zero largely followed this prediction, with a clear majority of uses associated with referents with the status *type identifiable*.

Table 8.7 provides the frequencies of zero use across cognitive statuses. *Referential* and *type identifiable* uses of zero represented nearly 90% of total uses in this study, while the use of zero – associated with referents of cognitive statuses higher than *referential*, and therefore not expected based on the hypothesis above – consisted of just over 10% of total zero use.

Table 8.7 also indicates a great deal of variability in zero use by learner for referents with the cognitive status *type identifiable*. Specifically, Pedro (Level 5)

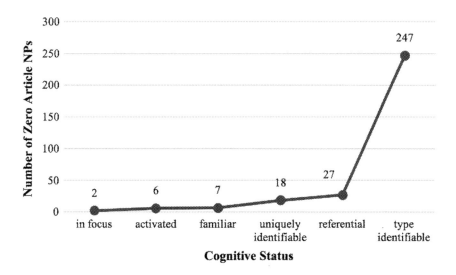

Figure 8.6 Zero article use by cognitive status

Table 8.7 Distribution of the zero article across cognitive statuses

Participant name	Course level	Zero NPs (%)	Cognitive status					
			INF (%)	ACT (%)	FAM (%)	UI (%)	REF (%)	TI (%)
Rosa	5	20	0	0	1	0	1	18
Ana	5	43	0	0	3	4	8	28
Maria	5	21	0	0	1	0	3	17
Pedro	5	82	1	1	1	4	6	69
David	4	38	0	2	1	1	1	33
Carmen	3	61	0	2	0	2	4	53
Juan	3	42	1	1	0	7	4	29
TOTALS		287	2	6	7	18	27	247
TOTAL AS PERCENT OF USES		100	0.65	1.95	2.28	5.86	8.79	80.46

and Carmen (Level 3) used zero for *type identifiable* referents at almost double the rates of other participants. For example, in Task 3, Pedro frequently repeated plural generic NPs, such as Ø *computer games* and Ø *kids* (27), leading to a particularly high frequency of zero use. Meanwhile, Carmen also repeated zero NPs frequently as shown in example (28) from Task 1.

(27) I am for Ø *computer games* and I think are good not just for Ø *kids*
(28) They think they can postpone Ø *happiness* until they achieve Ø *success*. But Ø *happiness* does not come from Ø *success*. Instead, Ø *success* comes from Ø *happiness*.

Again, since the Givenness Hierarchy makes no predictions for zero use in English, TLU for zero was calculated based on the hypothesis that zero is associated with the cognitive statuses *referential* and *type identifiable*. The resulting average TLU for the zero article for all participants was 76%, as shown in Table 8.5. However, there was variability in the accuracy of zero by learner and across tasks, as Juan (Level 3) had the lowest TLU for zero across the three tasks, with an average of 53% accuracy. In Task 2, for example, Juan used zero with singular NPs on multiple occasions, as can be seen in (29), leading to a question of whether he had perhaps acquired zero but had not fully acquired the need to mark count nouns as plural when using zero.

(29) some people don't have Ø *friend*

Maria (Level 5) had the second lowest accuracy with zero overall. However, in Maria's case, her tendency to overgeneralise *the* to *type identifiable* zero contexts affected her overall accuracy with zero as based on the TLU calculations utilised here, as shown in examples (30) and (31).

(30) I think that *the kids* can learn a lot from computer games
(31) everything in excess is bad, and right now *the kids* just want to spend their time just on front of their computer games

This overgeneralisation of *the* with generic NPs is again a possible indication of L1 Spanish transfer of syntactic rules governing generic reference.

Discussion

This small-scale exploratory study investigated whether the Givenness Hierarchy could be used to describe the distribution of articles in Spanish-speaking L2 English learners' writing. In particular, the first research question sought to discover whether the learners in this study used articles in ways that followed the predictions of the Givenness Hierarchy. Results indicate that the learners in this study did appear to transfer the cognitive statuses of the Givenness Hierarchy for both the definite and indefinite articles based on learners' patterns of use of these articles in the writing task data. However, transferring these discourse-pragmatic rules associated with cognitive status from Spanish to English did not ensure 100% accuracy with either the definite and indefinite articles. While some learners in this study exhibited near native-like use of one or both of these articles, others appeared to transfer Spanish language syntactic constraints to the use of the articles in L2 English, especially those constraints related to the construction of generic NPs. However, these findings require confirmation in future studies with greater numbers of participants and larger datasets. This is especially critical given that previous studies on Spanish-speaking learners' acquisition of L2 English generics have led to some conflicting results, as some studies provide evidence of negative transfer (Ionin, Montrul, & Crivos, 2013) while other studies have shown that Spanish-speaking learners construct generic NPs in L2 English in native-like ways (Snape et al., 2013).

In regard to the second research question, which examined the ability of the Givenness Hierarchy to describe the distribution of the zero article in L2 English writing, results showed that zero was most frequently associated with referents that have cognitive statuses of *type identifiable* and *referential*. This finding supports the hypothesis developed here that zero has the same distribution as the indefinite article. This hypothesis was based on Chesterman's (1991) suggestion that the zero article alternates with the indefinite article and is the most indefinite of all the articles in English. These findings also indicate that the zero articles in both English and Spanish may potentially share the same distribution across cognitive statuses, as do both the definite and indefinite articles. However, this finding needs to be confirmed by future L1 and L2 studies with larger datasets using both written and oral language data.

The decision to analyze the zero article as well as generic NPs was motivated by Gundel's (2003) assertion that the Givenness Hierarchy can account for the distribution of referring forms without the incorporation of additional syntactic constraints. Despite the fact that these NP types were excluded from Gundel et al.'s (1993) original data, Mulkern's (1996) work with proper nouns provides a basis for expanding the Givenness Hierarchy to include other forms. Likewise, Gundel et al. (2003) indicate that cognitive status can in fact be assigned to generic NPs, which suggests that the Givenness Hierarchy has the potential to describe the distribution of the entire set of article forms used to create generic reference in English: *the*, Ø, and *a/an*. Nevertheless, since generic reference in English is communicated by the same referring forms used in definite and indefinite reference, studies that specifically examine associations between referring forms and cognitive statuses for generic referents would expand the descriptive potential of the Givenness Hierarchy. Critically, future research should also address any such expansion by suggesting updates to the coding protocol developed by Gundel et al. (2006), an essential step given the overlapping nature of the forms and functions of articles. And, since L2 studies may have utilized the predictions of the Givenness Hierarchy to calculate TLU, steps must be taken to ensure that the resulting calculation is a fair reflection of learners' accuracy with referring forms when both generic and nongeneric uses are examined.

Conclusion

The research presented here represents a small step toward expanding the Givenness Hierarchy framework to account for a greater number of referring forms and reference types. It is believed that this study is the first to use the Givenness Hierarchy to examine the distribution of zero articles in L2 English learner discourse. As a result of the data collected here, important questions have arisen related to the possibility of including not only the zero article but also the generic reference more explicitly in the Givenness Hierarchy and coding protocol (Gundel et al., 2006). It is hoped that future research will not only seek to confirm the preliminary results discussed here in order to expand the Givenness Hierarchy and coding protocol, but will also explore the complex nature of generic reference in terms of the use of articles within the Givenness Hierarchy framework.

Appendix A

Prompt 1

The president of a big company once said that the most successful person he knew was his gardener. The gardener was a man loved by his family and respected by his friends, a man who worked hard and had a full life. Do you agree with this definition of success? Do you think the company president would agree to change places with the gardener? Would you? Explain your point and view and support it with details. (Adapted from Miller & Cohen, 2009, p. 67)

Prompt 2

When immigrants arrive in a new country, should they adapt and become part of the new culture or should they try to preserve their old culture? In what ways do you think immigrants need to adapt and change? What happens if immigrants choose not to change to fit into the new culture? Explain your ideas with examples and supporting details. (Adapted from Miller & Cohen, 2009, p. 122)

Prompt 3

Many parents and teachers think that it is bad for kids to play computer games. Other people think that children can learn a lot from computer games and possibly develop new skills. What do you think? Is playing video games good or bad for children? Explain your answer and give details to support your ideas. (Adapted from Haugnes & Maher, 2009, p. 132)

References

Amuzie, G. L., & Spinner, P. (2013). Korean EFL learners' indefinite article use with four types of abstract nouns. *Applied Linguistics, 34*(4), 415–434. doi:10.1093/applin/ams065

Blackwell, S. E., & Quesada, M. L. (2012). Third-person subjects in native speakers' and L2 learners' narratives: Testing (and revising) the Givenness Hierarchy for Spanish. In K. Geeslin & M. Díaz-Campos (Eds.), *Selected proceedings of the 14th hispanic linguistics symposium* (pp. 142–164). Somerville, MA: Cascadilla Proceedings Project.

Butler, Y. G. (2002). Second language learners' theories on the use of English articles: An analysis of the metalinguistic knowledge used by Japanese students in acquiring the English article system. *Studies in Second Language Acquisition, 24*(3), 451–480. doi:10.1017/S0272263102003042

Chesterman, A. (1991). *On definiteness: A study with special reference to English and Finnish.* Cambridge, UK: Cambridge University Press. doi:10.1017/CBO9780511519710

Chrabaszcz, A., & Jiang, N. (2014). The role of the native language in the use of the English nongeneric definite article by L2 learners: A crosslinguistic comparison. *Second Language Research, 30*(3), 351–379. doi:10.1177/0267658313493432

Crosthwaite, P. (2016). L2 English article use by L1 speakers of -ART languages: A learner corpus study. *International Journal of Learner Corpus Research, 2*(1), 68–100. doi:10.1075/ijlcr.2.1.03cro

Díez-Bedmar, M. B., & Papp, S. (2008). The use of the English article system by Chinese and Spanish learners. In G. Gilquin, S. Papp, & M. B. Díez-Bedmar (Eds.), *Linking up contrastive and learner corpus research.* Amsterdam, the Netherlands: Rodopi. doi:10.1163/9789401206204_007

Ekiert, M. (2004). Acquisition of the English article system by speakers of Polish in ESL and EFL settings. *Teachers College, Columbia University Working Papers in TESOL & Applied Linguistics, 4*(1), 1–23. doi:10.7916/D8P84BCK

García Mayo, M. P. (2009). Article choice in L2 English by Spanish speakers: Evidence for full transfer. In M. P. García Mayo & R. Hawkins (Eds.), *Second language acquisition of articles: Empirical findings and theoretical implications* (pp. 13–35). Amsterdam, the Netherlands: John Benjamins. doi:10.1075/lald.49.05pil

Grice, H. P. (1975). Logic and conversation. In P. Cole, & J. L. Morgan (Eds.), *Speech acts* (pp. 41–58). New York, NY: Academic Press.

Gundel, J. (2003). Information structure and referential givenness/newness: How much belongs in the grammar? In S. Müller (Ed.), *Proceedings of the 10th international conference on head-driven phrase structure grammar* (pp. 122–142), Michigan State University. Stanford, CA: CSLI Publications.

Gundel, J., Hedberg, N., & Zacharski, R. (1993). Cognitive status and the form of referring expressions in discourse. *Language, 68*(2), 274–307. doi:10.2307/416535

Gundel, J., Hedberg, N., & Zacharski, R. (2000). Statut cognitif et forme des anaphoriques indirects/'Cognitive status and the form of indirect anaphors' (F. Cornish, Trans.). *Verbum, 22*(1), 79–102.

Gundel, J., Hedberg, N., & Zacharski, R. (2003). Definite descriptions and cognitive status in English: Why accommodation is unnecessary. *English Language and Linguistics, 5*(2), 273–295. doi:10.1017/S1360674301000247

Gundel, J., Hedberg, N., & Zacharski, R. (2006). *Coding protocol for statuses on the Givenness Hierarchy* (Unpublished manuscript).

Haugnes, N., & Maher, B. (2009). *NorthStar reading and writing 2* (3rd ed.). White Plains, NY: Pearson Education.

Hawkins, J. A. (1978). *Definiteness and indefiniteness: A study in reference and grammaticality prediction.* London, UK: Croom Helm. doi:10.4324/9781315687919

Huebner, T. (1983). *A longitudinal analysis of the acquisition of English.* Ann Arbor, MI: Karoma Publishers.

Ionin, T., Montrul, S., & Crivos, M. (2013). A bidirectional study on the acquisition of plural noun phrase interpretation in English and Spanish. *Applied Psycholinguistics, 34*(3), 483–518. doi:10.1017/S0142716411000841

Ionin, T., Zubizarreta, M. L., & Maldonado, S. B. (2008). Sources of linguistic knowledge in the second language acquisition of English articles. *Lingua, 118*(4), 554–576. doi:10.1016/j.lingua.2006.11.012

Kim, H. Y. (2000). *Acquisition of English nominal reference by Korean speakers* (Unpublished doctoral dissertation). University of Hawaii, Manoa, HI.

Lim, H. (1999). El problema de la presencia y ausencia del artículo en español. *El español a las puertas del siglo XXI: Actas del XXXIV congreso internacional de la Asociación Europea de Profesores del Español* (pp. 103–119). Zaragoza, Spain: AEPE.

Liu, D., & Gleason, J. L. (2002). Acquisition of the article the by nonnative speakers of English: An analysis of four nongeneric uses. *Studies in Second Language Acquisition, 24*(1), 1–26. doi: 10.1017/S0272263102001018

Lyons, C. (1999). *Definiteness.* Cambridge, UK: Cambridge University Press. doi:10.1017/CBO9780511605789

Master, P. (1997). The English article system: Acquisition, function, and pedagogy. *System, 25*(2), 215–232. doi:10.1016/S0346-251X(97)00010-9

Master, P. (2002). Information structure and English article pedagogy. *System, 30*(3), 331–348. doi:10.1016/S0346-251X(02)00018-0

Miller, J., & Cohen, R. (2009). *NorthStar reading and writing 5* (3rd ed.). White Plains, NY: Pearson Education.

Mulkern, A. E. (1996). The game of the name. In T. Fretheim & J. K. Gundel (Eds.), *Reference and referent accessibility* (pp. 235–250). Amsterdam, the Netherlands: John Benjamins. doi:10.1075/pbns.38.14mul

Parrish, B. (1987). A new look at methodologies in the study of article acquisition for learners of ESL. *Language Learning, 37*(3), 361–383. doi:10.1111/j.1467-1770.1987.tb00576.x

Schleppegrell, M. (2004). *The language of schooling: A functional linguistics perspective.* Mahwah, NJ: Lawrence Erlbaum Associates. doi:10.4324/9781410610317

Snape, N., García Mayo, M., & Gürel, A. (2013). L1 transfer in article selection for generic reference by Spanish, Turkish and Japanese L2 learners. *International Journal of English Studies, 13*(1), 1–28. doi:10.6018/ijes/2013/1/138701

Stockwell, R. P., Bowen, J. D., & Martin, J. W. (1965). *The grammatical structures of English and Spanish.* Chicago, IL: University of Chicago Press.

Swierzbin, B. J. (2004). *The role of cognitive status in second language acquisition of English noun phrase referring expressions* (Unpublished doctoral dissertation). University of Minnesota, Minneapolis, MN.

Tacoronte, A. L. (2014). Sobre el artículo cero en español. *Linguistica Pragensia, 24*(2), 147–168.

Thomas, M. (1989). The acquisition of English articles by first- and second-language learners. *Applied Psycholinguistics, 10*(3), 335–355. doi:10.1017/S0142716400008663

9 Referent introducing strategies in advanced L2 usage
A bi-directional study on French learners of Chinese and Chinese learners of French

Ludovica Lena

Introduction

This study focuses on the acquisition of pragmatic principles relating to the structuring of information at the syntactic level. Specifically, we observe the patterns used to introduce referential entities into discourse by Chinese learners of L2 French and French learners of L2 Chinese. The research is based on the notion that French and Chinese native speakers use very similar syntactic strategies to fulfill this function. In French the most common pattern for referent introductions is the bi-clausal *il y a* 'there is' construction (from *avoir* 'have'), while Chinese speakers rely on presentational structures introduced by the semantically related existential verb *yŏu* 'have'. The aim of this study is to show that bi-directional combinations of the source and the target language may result in different outcomes.

Previous studies have shown the impact of the source language in organizing pragmatic information. Hendriks and Watorek (2008) show that adult learners structure their discourse in topic units through linguistic means that are modelled on those available in their source language. Lambert et al. (2008) studied the influence of the L1 in complex verbal task resolution, showing that learners' productions are characterized by systematic divergences in the structuring of information in speech, which reflects the influence of the source language regardless of the level of linguistic proficiency. In a study on English learners of L2 French, Leclercq (2008) shows that quasi-bilingual learners are still influenced by the conceptual structuring of the source language.

Specifically related to referent introductions, Lambert and Lenart (2004) pointed out that the L1 can strongly influence the way new referents may be introduced into discourse in the L2. Turco (2008) studied the acquisition of the syntactic structures used to introduce and identify referents by French advanced learners of Italian L2. She shows that these speakers can easily use the Italian split presentational structure '*c'è* SN *che*…' ('there is NP who…') that corresponds to the *il y a* presentational structure available in their source language. However, French learners of Italian seem to avoid the Italian V–S structure polysemy, using it only to introduce new referents into discourse. This is because the appearance of the verb–subject order (V–S) is conditioned by several factors such as the status of the referents, the semantic properties of the verb and the pragmatic context.

In general, it is known that the presence in the source language of a similar structure in the L2 should facilitate learners' usage in that L2, which has been shown to be the case for Spanish learners of Italian V–S structures (Chini, 2008), or French speakers when they produce the above-mentioned split presentational structures in Italian L2 (Turco, 2008) for referent introductions. Sometimes, however, L2 learners have been shown to over-rely on presentational structures when introducing new referents, favouring an explicit anchoring mode (Lambert & Lenart, 2004). For example, Leclercq (2008) observes in French learners' L2 English a number of forms that are not attested in a native speakers' corpus, such as the presentational 'I can see...' and the frequent use of relative clauses introduced by *who*. In general, French advanced learners tend to rely heavily on syntactic clefts, while native English speakers mostly use prosodic-type variations to structure information in speech.

Another good example is French speakers' use of the Italian split structure (even in case of unaccusative verbs), while L1 Italian speakers tend to employ V–S word order (Turco, 2008):

IT2_ FR1   *C'è la polizia che arriva*
            Lit: 'There is the police who arrives'
IT1   *Arriva la polizia*
            Lit: 'Arrives the police'

In our contribution, we propose to study how Chinese advanced learners adapt to pragmatic constraints in French as a target language and, conversely, how French advanced learners do the same in their L2 Chinese. We believe such an investigation is crucial, since the appropriation of pragmatic principles is often evoked as the last goal to be achieved before successful acquisition of the target language (Perdue, 1993). The main research questions that lead our study are the following:

RQ1) Does the presence in the target language of the same type of presentational structure (in particular the HAVE structure and the V–S order) in the source language trigger its use by learners?
RQ2) How do learners adapt to the pragmatic constraints specific to the presentational structures of the target language?
RQ3) Does directionality (FRL1>CHL2 vs CHL1>FRL2) play a role? In what manner and why?

The following section includes a brief theoretical presentation of the strategies available in the L1s, before I outline the methods used in the present study.

Referent introductions in French and in Chinese

Regarding the devices used by speakers to anchor new referential entities into discourse, the most well-described strategy in the relevant literature is that of the presentational structure, governed by the existential operator HAVE, in French (Léard, 1986; Lambrecht, 1988; Ashby, 1995 *inter alia*) as well as in Chinese

(Chao, 1968, p. 727; Li & Thompson, 1981, p. 509; Huang, 2013). In both languages, the HAVE structure can take either a 'simple' (HAVE + NP) or a 'complex' (HAVE + NP + VP) form, that is, the latter involving a second verb (V2), as seen for *arriver* in Example (1). In the latter case, the most obvious morphosyntactic difference between the HAVE structures of the two languages is the absence of a relative pronoun in Chinese.

(1) FR1   *ils sont tous les deux par terre*
            il y a *un attroupement*   [Existential structure]
            et **ya** *un policier* **qui** *arrive*   [Presentational structure]

            Lit: 'They're both lying on the ground
            there is a gathering
            and there is a policeman who comes'

In Chinese, what differentiates the existential and the presentational structure is the presence of a V2, of which the NP introduced by *yǒu* 有 is the semantic agent (2). Sometimes, a personal pronoun (namely, third-person pronoun *tā*) is inserted between the post-*you* NP and the V2, as in (3). When the prosodic profile is unitary (no pause intervening between the NP and the pronoun), we analyze such examples as presentational (i.e. 'complex') structures.

(2) CH1   看! 有人偷你的面包!
            Kàn! **Yǒu** *rén tōu nǐde miànbāo!*
            Look HAVE people steal your bread
            'Look! There's someone [who] stole your bread!'

(3) CH1   有一个人他送面包进来
            Yǒu yí-ge rén tā sòng miànbāo jìn-lai
            HAVE one-CL[1] people 3S send bread enter-come
            Lit: 'There is someone he delivered the bread inside'

In addition, the Chinese verb *yǒu* 有 is invariable, unlike the *il y a* sequence (*il y a, il y avait* lit: 'there *has*, there *had*' etc.) and in French the V2 needs to be conjugated as well:

(4) FR2_CH1   *Donc,* **il y avait** *une femme qui* **est passée** *devant*
                   une boulangerie
                   So it there had a woman REL.S is passed in.front.of a bakery
                   Lit: 'So, there was a woman who passed by a bakery'

Let us now turn to verb-subject (V–S) 'inverted' word order. That is, the postposition of the nominal subject to the verb, resulting in the non-canonical V–S word order. Notice that we speak of inverted or non-canonical word order just in terms of frequency, not implying any sort of derivation from a 'core' S–V structure. V–S formulations are, in the languages that concern us here, less frequently used and linked to specific information structure articulations. In both French and Chinese, V–S is typically used to introduce a new referential entity into discourse, and can take the form of a locative inversion when a locus noun phrase appears in preverbal position, or that of an absolute inversion.

(5) CH1   这个时候来了一位警察
          Zhège shíhou **lái-le yí-wei jǐngchá**
          this-CL moment come-PFV one-CL police
          就问发生什么事情
          jiù wèn fāshēng shénme shìqing
          then ask happen what matter
          'In that moment came a policeman and asked what happened'

Importantly, we are dealing here with a difference of register: while in Chinese, the V–S structure is a syntactic formulation that is commonly employed not only in the written language but also in the spoken register, the same cannot be said for French. Indeed, if French V–S structures are typical of the literary genre (ex: *Alors sont arrivés trois hommes en armes* 'Then arrived three armed man'; Marandin, 2003, p. 3), they are quite rare in the spoken language, where the entity-anchoring function is rather carried by bi-clausal presentational structures such as those described through this paper. In both languages, and cross-linguistically, predicates appearing in V–S structures are often motion verbs or verbs denoting appearance.

In sum, given that HAVE structures are the most commonly used syntactic device to express the discursive function of referent introductions in both Chinese and French L1, will this facilitate learners' production in the target language? In addition, considering that V–S structures are used in both languages, but with a difference in terms of their register and frequency of use, how do learners adapt to this constraint?

The current study: Method

Our study is based on a video-retelling task. We collected four corpora, composed of the retellings of 15 French native speakers; 15 Chinese native speakers; 15 French learners of L2 Chinese, and 15 Chinese learners of L2 French. The stimulus employed is an extract from Charlie Chaplin's silent film *Modern Times* developed as part of a European Science Foundation project (see Klein & Perdue, 1992). Following Turco (2008) and Sun (2008) *inter alia*, we selected the sequence comprising the bread robbery scene, where the appearance of several characters in the story enables us to observe how speakers encode them linguistically. Roughly, the storyline can be described as follows:

A hungry girl steals a loaf of bread on the street.
A lady who saw it said it to the baker.

168 *Ludovica Lena*

The baker runs after the girl,
who bumps into Charlie Chaplin,
and the two fall to the ground.
A policeman arrives with the baker.
Chaplin says he stole the bread.
The policeman brings him away.

We interrupted the video at this point and then added a final sequence (Chaplin comes out of the police station and the girl is outside, waiting for him. They are happy to meet again.) in order to study the expression of reintroduced referents which leave the stimulus for a period before returning later.

In sum, the participants had to introduce five characters:

1. Thief girl (main character)
2. Baker
3. Snitching lady
4. Chaplin
5. Police

In what follows, we present the results for these referent introductions, beginning with the L1 Chinese and L1 French groups.

The current study: Results

Referent introduction in the L1s

Table 9.1 shows the types of the structures employed by L1 French and L1 Chinese speakers when new referents are first introduced in the narration. Note that presentational structures coexist with utterances in which the relevant NP (i.e. the NP denoting the new referential entity) appears in its 'canonical' preverbal position.

Table 9.1 Distribution of the syntactic structures linked to referents introduction in the L1s and L2s

	French L1	Chinese L1	French L2	Chinese L2
HAVE structure	22	20	14	39
PERCEPTION Presentational	8	3	8	5
BE Presentational	7	2	1	3
V–S̲	3	4	–	–
S̲–V	17	19	29	9
V–O̲	15	14	15	15
Passive construction	–	10	4	–
Other	3	3	4	4
TOTAL	75	75	75	75

As expected, in the L1 groups referent introductions are mainly achieved by means of the presentational HAVE structure, as in the following examples:

(6) FRL1   *derrière elle **il y a** la voiture **qui** vient livrer le pain*
           behind 3S.F it there has the.F car REL.S comes deliver the.M bread
           'Behind her there is the car who delivers the bread'

(7) CHL1   旁边有面包店的师傅从他车里面搬货物进店里
           *pángbiān **yǒu** miànbāodiàn-de shīfu cóng tā chē lǐmiàn bān huòwù jìn diàn-li*
           side HAVE bakery-SUB master.worker from 3S car inside move merchandise enter shop-in
           'Next [to her] there is the baker who moves the merchandises from his car to the shop'

Other presentational structures are observed, namely: PERCEPTION presentationals, BE presentationals, and the postposition of the nominal subject to the verb, resulting in the verb-subject inverted word order. In PERCEPTION presentationals, the NP denoting the new referent is introduced by a verb of perception – namely a SEE type verb (Lambrecht, 2000):

(8) FR1   *Alors dans cette vidéo **on peut voir** une- une jeune fille **qui** se promène dans la rue*
           So in this.F video we can see a a young girl who REF walks in the.F street
           'So in this video we can see a young girl who walks in the street'

(9) CH1   我看到一个女儿，她看上是很饿
           *Wǒ **kàndào** yí-ge nǚ'ér, tā kànshàng shì hěn è*
           1S see one-CL girl 3S appear be very hungry
           'I see a girl, she looks very hungry'

Of course, the nature of the linguistic experience that we are dealing with – that is, one based on a visual stimulus – may trigger the choice of a PERCEPTION presentational, and between the perception verbs possible it is the vision verb SEE that is more likely to be used. However, the video stimulus is not the only reason triggering their use, since PERCEPTION presentationals are more common in French than in Chinese, and come in the *figées* forms *on voit* 'we see' or modalized *on peut voir* 'we can see'. In fact, such introductory elements of PERCEPTION, as *c'est* or the HAVE existential formula, allow French speakers to introduce the relevant NP – denoting the new referential entity – into discourse by avoiding the unmarked preverbal position – the position which is by default associated with topical entities. At the same time, this newly introduced NP can become the head of the following pseudo-relative clause governed by the relative pronoun *qui*. The following explains what these introductory formulas have in common:

Structure:	*[Introducer +*	*NP +*	*Pseudo-relative clause]*
Example:	il y a	une femme	qui se promène dans la rue
	there has	a lady	who walks in the street
	c'est		
	it is		
	on voit		
	we see		
	(…)		

We will see that, beyond the sentence level, French L1 speakers globally manage their discourse precisely by means of the relative pronoun *qui*, a strategy which is not fully mastered by L2 learners.

The label 'BE presentationals' embraces broad-focus *c'est* structures in French and those structures in which the relevant NP is introduced by the copular verb 是 *shì* 'be' in Chinese.[2]

CH1 首先呢是一个年轻的女孩子她看到橱窗里面
Shǒuxiān ne **shì** *yí-ge niánqīng-de nǚháizi* **tā** kàndao chúchuāng lǐmiàn
beginning NE be one-CL young-SUB girl 3S look window inside
Lit: 'At the beginning is a young lady she looks inside a window'
'The story begins with a young lady who looks into a shop window'

FR1 Alors **c'est** <u>une jeune fille</u> **qui** est pauvre
so it is a young lady who is poor
Lit: 'So it is a young girl who is poor'
'So this story is about a young girl who is poor'

It should be noted that broad-focus *c'est* structures in French are formally identical to narrow focus *c'est* structures, which typically serve to express identificational focus, that is, one in which the clefted NP stands in opposition with a set of alternative elements (*c'est moi qui ai volé la baguette* 'it was me who stole the bread'). We believe that this is a crucial factor when determining the avoidance of such structures by Chinese learners of French when introducing new referents into discourse in the L2: learners associate *c'est* structures with identificational focus, and thus the structure polysemy is not taken into consideration, following the 'unicity of functions' principle that has already been documented with regards to L2 learners' production (see Bartning & Kirchmeyer, 2003). We shall return to this issue later.

Regarding V–S order, both V–S in text-initial position and text-internal V–S clauses (Sasse, 2006, p. 285) are observed. A few cases are attested in the French L1 corpus, being mainly examples of a locative inversion:

FR1   *Devant elle s'approche <u>quelqu'un</u>*
        in.front 3S.F REF get.closer someone
        Lit:'In front of her approaches someone'

        De l'autre côté de la rue **vient** <u>Charlot</u> **qui** *marche*
        From the other side of the.F road comes Charlot REL.S walks
        Lit:'From the other side of the road comes Charlot who is walking'

Regarding the unmarked S–V word order, a closer look at the data tells us that the S–V configurations mainly include NPs whose referents bear a particular status with regard to their inferability. Between the S–V structures altogether, the vast majority involve a definite preverbal NP in L1 data (including preverbal bare nouns in Chinese which trigger a definite reading in this context).

We will now consider the distribution of presentational structures linked to each one of the five characters in the video (Table 9.2). For the sake of clarity, the characters are not necessarily discussed in chronological order.

The encoding of the first character appearing in the storyline, the thief girl, is the one who presents a higher degree of variability in both the L1s. In fact, even if we observe a preference for the PERCEPTION presentational in French L1, a wide range of structures are mobilized to introduce this referential entity. These include the the HAVE structure and the BE presentational (in both languages) and the V–S inverted word order (in Chinese). Note that the unmarked S–V word order is also observed in the Chinese L1 group.

The character of Chaplin is systematically expressed as a verbal object (V–<u>O</u>) in both languages by virtue of his semantic properties. In fact, he is the prototypical patient: as soon as Chaplin makes his appearance in the story, the girl bumps into him and they both fall on the floor.

As for the policeman and the baker, these two characters are likely to be introduced as definite NPs though a bridging operation. The baker is linked to the BAKERY context (*semantic frame*, Fillmore, 1982; *schema*, Chafe, 1987, p. 29). The police officer can be introduced as a 'given' entity by virtue of the extra-linguistic common knowledge. This brings variability with regards to speakers' choices:

FR1   *En même temps <u>la police</u>* **arrive**
FR1   *et juste après* **il y a** *<u>un policier</u>* **qui** *arrive*

As for the snitching lady, the encoding of this character is highly informative and gives us greater insights about referent introductions in Chinese and French L1s as well as the adaptations that will be needed by L2 learners of those languages. Recall that the snitching lady (a) appears in an unpredictable and sudden way and (b) brings a negative contribution to the story: she is the one who informs the baker about the robbery. As a matter of fact, the strategies adopted by the two groups of speakers when introducing this referent are radically different. On the one hand, this character is the one most systematically encoded by the HAVE

Table 9.2 The structures associated to the introduction of each character in the L1s

Linguistic structure	S-V		PERCEPTION		HAVE		BE		V-S		V-Q		Passive		Other	
CHARACTER	CH1	FR1	CH1	FR1	CH1	FR1	CH1	FR1	CH1	FR1	CH1	FR1	CH1	FR1	CH1	FR1
Thief girl	4	1	3	7	5	3	2	4	1	–	–	–	–	–	–	–
Baker	6	8	–	1	5	4	–	–	1	–	–	–	–	–	3	2
Snitching lady	1	3	–	–	4	12	–	–	–	–	–	–	10	–	–	–
Chaplin	–	–	–	–	1	–	–	–	–	2	14	13	–	–	–	–
Police	8	5	–	–	5	3	–	3	2	1	–	2	–	–	–	1
TOTAL	19	17	3	8	20	22	2	7	4	3	14	15	10	–	3	3

structure in French. On the other hand, Chinese speakers massively choose the passive construction where the relevant NP is introduced by the BEI 被 particle:

CH1   她被一个路人看到了
      Tā bèi yí-ge lùrén kàndao-le
      3S PASS one-CL passerby see-PFV
      'She was seen by a passerby'

FR1   *Sauf qu' entre temps il y a une passante qui l' a vu faire ça*
      except that in.the.meantime it there has a.F passerby.F REL.S OBJ has seen do that
      Lit:'But in the meantime there is a passerby who saw her doing that'

With regards to this referential entity, French speakers select the first characteristic (the 'out-of-the-blue' appearance[3]) while Chinese speakers focus on the negative contribution. Thus, the HAVE presentational structure is more suitable to express this kind of referential introduction in French, while the unfortunate nature of this referent's introduction offers the perfect context for employing the passive structure in Chinese where the post-BEI NP denotes the agent (cf. Hashimoto, 1988, p. 336). Once again, L2 learners of either language will be confronted by an interaction of semantic and pragmatic factors when introducing this referent.

Referent introduction in the L2s

As can be seen in Table 9.1 above, the strategies adopted by French learners of L2 Chinese and those of Chinese learners of L2 French appear to be strikingly different. In fact, Chinese learners use the HAVE presentational structures – and presentational structures in general – less frequently, more often choosing the unmarked S–V word order. Conversely, French speakers of Chinese L2 make extensive use of HAVE structures.

As it turns out, both strategies, i.e. avoidance and overuse, may equally result in a pragmatically infelicitous outcome. A good example is the encoding of the 'snitching lady' character (Table 9.3). In particular, recall that by virtue of her negative contribution to events and her sudden appearance, such a character is systematically encoded by the passive BEI construction in L1 Chinese and by means of the HAVE-presentational structure in L1 French accordingly. Besides 4 instances of the passive construction in Chinese learners' L2 French (not attested in the French L1 group), the S–V pattern is systematically employed to introduce this referent. On the other hand, French learners use extensively the *you* structure (14/15 introductions) in a way that reminds their L1 principles. Hence, in the learners' data, both the choice of an unmarked S–V word order and the HAVE presentational strategy fail to result here in a native-like formulation, and thus reflect a pragmatically inappropriate choice.

What remains is to explain why L2 learners' outcomes diverge from natives' in such a way, and, at the same time, why the L2 groups diverge one from another – that is, why Chinese speakers in L2 French and French speakers in L2 Chinese seem to make radically different choices when it comes to referent introductions,

Table 9.3 The structures associated to the introduction of each character in the L2s

Linguistic structure	S-V		PERCEPTION		HAVE		BE		V-S		V-Q		Passive		Other	
CHARACTER	CH2	FR2	CH2	FR2	CH2	FR2	CH2	FR2	CH2	FR2	CH2	FR2	CH2	FR2	CH2	FR2
Thief girl	–	5	5	5	8	4	2	1	–	–	–	–	–	–	–	–
Baker	3	7	–	3	9	5	1	–	–	–	–	–	–	–	2	–
Snitching lady	1	8	–	–	14	3	–	–	–	–	–	–	–	4	–	–
Chaplin	–	–	–	–	3	–	–	–	–	–	12	13	–	–	2	2
Police	5	9	–	–	5	2	–	–	–	–	3	2	–	–	2	2
TOTAL	9	29	5	8	39	14	3	1	–	–	15	15	–	4	4	4

despite their source and target languages providing a structure strongly associated with such a function. For the time being, let us explore the common properties that characterize the two learners' groups.

L2 learners' groups common characteristics

A lack of variety?

Recall that in L1 production, besides the HAVE construction, a wide range of presentational structures are found. In L1 Chinese, the V–S order is frequently used along with the *you* structure to anchor new referents into discourse. Moreover, when the semantic context demands it, the passive BEI construction is to be used. In L1 French, a full inventory of introductory formulas (as *il y a, c'est, on voit*) exist, and V–S order might be used as well.

When compared to the natives' production, L2 narratives stand out in that they manifest a relative lack of variety regarding the structures used to introduce new referents into discourse. That is, if almost all structure types are attested in the L2 productions, when one considers the general picture, the two learners' groups show a clear preference towards one linguistic pattern: the HAVE construction in French learners' L2 Chinese (39/75 introductions) and the S–V order Chinese learners' L2 French (29/75 introductions). This tendency is reflected in the avoidance of structures available in the L1 that would be equally felicitous in the L2 – an obvious example being the absence of V–S word order in both learners' groups.

Unicity of functions

A consequence of the previous point is that in L2 learners' production we observe the tendency to associate one precise function (here: referent introductions) to one single structure, following the principle of *unicity of functions* (Bartning & Kirchmeyer, 2003). Therefore, as mentioned above, when French learners in L2 Chinese seek for an L2 presentational structure allowing them to anchor new referents into the narration, the *you* structure will be picked up to carry this function. In other words, all the structures available in the source language for this purpose – and of which some may be felicitous in the target language – merge into the *you* structure in L2 Chinese.

Another good example concerns the *c'est* structure, which is chosen only to express identificational focus in Chinese learners' L2 French. The following are examples of the identificational focus *c'est* structure in Chinese learners' productions. Importantly, not a single learner fails to use this structure when the context requires it, nor do they misuse the S–V word order instead.

FR2_CH1   *le monsieur a dit que c'est lui qui a piqué la baguette*
          the.M gentleman has said REL.O it is him REL.S has stolen the.F baguette
          Lit:'The gentleman said that it was him who stole the baguette'

FR2_CH1   *ce n'est pas la fille qui a volé le pain*
          it NEG is NEG the.F girl REL.S has stolen the.M bread

        c'est <u>lui-même</u> **qui** a volé
        it is him self REL.S has stolen
        Lit:'It is not the girl who stole the bread, it is himself [the one] who stole [it]'

However, not one single example of presentational *c'est* (see the following example) is observed in their corpus.

FR1 *Donc, c'est <u>une- une fille</u> **qui** regarde des pâtisseries en vitrine*

In our view, several possible explanations arise. First, the identificational *c'est* structure corresponds to the narrow focus *shì* 是 structure in L1 Chinese. Secondly, the *c'est* configuration is prototypically associated with the expression of narrow identificational focus in French (see Lambrecht, 2001) contrary to presentational structures which, in some cases, commute with the unmarked S–V word order, and their felicitous use derives from a successful pragmatic consideration. Thirdly, as mentioned, learners associate one structure (i.e. the *c'est* structure) with one function (i.e. the expression of identificational focus) and are thus reluctant to use it in a different context (i.e. the introduction of new referential entities into discourse). This is also the case with learners' acquisition of V–S word order in Italian, the polysemy of which is problematic. Finally, as Bartning and Kirchmeyer (2003) have pointed out, 'continuative' relative clauses (expressing information that makes the story move forward) are acquired later than 'descriptive' relative clauses (i.e. expressing discourse-given background informational content). The narrow focus *c'est* structure typically includes a clefted focused element and a descriptive relative clause. On the other hand, presentational *c'est* structures involve by definition a 'continuative' relative clause. This could be a reason why Chinese learners produce the former kind of *c'est* structure, but not the latter.

Scarce usage of bridging

In both learner groups, the bridging of new inferable referents is not a common strategy. To begin with, French learners of L2 Chinese, as we said, massively use the *you* structure in order to introduce new referents into discourse. Only a very few cases of definite preverbal NPs are found, intervening to encode the referents of the baker and the police, as expected. It should be noted that French learners tend to underline the definitude of such NPs with the demonstratives这个 *zhè(-ge)* 'this' or 那(个) *nà(-ge)* 'that', as also seen for speakers of other article languages in Crosthwaite et al. (2018).

CH2_FR1   然后就那个警察来了
                Ránhòu jiù <u>nà-ge jǐngchá</u> lái-le
                after then that-CL police come-PFV
                'And then the police came'

Chinese learners, on the other hand, resort to the 'unmarked' S–V word order more often; however, preverbal NPs are mostly indefinite.

FR2_CH1 *A ce moment-là un homme livrait une- un plateau de pains dans la boulangerie*
at that time   a.M man deliver.IMP a.F a.M plate of bread into the.F bakery
'At that time, a man was delivering a plate of breads to the bakery'

Operating at the (morpho-)syntax/pragmatics interface, bridging is documented to be a difficult phenomenon for L2 learners to acquire (Crosthwaite et al. 2018) and our data confirms this. Note, incidentally, that the few cases of definite preverbal NPs in the L2 corpora properly concern the referents of the baker and the police officer, i.e. those referents that by virtue of a semantic frame and textra-linguistic common knowledge, respectively, are likely to be introduced by a bridging operation.

Summary

In this section, we discussed a number of characteristics that the two learner groups have in common: a lack of variety with regards to the choices of presentational structures; a tendency towards a 'unicity of functions,' where one function tends to be associated with only a single form; and the scarce usage of bridging as a strategy to introduce new referents. Now, we will turn to the main difference between the French learner group and the Chinese learner group, trying to explain why the former overuse presentational structure in their L2 productions while the latter, on the opposite, tend to avoid such structures in French L2 and reestablish the 'unmarked' S–V word order.

Explaining overuse and avoidance in L2 learners' production

As detailed above, Chinese speakers more often introduce new referential entities by using the canonical S–V word order, thus avoiding the HAVE structure in their L2 French. By way of explanation, we must acknowledge the structural complexity of French *il y a* structures compared to *yǒu*有 constructions, as the sequence *il y a* is not (entirely) fixed and demands agreement with the second verb (cf. example 24). This potential difficulty explains the preference manifested by Chinese learners towards simple vs. complex HAVE structures in L2 French as well as their general tendency to avoid bi-clausal presentational structures. Sometimes, Chinese learners might omit the relative pronoun *qui*, a formulation that is not attested in the French L1 corpus:

FR2_CH1 *pendant ce moment il y a le patron du magasin*
         ø était en train de transporter… les produits

In addition, we believe that Chinese speakers more often reestablish the S–V order in French because it is perceived as the 'canonical' word order of this language. In other words, we must take into account the role played by metalinguistic knowledge, both as educated learners of one's L1 and as educated learners of the target language.

French learners, on the other hand, strongly rely on the *yǒu*有 construction as a *ready-to-use device* that can help them to structure the discourse without demanding any syntactic adjustment or major global planning. As French overuse of presentational structures has been documented in other L2s (English, Italian), our study has showed that transfer of L1 patterns may occur even in an L2 such as Chinese, where the presentational structure does not involve a relative pronoun.

Secondly, *yǒu*有 structures seem to encompass the presentative function, which is achieved via a more diversified inventory of constructions in French L1. Thus, French learners seem to assign this function to the *yǒu*有 structure following a tendency towards the 'unicity of functions' typical of L2 production.

Our findings also suggest L2 learners do not employ V–S order. This is an interesting finding as studies on Chinese speakers of basic Italian (Chini, 2002) found that learners can correctly use the V–S order in L2 Italian. Valentini (1992, 2003) also finds the V–S order in beginning Chinese learners of Italian, and suggests that the L1 plays a major role in shaping the sentence word order, in that learners whose L1 allows a more flexible order (such as Chinese) would more easily acquire the use of correspondent V–S order sentences in the L2. However, we believe that our Chinese learners (that is, advanced learners who benefit from an enhanced L2 metalinguistic knowledge) do not produce V–S order in the French target language because they do not conceive it as a possible choice in the syntactic inventory of French. In other words, if the source language has a form (V–S in this case) which could be felicitously employed in the L2 under similar a context, learners seem to avoid its usage if such a form is not conceptualized as an alternative pattern to what is considered to be the prototypical L2 order, i.e. the S–V word order.

Insights from the expression of 'reactivated' referents

Contrary to the Chinese L1 group, French native speakers may use presentational structures (mostly the HAVE construction and sometimes the V–S order) to encode 'reactivated' referents, i.e. those referents that come back into the scene of discourse (that is, referentially 'known' but relationally 'focal'):

FR1   a.   ***il y a <u>la fille</u> qui l'attend à la sortie***
               it there has the girl who OBJ wait at the.F exit
               Lit:'There is the girl who waits for him at the exit'

       b.   ***et là au coin de la rue l'attend <u>la femme</u>***
               and there at.the corner of the.F road OBJ wait the.F woman
               Lit:'And there, at the corner waits for him the woman'

In this case, both learner groups follow the discursive principles of their source language, that is: Chinese learners never assign this function to the HAVE structure, while French learners do so.[4] It is worth highlighting that Chinese learners do produce examples where the NP encoded by the *il y a* structure is definite, therefore, it does not seem to be a constraint at the morphological level. However, the referent denoted by the definite NP is always one that appears for the first time into discourse:

FR2_CH1   *il y avait le personnel de la boulangerie qui vient de sortir quelque chose*
d'un- d'une grande voiture
Lit:'There was the employee of the bakery who just took something out of a big car'

Therefore, at the pragmatic level, learners fail to associate the HAVE structure with a function (namely the encoding of reactivated referents) that is not found in their L1. It might be the case that similarity in HAVE structures found across French and Chinese L1s influences L2 learners' production, in that the need for a conceptual rearrangement is less salient.

A look at speakers' global discourse planning

As previously noted, a characteristic that all French presentational structures have in common is the following *qui*-clause. Indeed, a crucial point here is the possibility to encode the newly introduced referent by a pseudo-relative clause (Hendriks, 2003, p. 300). This is the way French speakers manage their discourse by organizing sequences of relative clauses governed by the relative pronoun *qui* relating to one referent.[5]

FR1   *donc et on voit la personne ou le boulanger*
on sait pas trop qui c'est
qui- qui descend qui descend les les-
qui prend les pains ou les pâtisseries dans le camion
(qui est stationné devant la boulangerie)
et puis qui rentre dans la boulangerie

However, in Chinese, referential continuity is achieved by means of the personal pronoun *tā* and by zero anaph+or (marked by "Ø" in the text):

CH1   有一个女的 她 经过 一家面包店。
Yǒu yí-ge nǚde tā jīngguò yì-jia miànbāodiàn
然后她看到橱窗里面的点心,
ránhòu tā kàndao chúchuāng lǐmiàn de diǎnxīn,
她好像有一些饿,
tā hǎoxiàng yǒu yìxiē è
很想 吃,
Ø hěn xiǎng chī,

但是 可能没有钱买。
dànshì kěnéng Ø méi-yǒu qián mǎi

Thus, the point to be made here is that a successful acquisition of L2 pragmatic organization cannot be confined to the sentence level (i.e. the 'presentational' structure *per se*), but necessarily takes into consideration global discourse strategies as used by native speakers.

Concluding remarks

In this study we explored the strategies for referent introductions adopted by Chinese learners of L2 French and French learners of L2 Chinese. To begin with, given two languages, L1>L2 directionality may lead to quite different outcomes. In particular, a form/function pairing in the L1 does not always favour use of the corresponding form in the target language. On the one hand French speakers overuse HAVE structures in their L2 Chinese, even in clearly inappropriate contexts (that is, instead of passive BEI structures and to express reactivated referents). Thus, French learners tend to overuse presentational structures to introduce new referential entities, even in the case of a target language without relative pronouns – namely Mandarin Chinese. On the other hand, Chinese learners' systematic use of the S–V word order in French L2 is observed. In this case, we believe speakers' metalinguistic representation of the target language grammar plays a major role as well.

In general, the present study confirms previous claims in that although learners may be highly proficient, their patterns in information selection still partially reflect the ones found in their L1, both at the micro- and macro-planning levels. In addition, given that the introduction of new referents is not exclusively associated with marked syntactic structures (as the range of S–V results in our L1 corpora showed), the acquisition of presentational structures may be particularly challenging for the L2 learner. While the identificational focus structure (corresponding to English *it*-clefts) appears to be unproblematic in both learners' groups, on the contrary, learners' felicitous selection of presentational structures reflects a preference instead of a categorical choice. This, therefore, requires a prior and deep understanding of the pragmatic context, resulting in increased difficulty for L2 learners.

List of abbreviations used in glosses

1S	First person pronoun
3S	Third-person pronoun
ACC	Pretransitive marker *bǎ* 把
CL	Classifier
CRS	Current Relevant State particle *le* 了
F	Feminine gender
GEN	Genitive particle *de* 的
IMP	Imperfect
M	Masculine gender

NE	Pause particle *ne* 呢
NEG	Negation
PASS	Passive marker
PFV	Perfective aspect marker
PROG	Progressive aspect adverb *zai* 在
REF	Reflexive pronoun
REL.O	Relative object pronoun
REL.S	Relative subject pronoun
SUB	Subordinative particle *de* 的

Notes

1 See the end of the chapter for a list of abbreviations used in glosses.
2 We included the few cases of partially set expressions such as French *c'est l'histoire d'* NP 'it is the story of…' or 这个故事讲的是 NP 'What this story tells is…' in Chinese).
3 On the link between *il y a* presentational structures and the expression of an abrupt, 'surprising' event, see for instance Lambrecht (1988).
4 The means employed by Chinese learners to mark reactivated referents in French L2 (namely: demonstrative pronoun and dislocation) also directly reflect L1 strategies, and are not attested in native French corpus in this context.

> CH1 这个女生她就在外面等他
> *Zhè-ge nǚshēng tā jiù zài wàimiàn děng tā*
> this-CL girl 3S then be.located outside wait 3S
> Lit: 'This girl she was waiting for him outside'

5 Notice incidentally that such a discourse-organization strategy might be used even in the (rare) cases of V–S order, as seen in example 13 above.

References

Ashby, W. J. (1995). French presentational structures. In J. Amastae, G. Goodall, M. Montalbetti, & M. Phinney (Eds), *Contemporary research in romance linguistics* (pp. 91–104). Amsterdam, the Netherlands: John Benjamins.

Bartning, I., & Kirchmeyer, N. (2003). Le développement de la compétence textuelle à travers les stades acquisitionnels en français L2. *Acquisition et interaction en langue étrangère, 19,* 9–39.

Chafe, W. (1987). Cognitive constraints on information flow. In R. S. Tomlin (Ed.), *Coherence and grounding in discourse* (pp. 21–51). Amsterdam, the Netherlands: John Benjamins.

Chao, Y. (1968). *A grammar of spoken Chinese*. Berkeley, CA: University of California Press.

Chini, M. (2002). Ordres marqués et perspective du locuteur en italien L2. *Revue française de linguistique appliquée, 7*(2), 117–137.

Chini, M. (2008). Spunti comparativi sulla testualità nell'italiano L2 di tedescofoni e ispanofoni. In G. Bernini, L. Spreafico, & A. Valentini (Eds.), *Competenze lessicali e discorsive nell'acquisizione di lingue seconde* (pp. 301–339). Perugia, Italy: Guerra-Edizioni.

Crosthwaite, P., Yeung, Y., Bai, X., Lu, L., & Bae, Y. (2018). Definite discourse-new reference in L1 and L2: The case of L2 Mandarin. *Studies in Second Language Acquisition*, *40*(3), 625–649. doi:10.1017/S0272263117000353

Fillmore, C. J. (1982). Frame semantics. In Linguistic Society of Korea (Ed.), *Linguistics in the morning calm* (pp. 111–137). Seoul, Korea: Hanshin Publishing.

Hashimoto, M. J. (1988). The structure and typology of the Chinese passive construction. In M. Shibatani (Ed.), *Passive and voice* (pp. 329–354). Amsterdam, the Netherlands: John Benjamins.

Hendriks, H. (2003). Using nouns for reference maintenance: A seeming contradiction in L2 discourse. In A. G. Ramat (Ed.), *Typology and second language acquisition* (pp. 291–326). Berlin, Germany: Mouton de Gruyter.

Hendriks, H., & Watorek, M. (2008). L'organisation de l'information en topique dans les discours. *Acquisition et interaction en langue étrangère*, *26*, 149–171.

Huang, S. (2013). *Chinese grammar at work* (Vol. 1). Amsterdam, the Netherlands: John Benjamins.

Klein, W., & Perdue, C. (1992). Why does the production of some learners not grammaticalize? *Studies in Second Language Acquisition*, *14*(3), 259–272. doi:10.1017/S0272263100011116

Lambert, M., Carroll, M., & von Stutterheim, C. (2008). Acquisition en L2 des principes d'organisation de récits spécifiques aux langues. *Acquisition et interaction en langue étrangère*, *26*, 5–10.

Lambert, M., & Lenart, E. (2004). Incidence des langues sur le développement de la cohésion en L1 et en L2: Gestion du statut des entités dans une tâche de récit. *Langages*, *3*, 14–32. doi: 10.3917/lang.155.0014

Lambrecht, K. (1988). Presentational cleft constructions in spoken French. In J. Haiman & S. Thompson (Eds.), *Clause combining in grammar and discourse* (pp. 135–179). Amsterdam, the Netherlands: John Benjamins.

Lambrecht, K. (2000). Prédication seconde et structure informationnelle: La relative de perception comme construction présentative. *Langue Française*, *127*(1), 49–66.

Lambrecht, K. (2001). A framework for the analysis of cleft constructions. *Linguistics*, *39*(3), 463–516. doi:10.1515/ling.2001.021

Léard, J. M. (1986). Il y a...qui et C'est...qui: La syntaxe comme compatibilité d'opérations sémantiques. *Lingvisticae Investigationes*, *10*(1), 85–130. doi:10.1075/li.10.1.04lea

Leclercq, P. (2008). L'influence de la langue maternelle chez les apprenants adultes quasi-bilingues dans une tache contrainte de verbalization. *Acquisition et interaction en langue étrangère*, *26*, 51–69.

Li, C. N., & Thompson, S. A. (1981). *Mandarin Chinese: A functional reference grammar*. Berkeley, CA: University of California Press.

Marandin, J. M. (2003). Inversion du sujet et structure de l'information dans les langues romanes. In D. Godard (Ed.), *Langues romanes: Problèmes de la phrase simple* (pp. 345–392). Paris, France: Editions du CNRS.

Perdue, C. (Ed.). (1993). *Adult language acquisition: Cross-linguistic perspectives*. Cambridge, UK: Cambridge University Press.

Sasse, H.-J. (2006). Theticity. In G. Bernini & M. L. Schwartz (Eds.), *Pragmatic organization of discourse in the languages of Europe* (pp. 255–308). Berlin, Germany: de Gruyter.

Sun, J. (2008). Conceptualisation étendue du temps topique dans les narrations des apprenants sinophones en français langue étrangère. *Acquisition et interaction en langue étrangère, 26,* 71–88.

Turco, G. (2008). Introduction et identification d'un référent chez les apprenants francophones de l'italien L2. *Acquisition et interaction en langue étrangère, 26,* 211–237.

Valentini, A. (1992). *L'italiano dei cinesi: Questioni di sintassi.* Milan, Italy: Guerini e Associati.

Valentini, A. (2003). L'apprendimento della subordinazione avverbiale nell'italiano di sinofoni e le varietà di apprendimento. In E. Banfi (Ed.), *Italiano/L2 di cinesi: Processi acquisizionali* (pp. 66–78). Milan, Italy: Franco Angeli.

10 Nominal reference in L2 French

How do adult learners manage to understand the multifunctionality of determiners and their discourse counterparts?

Ewa Lenart

Introduction

The establishment of reference relations in language requires speakers to take into account multiple levels of structure and communicative constraints. Specifically, language learners must understand the close correlation between formal, semantic, and discourse constraints which govern sentence and text organisation in the target language. Furthermore, they must also learn to consider the boundaries of these constraints in relation to context and to shared knowledge. Consequently, the functionalist approach adopted in this study postulates a double computation in the grammar: formal rules and communicative/contextualisation rules (Lenart & Perdue 2004).

Frequently, L2 learners must express universal referential domains (entities, process, temporality, space, and modality) using the linguistic categories of a particular language. Yet, we know that linguistic categories are not universal (e.g. articles). So, if the mother tongue indeed influences our way of seeing the world, as partisans of linguistic relativity claim (*Sapir-Whorf hypothesis*, Whorf 1956; Gumperz & Levinson 1996), L2 learners strive to reconceptualise semantic concepts that are expressed differently (or not expressed at all) in one of their languages, in order to comply with the referential system of the target language (e.g. Slobin 1991, 1996; Stutterheim et al. 2012).

Reference to entities, typically expressed by nominals (NP, pronouns), forms the core of an utterance. In French, determiners obligatorily accompany nouns (excluding proper nouns and non-referential uses). They are multi-functional and reflect the interaction between internal processes (constraints related to the language system) and the external problem of reference. In order to identify a referent, the learner of L2 French must first understand this multifunctionality of the morphemes themselves, and the relations between the referent and the linguistic and extra-linguistic context.

Within the set of determiners, articles are purely surface phenomena which are far from a universal feature of language, and do not exist in many languages. Polish, the source language (SL) of our adult learners in this present study, is one such language. Therefore, Polish native speakers learning French are faced with the problem of acquiring those functions which are obligatorily encoded in French by articles or other determiners, but are only optionally expressed in Polish through other means such as word order (Lyons 1999).

This chapter examines the acquisition trajectory of Polish adult learners of L2 French at two levels of proficiency (beginners and advanced) through the interaction of sentence and communicative rules in the process of making reference to entities in a film-retelling task. My aim is to display how these learners use the linguistic strategies available in the L2 to ensure discourse cohesion in their oral narratives. Based on Ariel's Accessibility Theory (1988, 1990, 2004), I focus on the way the learners employ high, mid, and low accessibility markers to maintain and shift reference to the protagonists of the story. Analysis of reference resolution and referential movement is traceable thanks to the *quaestio* model (Klein & Sttuterheim 1991), which we use as a bridge between the communicative intentions of speakers and their linguistic formulation.

In the following sections, we will present, from the functionalist point of view, what is the learner's verbal task, and how complex is the choice of an appropriate determiner or other linguistic means to refer to entities in French. Then, relying on the Accessibility Theory and the *quaestio* model, we will show how L2 French learners manage to construct a cohesive discourse and the features specific to their interlanguage, from the beginner to the advanced levels of proficiency.

The learner's problem of arranging words[1]

The functionalist approach maintains that it is necessary to analyse the interaction between the different levels of language organisation (phonology, morphosyntax, lexicon, discourse/pragmatics) and the contexts of their use. Consequently, functionalists postulate two types of computation in grammar, namely formal rules and communicative (contextualisation) rules. Formal rules refer to the conditions for correct sentence formation – how minimal units of meaning are combined to form larger constituents up to the level of the sentence. Communicative rules deal with the conditions under which a sentence can be actualised in a situational and discourse context. Among other aspects necessary for successful communication, contextual information has to allow for referential interpretation of deictic and anaphoric terms.

Double computation provides a way to define the language learner's task: how they gradually master sentence organisation and the rules of sentence contextualisation. That is, how the learner combines vocabulary items in contextualised utterances. Therefore, two sets of factors determining the acquisition process must be taken into consideration – formal and communicative. To underline the importance of the linguistic and extra-linguistic context, we can give the example of a correct linguistic form that can be inadequate in context and considered a *covert error* (Corder 1971). If a speaker utters *il est parti* ("he left") out of the blue, and we cannot retrieve the referent of the pronoun *il* from the context, *il* is an erroneous form from the communicative point of view, although the linguistic string is correct from a morphosyntactic perspective. Yet, we can only determine that the learner succeeds or fails in achieving their communicative goals through the analysis of the implementation of linguistic means in a given context. The speaker refers to an entity so that the interlocutor can identify it. The speaker must therefore calculate, according to the communicative situation, what has just been said, and the presupposed (general and/or shared) knowledge of the addressee, in order to choose the appropriate linguistic means for the context in question.

Ariel, in her Accessibility Theory (1988, 1990, 2004), highlighted the importance of the speaker's choice of referring expression to enable the addressee to retrieve the intended referent. The choice among linguistic means signals different degrees of the cognitive accessibility of the referent. A definite NP, for example, is a high accessibility marker, and a pronoun is a low accessibility marker. Consequently, discourse cohesion relies on the speakers' pragmatic competence as well as their knowledge of appropriate linguistic means (Lenart & Perdue 2004). L2 learners possess this pragmatic competence through the knowledge of their L1 but have to learn the appropriate sentence organisation and the appropriate NP range (nominal/pronominal) for reference (to entities) in the L2.

Various studies have analysed discourse cohesion in different L1–L2 language pairs. Many found over-explicitness in L2 discourse, especially at intermediate proficiency (e.g. Chinese learners of German, Hendriks 2003; German learners of Italian, Chini 2005; French learners of Swedish and Swedish learners of French, Gullberg 2003; French learners of English and English learners of French, Leclercq & Lenart 2013; Chinese learners of English, Ryan 2015). L2 learners tend to use more explicit linguistic means than native speakers, and thus violate the principle of economy (Levinson 2000). Therefore, over-explicitness seems to be a property of interlanguage in general, not just a particular language feature. Frederiksen and Mayberry (2015) list a number of studies who found over-explicitness and tried to provide explanations in the form of markedness and transfer strategies (Muñoz 1995; Polio 1995), communicative strategies (Williams 1988), and process-oriented learner strategies (Carroll & Lambert 2003; Gullberg 2003, 2006).

In the early levels of L2 acquisition, learners lack sufficient linguistic means in their L2, and must rely on their pragmatic knowledge for discourse organisation. Their production reflects the most neutral conceptualisation of the discourse task. Namely, to produce a narrative, learners apply a triple constraint: following the chronological order strictly, keeping the perspective of the controlling actor/agent, and constructing anaphoric chains through this referent. This plan (a high-level process) makes it possible to perform a minimal discourse task with rudimentary linguistic means (cf. Klein & Perdue 1992). Interlanguage becomes more complex and more target-like with acquisitional grammaticalisation (Giacalone-Ramat 1993). However, when conceptualisation in different referential domains differs between the source and target languages, L2 learners struggle to reconceptualise the concept in question. This is illustrated with reference to definiteness in French and Polish.

Using the example of Polish speakers learning L2 French (beginners and advanced), we will examine how proficiency and crosslinguistic factors impact the choice of NP (determiners, pronouns, zero anaphora) to refer to entities and allow learners to build a coherent discourse. We expected both groups to first rely on communicative/pragmatic rules to be understood by the interlocutor, but that differences would arise due to the linguistic skills at their disposal. The lack of necessary linguistic means in the L2 would prevent the beginners from abiding by the communicative rules of the target language. In contrast, the advanced learners would endeavour to follow both communicative and grammatical rules, but the cognitive efforts involved in a complex verbal task could influence their choice of linguistic means. We also assumed that the source language would have an impact on discourse organisation in both groups. I now explore these hypotheses in more detail.

Reference to entities

An entity (an object of the world) passes into discourse through a process of referencing. Lyons (1977) proposes three major types of linguistic expression to accomplish the act of reference: the definite noun phrase, the proper noun, and the pronoun. To these three categories, we add the indefinite phrase and zero anaphora, which perform very specific and distinct functions in discourse.

In French, reference is partly linked to nominal determination. While the noun gives to the NP its notional substance and categorical status, determiners participate in the actualisation of the noun by designating particular instantiations of the notion lexically associated with the noun. The minimal canonical structure of the NP in French is a noun preceded by a determiner (det+N).[2] French determiners are distinguished into definite and indefinite determiners – the first include the definite article, demonstratives, and possessives, although the latter are not incompatible with the feature [-def]; while indefinites include the indefinite article and other forms, such as *aucun* ("none"), *plusieurs* ("several"). These elements signal the grammatical category of definiteness. The definite article *le/la/les* indicates that the referent of the NP is identifiable and belongs to the speaker's universe of discourse. Demonstrative and possessive markers share some properties with the definite article, but are characterised frequently by *deixis*, spatial (reference to context/co-text), and personal (reference to person), respectively. When the relation with the person possessed is clear in a given context, the definite article can replace a possessive. The article *un/une* occupies a special place among indefinite determiners. Its impact on meaning is quite diverse. According to Van de Velde, "a definite article relies on a [preceding] indefinite article with which it holds anaphoric relations [...]. The indefinite article itself ensures the transfer from concept to object, but nothing more. In particular, it does not imply the [real-world] existence of the discourse entity (a mental concept) that it helped create. It takes on a *thetic* or *hypothetical* value, depending on context" (1997: 84) (my translation).[3]

When a referent is introduced into the discourse and is accessible through other segments of the text, co-referential relations are realised through anaphoric relations expressed by determiners (in a broad sense), third person pronouns, possessives, and demonstratives. Every linguistic marker forms a link in a reference chain (anaphoric chain) used to instantiate the referent, thereby ensuring textual continuity and, consequently, textual cohesion. In French, a noun, accompanied by a determiner, or a pronominal, realises the subject paradigm. Personal pronouns present a binary gender opposition (masculine and feminine: *il/elle* "he/she"), while the relative marker *qui* ("who/what") has only one form (in the case of simple relative pronouns). In some (rare) co-referential contexts, the subject may not be expressed morpho-phonologically on the surface (zero anaphora Ø). The internal realisations of the object paradigm, which is post-verbal, can be multiple (as for the subject paradigm). The pronominal forms reflect variations of case marking: *le/la* (him/her) for the direct object (accusative), and a single form *lui* (him/her) for masculine and feminine indirect object (dative). In French, object pronouns usually precede the verb.

Other factors are important in the choice of NP form, among them, the degree to which a referent can be presupposed in a given discourse context. Several authors (including the frequently cited Givón 1983) use the following continuum, which is argued to be universal (cf. Hickmann 2003, for detailed discussion):

Nominal expressions   Pronominal expressions
Indefinite NP > definite NP   >   Explicit pronoun > zero pronoun

Ariel's Accessibility Theory (1990, 2004) relies on a cognitive concept of accessibility ("specific degree of mental accessibility", 2004: 92), which is intended to bridge between the structure of memory and linguistic marking of a referent. Accessibility enables the addressee to retrieve the necessary information from short- or long-term memory (depending on linguistic and extra-linguistic context, and shared general knowledge) to understand the speaker's message. Ariel broadly distinguishes between three broad levels of accessibility, high, medium, and low, and correlates these with linguistic markers. Thus, (subject and object) pronouns and zero anaphora are markers of high accessibility (HAM), NPs with demonstrative or possessive markers are mid-accessibility markers (MAM), and definite NPs are low accessibility markers (LAM). Indefinite NPs in English (and in French) are used to introduce into discourse entities that are not accessible to the addressee. This type of NP is not listed in Ariel's category of referential expressions, nor in Lyons' (1977). Once introduced, the new entity becomes accessible and one can refer to it through anaphoric expressions. The use of subject or object pronouns implies that the interlocutor knows the referent chosen by the speaker. In French, an SVO language, in which the subject is generally more salient than the object, subject pronouns are also considered more accessible than object pronouns. According to Ariel's theory, zero anaphora marks higher accessibility than pronouns, allowing for tight discourse cohesion to be established. Zero anaphora is also at the top of Givón's (1983, 1989) topicality scale, established to code topic accessibility[4] and assumed to be valid for all languages.

To summarise, the same linguistic phenomenon varies in importance depending on language. For local accessibility marking of the referent (*identifiability*), using a determiner is obligatory in French, but not in Polish, the source language of our learners. Maintained reference reflects a linguistic problem of pronominalisation, specifically with respect to obligatory or optional conditions under which a full NP can/must be replaced with a pronoun, both to avoid repetition of the NP and to signal that referents are mutually known. Another difference concerns the use of zero anaphora for subjects. French is prototypically an obligatory subject language (except in some co-referential contexts where zero anaphora can be used). In Polish, the subject is optional and can remain implicit, while verbal morphology indicates person, number, and, in the past tense, gender of the subject referent in non-contrastive contexts. Zero anaphora is the rule for maintained reference.

So, the establishment of reference goes hand in hand with the discourse organisation of the information in different referential domains, here, in the domain of entities. The speakers' task is to select and linearise information to express their communicative intentions that involve the production of a discourse (a *complex verbal task*, Levelt 1989). Klein and Stutterheim (1991) propose a *quaestio* model that is not constrained by any particular language and links two levels of analysis – sentence and discourse. It also demonstrates the twofold L2 learner's task: how the learner must master both formal and communicative factors in order to build a coherent and cohesive discourse. I discuss this further in the next section.

The *quaestio* model

Klein and Stutterheim's *quaestio* model (1991) follows the tradition of Henri Weil's treaty on word order (1844), in that the organisation of a text follows the order of ideas. "Ideas" are organised from a "starting point", which corresponds to the knowledge shared by interlocutors, and tend towards a "goal", that is to say towards information not shared by the interlocutor. Thus, the "march of ideas" goes from the known to the unknown, and, through utterances, the ideas follow a "parallel march" or a "progressive march". Aristotle, in his dialectic, already proposed the principle of information organisation – first to say "being" and then "how is being": *prius esse, quam tam esse*.

The starting point in the organisation of a long text is governed by a *quaestio* – the general question to which the text provides an answer. The movement of information in a coherent text is therefore constrained, on the global level (discourse) and on the local level (utterance), by this *quaestio*, to which the specific type of discourse responds. For narratives, the *quaestio* is: *what happened (for p) in t i+1?*, where p denotes a protagonist, t a time interval, and $i+t$ specifies the time interval "after". The *quaestio* defines the main structure – the plot of the discourse – and the information to be expressed as part of the topic constituent or the focus of every utterance. The *quaestio* (and the *quaestiones* in the background) raises a range of possibilities for the answer. Local *quaestiones* are closely linked to the global *quaestio*, but impose different structures. Each utterance specifies only one of the possibilities of the range. This specification is called focus (F) – which is not given by the *quaestio*. The rest of the answer, that is, what is constrained by the *quaestio*, constitutes the topic (T). This topic/focus distinction, therefore, applies to contents (meanings) that must be organised into linguistic means in a particular language. Yet, the information/referential movement determined by a discourse specific *quaestio* is visible through textual marks of cohesion: connectors, anaphors, order of words, etc., and concerns the introduction, maintenance, and shift of reference (or continuation).

In short, the *quaestio* links the communicative intentions of the speaker and their linguistic formulation that determine the selection and linearisation of information. At the same time, in order to manage referential movement (in the domain of entities), the speaker must take into account intrinsic features of the NP, expressions that denote p (protagonist), (singular or plural, masculine or feminine – when this information is grammatically encoded), the syntactic function of the referential expression, and the informational status (topic, focus). The linguistic form used must allow the interlocutor to retrieve all of this information. Therefore, the speaker must calculate the state of knowledge of his addressee at every moment in the production of the discourse.

As we can see, there are different levels of analysis (NP internal structure, information organisation, and referential movement), even if the same constituent can realise all of them. The transition from a referent to the linguistic expression refers to the expression of definiteness and information organisation, and concerns morphosyntactic, semantic (semantic-referential), and pragmatic (enunciative-hierarchical) analysis. These different levels are interrelated. The *quaestio* model creates (artificially) a context of interpretation and makes possible the sentence and discourse levels of analysis. It also allows interlanguage and interlearner comparisons of production, as well as an assessment of the general acquisition trends specific to each acquisition context (learner/language/context).

Thus, the use of an indefinite article reflects a linguistic operation in which the existence of something is indicated for the first time; that is, the indefinite article brings an entity to existence in the interlocutors' discourse model, simultaneously indicating the non-identifiability of the referent. The indefinite NP often appears in (spoken) French accompanied by existential or presentational structures that place the entity in focus position. Blanche-Benveniste calls this an "auxiliary device of nominal determination" (1997: 93); Lambrecht (1986) talks about "the Principle of the Separation of Reference and Role". According to both, the act of introducing a referent (a topic) and the predication about it are two separate operations. The entities introduced into a discourse are linked together by causal and temporal relations. Maintaining reference to these entities is ensured by anaphoric links, the choice of which depends on the degree of accessibility of the referent and the linguistic means available in the specific language. Thus, the referent of an NP *un chien* ("a dog"), introduced into the discourse with an existential/presentative structure, can be maintained by a pronoun (*il/elle/qui*), zero anaphora (Ø), or by a nominal recovery, that also accompanies the change of information status, for example: *c'est l'histoire d'un chien; le chien sort de sa niche* ("this is a story about a dog; the dog comes out of his kennel"), where *le chien* becomes the topic of the second utterance. Therefore, referential movement in the domain of entities reflects the organisation of information (local referent accessibility marking at the NP level) and a global status marking of the NP (topic/focus). The topic/focus opposition does not always coincide with the given/new opposition, as focus does not necessarily refer to something new from the referential point of view (Trévisiol, Watorek, & Lenart 2010). Local and global marking are interdependent and analysed, on the discourse level, according to referential movement, namely the introduction, maintenance, shift, or reintroduction of a referent.

Consequently, the L2 learner's task is twofold: to master the internal structure of the NP on the sentence level, and its appropriate use in context on the discourse level. The learner's acquisition trajectory differs depending on their SL, and the psychotypological distance between the SL and the target language (TL)[5] (cf. Kellerman 1977, 1978; Gass 1979; Ringbom 1987; Odlin 1989; Singleton 1987). To exemplify this process, in the following section, I will show how Polish learners of L2 French manage to perform a complex discourse task by producing oral narratives in the L2.

The acquisition trajectory of Polish adult learners of L2 French

Data and methodology

Our data consist of oral narratives by Polish adult learners of L2 French (beginners and advanced, ten learners per group) and by a control group of ten native French adults. The beginner level corresponds to the "basic variety", characterised by the structuring of utterances around non-inflected verbs (*infinite utterance organisation*). Overall, at this level of proficiency, inflectional morphology and subordination are absent; if there is a flectional form, it often does not have the functional value that it takes in the TL (cf. Klein & Perdue 1992, 1997). However, the learner is minimally autonomous from the communicative point of view. Then, at the *finite utterance structure* level ("post-basic varieties"), morphological inflection and syntactic complexity are variable. In the advanced learner variety, L2 syntax is appropriate, but morphology still causes some difficulties (cf. Bartning 1997).

The narratives were elicited via a five-minute silent cartoon presenting the adventures of two protagonists, a dog, called Reksio, and his master, a little boy. The protagonists are engaged in common activities such as waking up, getting dressed, walking, and skating. The realisation of these activities is thwarted by obstacles: they wear their clothes upside down, skid on the icy ground, then, more dramatically during a skating party, the ice cracks and the child falls into the water and must be rescued. Thanks to the dog's intervention, order is restored, and the child and the dog return home, as they were at the beginning of the story.

192 Ewa Lenart

Each participant watched the cartoon alone and was then invited to tell the story, with the following prompt: *You've just watched a cartoon that I don't know. Could you tell me the story?* The investigator was instructed not to intervene, except for gestures of interest. This context of unshared knowledge enables the study of learners' discourse competence in terms of how reference to entities is managed.

A narrative is constructed following the chronological sequence of events, sometimes reinforced by temporal connectors such as (*et*) *après* ((and) after), *et tout de suite* ("and immediately"). Among advanced learners, ambiguous forms are rare and discourse organisation is more in line with native speaker' practices. The use of inappropriate forms reflects the specificities of their acquisition level, as well as the influence of their SL, Polish. These differences are also reflected in the length of the narratives (respectively an average of 15 and 40.7 utterances for beginner and advanced learners, compared to 99.2 for native speakers), with a significant standard deviation in each group (respectively 7.2 for beginners and 9.7 for advanced; 45.2 for the natives).

Here, I briefly review the typological properties of the two languages (source: Polish; target: French), and the discourse organisation of narratives in French for the reader. In French, a prototypical noun is accompanied by an article, or other determiner, which, at the formal level, marks gender (singular) and number; this does not apply to proper nouns referring to animate entities or to nouns in a non-referential use (N attribute, for example). The establishment of reference and the introduction of an entity into the universe of discourse are associated with the presence of the indefinite article (*un* N). The distinction between new and given/familiar referents is, therefore, mainly marked by determiners (local marking on the NP level): a new entity is introduced with an indefinite NP; other nominal and pronominal forms mark given/familiar referents. Table 10.1 illustrates the division of forms into three categories following Ariel's (1990, 2004) hierarchy.

In spoken French, the local marking of new information (*un* N) is associated with global marking (sentence level) through the use of presentational or

Table 10.1 Types of reference markers in L1 French and L1 Polish

	French	Polish
High accessibility markers	Subject pronouns: *il* (*elle*)/*qui*/Ø Object pronouns: *le*/*lui*/*la*	Subject pronouns: Ø/*on* (*ona*)/*który* (*która*) (Ø/il; he (elle; she)/qui; who) Object pronouns: *jemu*/*jej* (lui; him/her)
Mid accessibility markers	NP with demonstrative or possessive: *ce*/*son chien* (this/his (her) dog)	NP with demonstrative or possessive: *ten*/*jego* (*jej*) *pies* (ce; this/son; his (her) dog)
Low accessibility markers	NP with definite article: *le chien* (the dog)	NP without any determiner: *pies* (dog)

existential structures: *c'est un chien/c'est l'histoire d'un chien* (it's a dog/it's the story of a dog); *il y a un chien* (there's a dog). French relies on a relatively rigid word order, which indicates grammatical function of each constituent (SVO). The subject is most often preverbal, agent, and topic. The obligatory subject pronoun (*il/elle*) marks maintained reference. In some contexts, the subject can be omitted (Ø), when it is identical in two declarative sentences that immediately follow each other.

Polish does not have articles, nor presentational structures, and relies, in a discourse context, on a relatively flexible word order. Nouns without any determiner (ØN) can fulfil the function of introduction, maintained or shifted reference. Ø is the most used form for maintained reference. The main problem for Polish learners of L2 French is therefore to understand the marking of definiteness, and how to express it in accordance with norms of the target language.

Results

Introduction of protagonists

Introducing an entity in the absence of shared knowledge informs the interlocutor that the referent is not accessible (not identifiable). The beginners use multiple forms (ex. 1) ranging from a proper noun (*Reksio*) to a noun without any determiner (ØN), through a numeral *un* (one) or the definite article *le* (the). The second protagonist is most often introduced with a possessive, Ø adj N or an extended NP:

(1)   (Es)[6] chien avec un garçon ((es) dog with a boy);
      Le chien est blanc rosso petit (the dog is white rosso small);
      Et après il (amusE) avec son ami (and after he (amusE) with his friend);
      Je (vwar) petit chien qui s'appelle Reksio
      (I (vwar) little dog who is called Reksio);
      Je regarde un film Reksio et Reksio il est un chien
      (I watch a film Reksio and Reksio he is a dog);
      Après on (vien) pour la maison ami (then we (vien) for the house friend).

Evidently, nominal determination is not functional at the beginner level, neither from a formal nor from a communicative point of view. The use of ØN, for example, shows that communicative inadequacy can result from formal inadequacy. When learners use a bare noun without any determiner, they do not appropriately indicate the accessibility of the referent. The use of a definite article to indicate non-accessibility of the referent goes contra to the communicative rules of the L2. In the data, there are also forms containing other types of formal errors, such as gender errors (*cette film* (this [feminine instead of masculine] movie), *cette boy* (this [idem] boy), *la escalier* (the [idem] stairs), *une moment* (a [idem] moment). Beginners use the following NP configurations: ØN/adjective+N/numeral+N (Ø *chien*/*petit chien*/*un chien*) or determiner+N (*le chien*). Note that there are no occurrences of the definite and indefinite articles in the same narrative. This pattern indicates that the category of definiteness is not yet functional at the beginner level.

At the advanced level, local reference marking is generally appropriate. The introduction of the first protagonist is marked by an indefinite article, and the second protagonist by an anaphoric possessive. However, some introductory structures differ from those used by native speakers:

(2) ce film présente le héros principal (this movie presents the main hero)
dans ce film il y a un chien (in this movie there is a dog)
il s'agit d'un chien (it's about a dog).

Maintained reference

The beginners' narratives are very short with few occurrences of maintained reference. The learners limit themselves to mentioning the most salient events given the linguistic means at their disposal. Half of the beginners mark maintained reference with a pronoun, as expected in the TL, but also with Ø and with a full NP. Some occurrences of pronouns do not allow reference retrieval and must be considered covert errors. The use of a nominal form is common among beginners to avoid potential ambiguity. This is sometimes linked to the presence of the other entity in focus:

(3) Et vite cette garçon (sor). (Se) très froid. Est-ce que il donne lui manteau ou quelque chose. Cette garçon donne le manteau.
(And quickly this boy (sor). (Se) very cold. Does he give him coat or something? This boy gives the coat.)

(4) Et garçon (return) à la maison. Le garçon à la maison (bwa).
(And boy [return] to the house. The boy in the house [bwa])

This phenomenon is interesting in comparison with the over-explicitness phenomenon observed in the interlanguage of intermediate and advanced learners, as noted previously in this chapter. However, we do not know if this phenomenon is related to a communicative strategy or to a pronominalisation problem. The beginners must perform the discourse task at minimal cognitive cost, and the use of a nominal form seems to be cognitively less expensive than the use of a pronoun.

Advanced learners are beginning to construct (double) referential chains. Maintained reference in topic position is mostly ensured by the pronoun *il*, but also by Ø anaphora:

(5) Il se lève. Il sort de sa maison plutôt niche. Il voit une flaque glacée. Bon il glisse. Puis Ø tombe. Ah puis il monte l'escalier et Ø va chercher son maître.
(He gets up. He leaves his house rather kennel. He sees an icy puddle. So he slips. Then falls. Ah then he goes up the stairs and goes to get his master.)

Pronominalisation errors are rare and are formal/grammatical in nature – *Reksio veut lui* aider* (Reksio wants to help him). The inappropriate use of the subject pronoun is also marginal in comparison with the beginner learners.

Shift/reintroduction of referent

Given that the two protagonists are already introduced in the narrative, we would expect to find local marking in the form of definite NPs. However, in beginner L2 production, most NPs are found without any determiner (30.5% for *chien* [dog] and 49.9% for *garçon* [boy]). NPs with determiners are used by the learners in dislocations, dislocations with a proper name (*Reksio il*) or with a possessive (*son monsieur il*). Maintained and shift reference are mainly topical (6). Entities in focus are relatively rare (7):

(6) Et après <u>ami de Reksio</u> tombe à l'eau (and then friend of Reksio falls in water)
Et <u>Reksio il</u> aide sortir de l'eau (and Reksio he helps get out of the water)
(7) <u>Chien</u> aide <u>garçon</u> (dog helps boy)
Et <u>garçon</u> (return) à la maison (and boy [return] at the house)

Advanced learners have a larger repertoire of determiners at their disposal, but their choices are different from those of native speakers', notably in the frequent use of possessives and the marking of definiteness by demonstratives:

(8) <u>Son maître</u> est un petit garçon (his master is a little boy)
Et <u>ce garçon</u> sort de la maison (and this boy comes out of the house)
Il est très glissant en au dehors (it is very slippery on the outside)
<u>Ce garçon</u> tombe de l'escalier (this boy falls from the stairs)

Figures 10.1 through 10.5 show the reference markers used and their frequencies.

Discussion

The data show our beginner learners manage to produce an understandable story despite the lack of formal linguistic means in the L2. They achieve this through sufficient discourse knowledge mastered in their L1, and through other methods to build inter-utterance links using the principle of chronological presentation of events, agent first. The high frequency of nominal forms (MAM and LAM) shows that they do not use the most economical linguistic means available in the L2, but manage to be effective in signalling a referential shift or ensuring referential continuity.

The question is – can we consider this strategy as an example of over-explicitness? That depends on what we consider. In one way, yes, since this strategy ensures discourse cohesion; but the answer must be negative if we assume that the over-explicitness must be accompanied by a correct use of linguistic means

196 *Ewa Lenart*

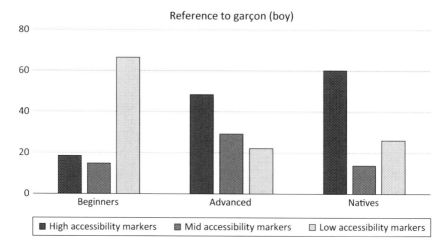

Figure 10.1 Types of reference markers used by Polish learners of L2 French and by French speakers: reference to garçon (boy)

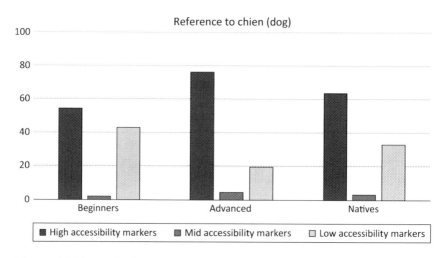

Figure 10.2 Types of reference markers used by Polish learners of L2 French and by French speakers: reference to chien (dog)

showing mastery of formal rules. Thus, 30.5% of NPs referring to *dog* and 49.9% of those referring to *boy* are used without any determiner (ØN). A particularly varied and problematic set of strategies is used by the beginners for the introduction of the first referent, who is also the anchor of the narrative (proper noun, ØN, numeral, definite article). This variety clearly demonstrates that nominal determination is not functional in the beginner level; the formal and communicative rules

Nominal reference in L2 French 197

Beginners: all reference markers

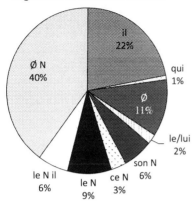

Figure 10.3 All reference markers used by beginners

Advanced: all reference markers

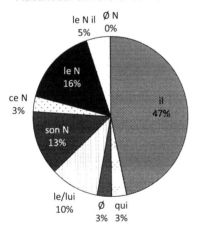

Figure 10.4 All reference markers used by advanced learners

of the TL are not followed. In French, bare nouns do not mark the accessibility of the referent (or lack thereof); definite NPs do not mark the absence of accessibility either, and are not used for referent introduction.

The narratives of advanced learners display a qualitative shift in the organisation of referential movement, and local marking that is very similar to native speaker strategies. The first protagonist is introduced with the indefinite article, the second with a possessive followed by an indefinite NP in apposition. Advanced learners mark definiteness (*maintained reference*) through demonstratives and

Natives: all reference markers

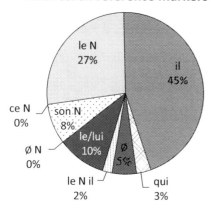

Figure 10.5 All reference markers used by native speakers

possessives (MAM), but do so more than the native speakers. Two types of inappropriate uses occur in their interlanguage: redundant NP repetitions in (immediate) co-referential contexts (that we can qualify as over-explicitness), and inappropriate uses of pronominal forms (a marginal phenomenon in comparison to the beginners).

Quantitative and qualitative analysis of determiner evolution between the beginner and advanced levels indicates that acquisition starts with quantification (which may be communicatively more important, cf. Perdue 1984), followed by qualification, and finally the definite/indefinite opposition that marks identifiability/accessibility of the referent. The first qualifying element would be an adjective, accompanied by an article at the intermediate level: *petit chien* (little dog) → *un/le petit chien* (a/the little dog). This order confirms the NP acquisition order established for L2 German by Klein and Dittmar (1979), who highlighted that while all languages have quantifiers, only some of them have qualifiers.

The typological properties of Polish could also influence learner choices. One such influence may be the absence of referential marking (Ø*, ØN*) in beginner production. However, this phenomenon was also observed in learners whose interlanguage shows neither articles nor pronouns. Furthermore, as this phenomenon was also observed in learners with different L1s (with or without articles, obligatory or optional subject language), it is more likely to be a process specific to the basic variety more generally (cf. Klein & Perdue 1992). The influence of Polish is demonstrable in the choice of word order: having preverbal nominal elements (other than the subject) to emphasise the process (*le garçon à la maison [bwa]*) (the boy at home [bwa]), post-verbal subject (*à cette maison habite petit garçon*) (at this house lives young boy), and the possibility of placing the object pronoun in post-verbal position (*il donne lui un manteau ou quelque chose*) (he gives him a coat or something).

In both groups, ambiguous forms are rare from the communicative point of view (contextual rules). When beginner learners lack the formal means to efficiently express referential movement, they reserve Ø or pronominal forms (HAM) for those contexts where the referent is immediately recoverable, and use full NPs (LAM, MAM) where they must specify more information. At the advanced level, the learners use dislocated forms and demonstratives more than the natives. They seem not to be sensitive to register distinctions in the L2 regarding dislocation (which is reserved for informal speech in French), and/or to over-explicitness of reference in the case of demonstratives. Over-explicitness has been reported in Hendriks (2003) and in other studies (see above). Adult learners optimise the means at their disposal to construct a narrative in a way that is understandable to the interlocutor, whatever their language of expression. This strategy should be common to all learners. However, while Chini (2005) and Ahrenholtz (2005), for example, attribute this strategy to intermediate learners, we also observed it in the advanced learners, regardless of the properties of the L1 (see Leclercq & Lenart 2013). We can conclude, therefore, that maintaining discourse cohesion is a costly process even at the advanced level, and over-explicitness is a way to reduce the cognitive overload involved in the discourse task.

Conclusion

This study of the acquisition of nominal reference has shown recurrent phenomena characteristic of adult L2 learners. Adult learners conducting a complex discourse task in L2 have more difficulty with the formal rules of the L2 than with communicative rules. Thanks to their communicative experience in the L1, they have more or less universal cognitive abilities to construct a narrative and are able to make the conceptual transfer necessary in relation to the task (adopting the perspective of their interlocutor). At the same time, the level of language proficiency, and typological properties of the L1–L2 language pair, influence the frequency of the nominal forms used (bare nouns in beginners and MAM in advanced). In line with Klein and Perdue (1997) and the longitudinal and transversal studies by Bartning (1997) and Bartning and Schlyter (2004), once learners have moved beyond a common organisation at initial proficiency levels (*basic variety*), their trajectories tend to vary as learners grammaticalise their interlanguage. Consequently, advanced levels show heterogeneity, due in particular to the influence of the SL. In the present study, the absence of a grammatical category in the SL (e.g. grammatical definiteness) seems to influence the way the Polish learners mark the accessibility of the referent in L2 French. They must adjust their understanding of definiteness since the marking associated with this concept does not have the same degree of prominence in both languages. In any case, the adult learner enters into a new language through the bias of their L1, which influences the acquisition process. Yet, the successful completion of any complex discourse task still implies a required degree of communicative competence that adult L2 learners do in fact possess, as I have shown through a triple-level analysis of nominal determination, information structure, and referential movement.

Notes

1 Title of a chapter by Klein and Perdue (1989).
2 Occasionally a bare noun is possible, as in certain proper or common nouns in specific structures/contexts: *avec courage* ("with courage"), *avoir raison* ("to be right").
3 « Tout article défini est appuyé sur un article indéfini avec lequel il entretient une relation anaphorique. [...] L'article indéfini lui-même assure le passage du concept à l'objet, mais ne fait rien d'autre: en particulier il ne confère aucune existence à l'objet du discours (de pensée) qu'il a permis de constituer. Il prendra, selon le contexte, une valeur « thétique » ou « hypothétique ».
4 *Most continuous/accessible topic* – zero anaphora – unstressed/bound pronouns or grammatical agreement – stressed/independent pronouns – R-dislocated DEF-NPs – neutral ordered DEF-NPs – L-dislocated DEF-NPs – Y-moved NPs ('contrastive topicalisation') – cleft/focus constructions – cleft/focus constructions – referential infinite NPs – *most discontinuous/inaccessible topic*.
5 From the psychotypological perspective, learner perceptions and decisions (conscious or not) influence the acquisitional trajectory.
6 The data come from the project APN 2JE 454 *Discourse construction by L1 child and L2 adult learners of languages* (cf. Watorek 2004). The sequences in brackets () provide phonetic transcription adapted to the project when a sequence is ambiguous.

References

Ahrenholz, B. (2005). Reference to person and objects in the function of subject in learner varieties. In H. Hendriks (Ed.), *The structure of learner varieties* (pp. 19–64). Berlin, Germany: de Gruyter.

Ariel, M. (1988). Referring and accessibility. *Journal of Linguistics*, 24(1), 65–87. doi:10.1017/S0022226700011567

Ariel, M. (1990). *Accessing noun phrase antecedents*. London, UK: Routledge.

Ariel, M. (2004). Accessibility marking: Discourse functions, discourse profiles, and processing cues. *Discourse Processes*, 37(2), 91–116. doi:10.1207/s15326950dp3702_2

Bartning, I. (1997). L'apprenant dit avancé et son acquisition d'une étrangère. Tour d'horizon et esquisse d'une caractérisation de la variété avancée. *Acquisition et interaction en langue étrangère*, 9, 9–50.

Bartning, I., & Schlyter, S. (2004). Itinéraires acquisitionnels et stades de développement en français L2. *Journal of French Language Studies*, 14, 281–299. doi:10.1017/S0959269504001802

Blanche-Benveniste, C. (1997). *Approches de la langue parlée en français*. Paris, France: Ophrys.

Carroll, M., & Lambert, M. (2003). Information structure in narratives and the role of grammaticised knowledge. In C. Dimroth & M. Starren (Eds.), *Information structure and the dynamics of language acquisition* (pp. 267–287). Amsterdam, the Netherlands: John Benjamins.

Chini, M. (2005). Reference to person in learner discourse. In H. Hendriks (Ed.), *The structure of learner varieties* (pp. 65–110). Berlin, Germany: de Gruyter.

Corder, S. P. (1971). Idiosyncratic dialects and error analysis. *International Review of Applied Linguistics*, 9(2), 147–160. doi:10.1515/iral.1971.9.2.147

Frederiksen, A. T., & Mayberry, R. I. (2015). Tracking reference in space: How L2 learners use ASL referring expressions. In E. Grillo & K. Jepson (Eds.) (pp.

165–177). *BUCLD 39: Proceedings of the 39th annual Boston University Conference on Language Development*. Somerville, MA: Cascadilla Press.

Gass, S. M. (1979). Language transfer and universal grammatical relations. *Language Learning*, 29(2), 327–344. doi:10.1111/j.1467-1770.1979.tb01073.x

Giacalone-Ramat, A. (1993). Sur quelques manifestations de la grammaticalisation dans l'acquisition de l'italien comme deuxième langue. *Acquisition et interaction en langue étrangère*, 2, 173–200.

Givón, T. (1983). Topic continuity in discourse: An introduction. In T. Givón (Ed.), *Topic continuity in discourse. A quantitative cross-language study* (pp. 1–41). Amsterdam, the Netherlands: John Benjamins.

Givón, T. (1989). *Mind, code and context: Essays in pragmatics*. Hillsdale, NJ: Erlbaum.

Gullberg, M. (2003). Gesture, referents and anaphoric linkage in learner varieties. In C. Dimroth & M. Starren (Eds.), *Information structure and the dynamics of language acquisition* (pp. 311–328). Amsterdam, the Netherlands: John Benjamins.

Gullberg, M. (2006). Handling discourse: Gestures, reference tracking, and communication strategies in early L2. *Language Learning* 56(1), 155–196. doi:10.1111/j.0023-8333.2006.00344.x

Gumperz, J. J., & Levinson S. C. (Eds.). (1996). *Rethinking linguistic relativity*. Cambridge, UK: Cambridge University Press.

Hendriks, H. (2003). Using nouns for reference maintenance: A seeming contradiction in L2 discourse. In A. Giacalone Ramat (Ed.), *Typology and second language acquisition* (pp. 291–326). Berlin, Germany: de Gruyter.

Hickmann, M. (2003). *Children's discourse: Person, space and time across languages*. Cambridge, UK: Cambridge University Press.

Kellerman, E. (1977). Towards a characterization of the strategy of transfer in second language learning. *Interlanguage Studies Bulletin*, 2(1), 58–145.

Kellerman, E. (1978). Giving learners a break: Native language intuitions as a source of predictions about transferability. *Working Papers in Bilingualism*, 15, 309–315.

Klein, W., & Dittmar, N. (1979). *Developing grammars. The acquisition of German syntax by foreign workers*. Berlin-Heidelberg, Germany: Springer-Verlag.

Klein, W., & Perdue, C. (1989). The learner's problem of arranging words. In E. Bates & B. MacWhinney (Eds.), *The cross-linguistic study of sentence processing* (pp. 292–327). Cambridge, UK: Cambridge University Press.

Klein, W., & Perdue, C. (1992). *Utterance structure: Developing grammars again*. Amsterdam, the Netherlands: John Benjamins.

Klein, W., & Perdue, C. (1997). The basic variety (Or couldn't natural language be much simpler?) *Second Language Acquisition Research*, 13(4), 310–347. doi:10.1191/026765897666879396

Klein, W., & von Stutterheim, C. (1991). Text structure and referential movement. *Sprache und Pragmatik*, 22, 1–32.

Lambrecht, K. (1986). *Topic, focus and the grammar of spoken French*. Berkeley, CA: University of Berkeley-UMI.

Leclercq, P., & Lenart, E. (2013). Discourse cohesion and accessibility of referents in oral narratives: A comparison of L1 and L2 acquisition of French and English. *Discours*, 12, 3–31. doi:10.4000/discours.8801

Lenart, E., & Perdue, C. (2004). L'approche fonctionnaliste: Structure interne et mise en œuvre du syntagme nominal. *Acquisition et interaction en langue étrangère*, 21, 85–122.

Levelt, W. J. M. (1989). *Speaking. From intention to articulation*. Cambridge, MA: The MIT Press.

Levinson, S. C. (2000). *Presumptive meanings: The theory of generalized conversational implicature*. Cambridge, MA: The MIT Press.

Lyons, C. (1999). *Definiteness*. Cambridge, UK: Cambridge University Press.

Lyons, J. (1977). *Semantics*. Cambridge, UK: Cambridge University Press.

Muñoz, C. (1995). Markedness and the acquisition of referential forms: The case of zero anaphora. *Studies in Second Language Acquisition*, *17*(4), 517–527. doi:10.1017/S0272263100014431

Odlin, T. (1989). *Language transfer: Cross-linguistic influence in language learning*. Cambridge, UK: Cambridge University Press.

Perdue, C. (Ed.). (1984). *Second language acquisition by adult immigrants: A field manual*. Rowley, MA: Newbury House.

Polio, C. (1995). Acquiring nothing? The use of zero pronouns by nonnative speakers of Chinese and the implications of the acquisition of nominal reference. *Studies in Second Language Acquisition*, *17*(3), 353–377. doi:10.1017/S0272263100014248

Ringbom, H. (1987). *The role of the first language in foreign language learning*. Clevedon, UK: Multilingual Matters.

Ryan, J. (2015). Overexplicit referent tracking in L2 English. Strategy, avoidance, or myth? *Language Learning*, *65*(4), 824–859. doi:10.1111/lang.12139

Singleton, D. (1987). The fall and rise of language transfer. In J. Coleman & R. Towell (Eds.), *The advanced language learner* (pp. 27–53). London, UK: CILT.

Slobin, D. I. (1991). Learning to think for speaking: Native language, cognition, and rhetorical style. *Pragmatics*, *1*(1), 7–25. doi:10.1075/prag.1.1.01slo

Slobin, D. I. (1996). From "thought and language" to "thinking for speaking". In J. J. Gumperz & S. C. Levinson (Eds.), *Rethinking linguistic relativity* (pp. 70–96). Cambridge, UK: Cambridge University Press.

Stutterheim, C., Andermann, M., Carroll, M., Flecken, M., & Schmiedtová, B. (2012). How grammaticized concepts shape event conceptualization in language production: Insights from linguistic analysis, eye tracking data and memory performance, *Linguistics 50*(4), 833–867. doi:10.1515/ling-2012-0026

Trévisiol, P., Watorek, M., & Lenart, E. (2010). Topique du discours/topique de l'énoncé – réflexions à partir de données en acquisition des langues. In M. Chini (Ed.), *Topic, information structure and acquisition* (pp. 177–194). Milan, Italy: Franco Angeli.

Van de Velde, D. (1997). Articles, généralités, abstractions. In W. De Mulder, N. Flaux, & D. Van de Velde (Eds.), *Entre général et particulier: Les déterminants* (pp. 83–136). Lille, France: Artois Presses Université.

Watorek, M. (Ed.). (2004). Construction du discours par des enfants et des apprenants adultes [Special issue]. *Langages*, *155*(3).

Whorf, B. L. (1956). *Language, thought, and reality: Selected writings of Benjamin Lee Whorf* (Ed. J. B. Carroll). Cambridge, MA: The MIT Press.

Weil, H. (1844). *De l'ordre des mots dans les langues anciennes comparées aux langues modernes*. Paris, France: L'Imprimerie de Crapelet.

Williams, J. (1988). Zero anaphora in second language acquisition: A comparison among three varieties of English. *Studies in Second Language Acquisition 10*(3), 339–370. doi:10.1017/S0272263100007488

11 Afterword
New directions in L2 reference research

Jonathon Ryan and Peter Crosthwaite

As outlined in the Foreword and Introduction to this volume, reference has proven to be a rich vein for SLA inquiry, attracting the interest of researchers from a broad range of theoretical perspectives and research agendas including those exploring cross-linguistic influence, developmental pragmatics, interlanguage, error analysis, constraints on transfer, influence of universal grammar, developmental trajectories in NP marking, and cognitive accounts of acquisition, production, and processing. This volume has contributed to this inquiry by exploring aspects of L2 reference through the use of new methodological advances, through expanding the range of L1/L2 pairs for investigation, and by working with a broad range of data sources.

On occasion, when a focused line of research enquiry has been pursued for a considerable number of years, an edited volume can seem to function as a full-stop, an indication that the field has been sufficiently scoped and the main issues resolved. At other times, as we wish to emphasize here, an edited volume will not only consolidate and extend the field, but highlight new directions of inquiry. In this concluding chapter, we outline some of these new directions while adding our own further reflections. We focus here specifically on research opportunities relating to varying types of referential phenomena, theoretical frameworks in RE selection, data types, elicitation tasks, languages, participants, and applications for teaching.

Theoretical frameworks in examining RE selection

In accounting for the selection of referring expressions (REs), there are currently four main theoretical frameworks, three of which have been adopted by studies in the present volume and elsewhere: the topic continuity scale and iconicity principle (Givón, 1983) in **Yuko Nakahama's** chapter, the Givenness Hierarchy (GH) (Gundel, Hedberg, & Zacharski, 1993) in the chapter by **Jennifer Killam**, and Accessibility Theory (AT) (Ariel, 1990) in the chapters by **Ewa Lenart**; **Jo Lumley**; **Jonathon Ryan**; and **Peter Crosthwaite** and **Min Jung Jee**. For the purposes of L2 research, each has its own particular merits and drawbacks, and each enriches our understanding of reference. For instance, GH makes strong predictions about the comparable cross-linguistic uses of determiners and pronouns and thus seems especially suited to exploring cross-linguistic influence.

It boasts a well-refined coding system and has been the framework for sustained linguistic research over many years. It is, however, less suited to exploring the issue of L2 over-explicitness due to the nature of its inferential hierarchy, which (to an extent) permits the use of forms associated with lower cognitive statuses (see Ryan, 2015). In the case of AT, its advantages include that it encompasses all referential definite NP types and is suitable for exploring the recurring L2 phenomenon of over-explicitness, yet it appears to offer fewer clear, readily testable hypotheses than the precise, categorical predictions of GH.

The fourth main theoretical approach encompasses a set of frameworks which take the seminal work of Grice (1989) as their starting point. These are conspicuously absent from studies of L2 reference. They include the neo-Gricean approaches of Levinson (2000) and Huang (2000), and the post-Gricean approach of Sperber and Wilson's (1986) Relevance Theory. Although the neo- and post-Gricean approaches are rather different in terms of their underlying arguments, both positions arrive at broadly similar accounts of how reference works. For instance, in Levinson's heuristics-based account, a default inference is that a minimal form points to local co-reference, a non-minimal RE points to a non-coreferential reading, and an expression that is unusual in some other way is purposefully designed to exclude the other, more ordinary inferences. Relevance Theory is similarly inference-driven, and assumes that although REs are typically semantically underdetermined, they will be processed in relation to the current state of one's understanding of the preceding discourse and other world knowledge (see also Scott, 2013; Wilson, 1992).

For two key reasons, these neo- and post-Gricean approaches appeal as a further framework to be adopted in L2 reference. Firstly, they are not theories of reference *per se* but represent far more generalized accounts of pragmatic processes, capable of accounting for a very wide range of contextual meaning. As such, their adoption offers the possibility that findings about L2 reference could generate insights into broader L2 pragmatic processes. Secondly, they appeal in terms of providing the simplest explanation (the principle of Occam's razor); as Bach (1998) has argued, both AT and GH propose features that may prove to be superfluous to accounts of RE resolution, most obviously in relation to the proposed grammaticized relationship between RE types and accessibility/cognitive status, but also in their assumptions about the structure of memory. Bach argues that REs may simply encode semantic information, and that reference resolution simply arises out of general principles of context, speaker intention, and inferencing (although see Ariel, 2008, pp. 44–53 for counter evidence and arguments).

To date, however, neo- and post-Gricean frameworks have not yet been fully applied in explorations of L2 reference. The major stumbling block is the lack of a suitable coding system for even moderate-sized L2 data sets. Although related ideas have been applied in the development of algorithms for anaphora production and resolution, these are predicated on felicitous (L1) use. A suitable L2 system would, in the first instance, provide for independent analysis of the discourse status of the referent, thereby enabling predictions of a set of suitable REs; secondly, it would provide for analysis of the RE actually used, thereby enabling comparisons with the predicted RE. This is considerably more complex than required for AT and GH coding systems as it requires analysis of lexical-semantic features and of the implicatures derived from the semantic weight (or "un-ordinariness") of the RE, rather than simply coding for pronoun and determiner type. It is not difficult to think of some tentative first steps in devising a prototype system, and this could prove to be a fruitful research path.

Data types and elicitation instruments

The data, participants, and elicitation instruments reported in the present volume represent a microcosm of those found within the broader field, where narrative elicitation tasks (as picture sequence or film retellings) have proved a rich source of data. For example, the widespread use of *Modern Times* has undoubted advantages arising from ready cross-linguistic and cross-study comparisons. Indeed, there are arguably grounds for eventually conducting a meta-analysis of such studies, as this may enable a broad overview of reference from beginner to advanced levels, across multiple L1 and L2 pairings, and in both speaking and writing. However, there may be much to be gained from extending the research focus to alternative genres/registers, such as casual conversation, institutional discourse, academic writing, computer-mediated communication, or – as in **Jonathon Ryan's** chapter – interviews. Within such data, there may prove to be a much fuller picture of L2 reference to be glimpsed. It would also be of interest to investigate reference from the perspectives of new, emerging genres and registers, which could involve the use of alternative elicitation instruments including virtual reality, multimodal, or group-oriented materials.

Languages and participants

While the present volume has provided a wide range of previously underexplored L1/L2 pairs for analysis, there are still intriguing gaps to be explored outside the major European and north-east Asian languages; moreover, a rough calculation suggests that not much more than a quarter of the world's population are L1 speakers of one of these languages. As Garde (2013) demonstrates, reference systems can differ remarkably from how they appear in these languages, and even seemingly universal principles such as accessibility marking and the principle of achieving clarity may take a backseat to other cultural factors, as is often the case for example with Australian Aboriginal languages (e.g. Walsh, 2016). Thus, it seems rather likely that some of the current assumptions about common features of L2 reference could be overturned through future studies in which the source or target language has a radically different system of RE use.

A related issue is that of sampling. A recent call for papers (Andringa & Godfroid, 2019) drew attention to the staggering reliance in SLA (as elsewhere) on samples from WEIRD (Western, Educated, Industrialized, Rich, Democratic) populations, with consequent risks of highly skewed data. Specifically within the field of L2 reference, this is paralleled in the heavy reliance on samples drawn from tertiary institutions, alongside a handful involving young learners; among the studies reviewed for this chapter, it appeared that only works derived from the ESF study (Broeder, 1991; Klein & Perdue, 1992) report on cases outside these limited specifications. Among those populations not represented are the billions who have not received a full secondary – let alone tertiary – education or otherwise been exposed to the same linguistic environments as the tertiary students typically sampled. Yule (1997, p. 26) has even argued that "the frequent assumption of perfect L1 linguistic competence of native speakers found in linguistic studies of L2 acquisition cannot be extended to studies of referential communication."

An even greater oversight may be the neglect of the estimated 781 million people with limited L1 literacy (UNESCO, 2015). While it is difficult to disentangle the effects of literacy from those of schooling and urbanization (Scribner & Cole, 1981), evidence appears to point to language processing being – not better or worse – but *different* among those who acquired and those who did not acquire literacy in childhood; this is evidenced in both neuropsychological evidence (Ardila et al., 2010) and more importantly in the small body of relevant SLA research (see especially Tarone, Bigelow, & Hansen, 2009). As Tarone et al. (2009) argue, a number of key assumptions about SLA may need to be revised in light of findings relating to low-literacy L2 learners. It remains entirely unclear how current perspectives on L2 reference may require revision as this line of inquiry unfolds.

In short, then, there remain strong reasons to conduct further exploratory studies, and also to replicate studies with non-WEIRD samples and with participants from underrepresented source and target languages.

Referential phenomena

As reflected in the present volume, studies of L2 reference have overwhelmingly focused on referent tracking (anaphoric reference), which is probably a fair indication of its practical and theoretical importance, positioned as it is at the intersection of grammar, pragmatics, and discourse. There is, however, much of interest to be learned about other referential phenomena. As noted in the introduction, **Jo Lumley's** chapter appears to be the first publication to explore the interaction between referent accessibility, social status, and RE selection, which is an area particularly ripe for further investigation.

It is also notable that L2 reference has overwhelmingly focused on the referring expression (RE) as the sole unit of analysis (Ryan, 2016), despite evidence of the complex ways in which referents with very low accessibility may be introduced and re-introduced incrementally over several turns (Smith, Noda, Andrews, & Jucker, 2005). Although very few L2 studies have applied such frameworks, indications are that this area is problematic for language learners (Ryan, 2016). Research into other interactional aspects of L2 reference is also lacking yet seem similarly promising (see, for example, Geluykens, 1994, for L1 referential repair). Similarly, since Gullberg's (2006) seminal work on gesture in L2 reference, there have been few studies to advance this line of inquiry despite the considerable recent advances in the study of L1 gestures. For instance, it is now known that L1 speakers use gestures which reflect contrasting perspectives when introducing and maintaining reference: that of an observer and of the character, respectively (Debreslioska, Özyürek, Gullberg, & Perniss, 2013); there is also evidence of a processing cost to the production of unnecessary (congruent) gestures (Debreslioska, van de Weijer, & Gullberg, 2019. Both suggest intriguing lines of SLA research.

Applications for teaching

A final avenue of exploration we would like to touch on here is the relative lack of attention to the teaching and learning of reference in the L2 classroom. Given the reported difficulties for L2 learners in terms of both introducing and coherently maintaining reference, it is surprising that treatments of reference in many L2 textbooks, standardized tests (e.g. IELTS), and L2 teaching curricula worldwide have not yet moved beyond classifying reference as just one component of simple text cohesion. In other words, we have not moved beyond the Hallidayian concept of coherence in text to one of coherence as shared in the common ground. This causes the complex interaction of syntax, pragmatics, and discourse (necessarily entailed within the production of reference) to play second fiddle to other forms of "cohesion" such as discourse markers or sentence connectives in many L2 writing textbooks (Cho & Shin, 2014). In fact, Celce-Murcia and Yoo (2014) have suggested that "we need to reanalyze virtually all [of English] grammar at the discourse level in order to be able to teach our students the grammar that will serve them when they read and write" (2014, p. 19).

It is also worth noting the constraining influence of the classroom on the types of referential phenomena that learners might be exposed to incidentally. It is usually the case that the teacher and students collectively experience little together outside the classroom and so spoken references are likely to be restricted to class members, a handful of institutional figures, and celebrities or those in public service, all of whom will be known by name or role. Missing from this list are the numerous categories of individuals that may require more complex introductions or other disambiguation, such as the associates, acquaintances, and clients that may be dimly recalled by the hearer, and even strangers who have been jointly encountered and are relevant to storytelling.

However, there has been precious little subsequent research in the SLA literature about how to teach the principles required for complex referent introductions or coherent referential movement in the L2. One exception comes from Crosthwaite (2017), focusing on the teaching of referential movement specifically to Asian learners of English writing, who recommends four "solutions" language teachers can use to improve certain representational deficits commonly experienced by such learners. These solutions include:

- Explicit teaching on English article semantics using Bickerton's (1981) framework, so as to assist learners with the complexities of definiteness marking;

- Making learners from topic-prominent languages explicitly aware of the overt nature of subject-prominent reference through the use of target gap-fills and narrative reconstruction tasks (and vice-versa for subject-prominent language learners acquiring topic-prominent languages);
- Asking learners to describe out loud what they are referring to when using pronouns or describing the functions of various pronouns in pre-set example texts, and;
- Allowing students much more experience of building extended discourse texts, so as to allow them to experience the full range of possible referential contexts (i.e. co-reference; re-introductions) they might be exposed to during lengthier L2 production.

While many studies of L2 reference have talked about the "implications" for pedagogy arising from understanding L2 reference across specific L1/L2 pairs (e.g. Kang, 2005), actual "strategies" arising from such research is, unfortunately, still rare. Further pedagogical solutions need to be discussed that help learners overcome representational deficits specific to other L1/L2 pairs, how to appropriately introduce and continue reference for referents of a wide range of types and numbers, how to maintain coherent reference across extended multi-party discourse, or how the L1 (perhaps in the form of oral or written corrective feedback) may reasonably be used to assist L2 learners in understanding the principles of L2 target reference.

Final comment

To reiterate the point made at the beginning of this chapter, the present volume builds on a substantial body of research into L2 reference and in so doing reaffirms a number of robust and coherent findings, yet collectively the studies here also highlight a sense of there being much further territory remaining to be explored. Undoubtedly, researchers will continue to be drawn to L2 reference, not only by the mysteries of RE systems and SLA processes, but also by the perhaps unmatched opportunities to apply cross-disciplinary and interdisciplinary insights and frameworks: reference was one of the central topics of interest in 20th Century philosophy, has been a major area of inquiry in cognitive psychology and various branches of linguistics, is a topic of interest within sociology (and its offshoot conversation analysis), anthropology and increasingly of course applied linguistics. We conclude with two predictions. The first is that studies of L2 reference will increasingly be enriched by broader interdisciplinary perspectives, such as those within the fields of philosophy and anthropology which have had less application to date. Secondly, and more speculatively, we predict that findings based on L2 reference and applied linguistics perspectives will begin to have greater cross-disciplinary influence, which will be afforded by both the inherently interdisciplinary footing of applied linguistics and its data-driven approach.

References

Andringa, S., & Godfroid, A. (2019). Call for participation. *Language Learning*, 69(1), 5–10. doi:10.1111/lang.12338

Ardila, A., Bertolucci, P. H., Braga, L. W., Castro-Caldas, A., Judd, T., Kosmidis, M. H., Rosselli, M. (2010). Illiteracy: The neuropsychology of cognition without reading. *Archives of Clinical Neuropsychology*, 25(8), 689–712. doi:10.1093/arclin/acq079

Ariel, M. (1990). *Accessing noun phrase antecedents*. London, UK: Routledge.

Ariel, M. (2008). *Pragmatics and grammar*. Cambridge, UK: Cambridge University Press.

Bach, K. (1998). [Review of the book Reference and referent accessibility by T. Fretheim & J. K. Gundel (eds)]. *Pragmatics and Cognition*, 6(1/2), 335–338. doi:10.1075/pc.6.1-2.17bac

Bickerton, D. (1981). *Roots of language*. Ann Arbor, MI: Karoma Press.

Broeder, P. (1991). *Talking about people: A multiple case study on adult language acquisition*. Amsterdam, the Netherlands: Swets & Zeitlinger.

Celce-Murcia, M., & Yoo, I. W. H. (2014). Discourse-based grammar and the teaching of academic reading and writing in EFL contexts. *English Teaching*, 69(1), 3–21. doi:10.15858/engtea.69.1.201403.3

Cho, H. Y., & Shin, J. (2014). Cohesive devices in English writing textbooks and Korean learners' English writings. *English Teaching*, 69(1), 41–59. doi:10.15858/engtea.69.1.201403.41

Crosthwaite, P. (2017). Managing referential movement in Asian L2 writing: Implications for pedagogy. *Writing and Pedagogy*, 8(3), 537–558. doi:10.1558/wap.27695

Debreslioska, S., Özyürek, A., Gullberg, M., & Perniss, P. (2013). Gestural viewpoint signals referent accessibility. *Discourse Processes*, 50(7), 431–456. doi:10.1080/0163853x.2013.824286

Debreslioska, S., van de Weijer, J., & Gullberg, M. (2019). Addressees are sensitive to the presence of gesture when tracking a single referent in discourse. *Frontiers in Psychology*, 10(1775), 1–14. doi:10.3389/fpsyg.2019.01775

Foster, P., & Skehan, P. (1996). The influence of planning and task type on second language performance. *Studies in Second Language Acquisition*, 18(3), 299–323. doi:10.1017/S0272263100015047

Garde, M. (2013). *Culture, interaction and person reference in an Australian language*. Amsterdam, the Netherlands: John Benjamins.

Geluykens, R. (1994). *The pragmatics of discourse anaphora in English: Evidence from conversational repair*. Berlin, Germany: Mouton de Gruyter.

Givón, T. (Ed.). (1983). *Topic continuity in discourse: A quantitative cross-language study*. Amsterdam, the Netherlands: John Benjamins.

Grice, P. (1989). *Studies in the way of words*. Cambridge, MA: Harvard University Press.

Gullberg, M. (2006). Handling discourse: Gestures, reference tracking, and communication strategies in early L2. *Language Learning*, 56(1), 155–196. doi:10.1111/j.0023-8333.2006.00344.x

Gundel, J. K., Hedberg, N., & Zacharski, R. (1993). Cognitive status and the form of referring expressions in discourse. *Language*, 69(2), 247–307. doi:10.2307/416535

Huang, Y. (2000). *Anaphora: A cross-linguistic approach.* Oxford, UK: Oxford University Press.

Kang, J. Y. (2005). Written narratives as an index of L2 competence in Korean EFL learners. *Journal of Second Language Writing, 14*(4), 259–279. doi:10.1016/j.jslw.2005.10.002

Klein, W., & Perdue, C. (1992). *Utterance structure: Developing grammars again.* Amsterdam, the Netherlands: John Benjamins.

Levinson, S. C. (2000). *Presumptive meanings: The theory of generalized conversational implicature.* Cambridge, MA: MIT Press.

Ryan, J. (2015). Overexplicit referent tracking in L2 English: Strategy, avoidance, or myth? *Language Learning, 65*(4), 824–859. doi:10.1111/lang.12139

Ryan, J. (2016). Introducing referents for recognition: L2 pragmatic competence and miscommunication. *Journal of Pragmatics, 97,* 55–73. doi:10.1016/j.pragma.2016.04.005

Scott, K. (2013). Pragmatically motivated null subjects in English: A relevance theory perspective. *Journal of Pragmatics, 53,* 68–83. doi:10.1016/j.pragma.2013.04.001

Scribner, S., & Cole, M. (1981). *The psychology of literacy.* Cambridge, MA: Harvard University Press.

Smith, S. W., Noda, H. P., Andrews, S., & Jucker, A. H. (2005). Setting the stage: How speakers prepare listeners for the introduction of referents in dialogues and monologues. *Journal of Pragmatics, 37*(11), 1865–1895. doi:10.1016/j.pragma.2005.02.016

Sperber, D., & Wilson, D. (1986). *Relevance: Communication and cognition.* Oxford, UK: Blackwell.

Tarone, E., Bigelow, M., & Hansen, K. (2009). *Literacy and second language oracy.* Oxford, UK: Oxford University Press.

UNESCO. (2015). *Education for all 2000–2015: Achievements and challenges.* Paris, France: UNESCO.

Walsh, M. (2016). Ten postulates concerning narrative in Aboriginal Australia. *Narrative Inquiry, 26*(2), 193–216. doi:10.1075/ni.26.2.02wal

Wilson, D. (1992). Reference and relevance. *UCL Working Papers in Linguistics, 4,* 167–191.

Yule, G. (1997). *Referential communication tasks.* Mahwah, NJ: Lawrence Erlbaum.

Index

Accessibility Theory 4, 16–17, 19, 77, 100–101, 185–186, 188, 192, 203–205
accuracy 76, 115, 148, 150, 155–156, 159–160
accusative 76, 84–86, 165, 188
activated 95, 122–123, 133, 137, 143, 145, 147, 152
addressee *see* interlocutor
adult 69, 71
agent 5, 166, 173, 186, 193, 195
ambiguity xv, 1, 5, 12, 77, 109–110, 112, 121–123, 134, 137, 194, 199
animacy 81, 192
antecedent 18–20, 51, 101, 105, 112–113, 120–126, 132–137
Ariel, M. 4, 17, 19, 77, 100–101, 185–186, 188
avoidance 31, 102, 169–170, 173, 175, 177, 189

Bach, K. 100, 204
beginners 80–90, 93–96, 123–124, 127–135, 191–199
bi-clausal 164, 167, 177
bridging 7, 146, 171, 176–177

causal 2, 5, 40–41, 45, 48–49, 190
Chafe, W. 3, 43, 59, 171
chains 8, 132–133, 186, 188, 194
characters (fictional) 16, 29–31, 87, 95
children xiv, 1, 76
Chinese: language xv, 58, 165–175, 178–180; learners 7, 102, 124, 164, 167, 170, 176–177, 179, 180, 186; second language 7, 31, 58, 79, 164–165, 168, 173–176, 178, 180
Chini, M. 12, 101–102, 114
Chomsky, N. 2, 4

chronological 40, 48, 186, 192, 195
classroom 39, 51, 207
coding 19, 32, 60–61, 104–106, 150, 160–161, 204–205
coherence xiii, 1–3, 5–6, 56–57, 79, 187, 189, 207–208
cohesion 3, 17, 18, 20–22, 30, 32, 109, 156
competition 4, 18–21, 30, 101, 109
complexity: activity 5–6, 30, 32, 112–113; communicative 1, 206–207; event 41, 45–47; language and linguistic 60, 86, 95, 112, 115, 146, 148, 161, 166, 177, 199; task 8, 59, 69, 71
conceptual 76, 164, 178–179, 184, 186–187, 199
continuity: referent 4, 179, 188, 195; topic 57–59, 62–63, 65, 68, 119–137
conversation 18, 51, 105, 115
corpora 75, 80–81, 96, 119, 124–126, 131, 136–137, 167
cross-linguistic (CLI) 56, 58–60, 64, 67–71, 101–103, 203–205

definiteness 56–59, 62, 64–65, 101, 187, 190, 193, 195, 197, 199, 207
deixis 39, 42–43, 45–55
demonstratives 3–5, 39–53, 77–79, 92, 96, 151, 176, 187–188, 195, 197, 199
developmental trajectories 4, 101, 103, 185, 191, 199, 203
discontinuous 3, 57–58
discourse-new *see* introductions
dislocation 3, 57, 61, 70, 181, 195, 199
distance: antecedent 3–4, 17–20, 50–51, 101, 105, 109, 125; social 17, 20

economical 110, 113–114, 186, 195
education 206
elicitation xvi, 8, 59, 100, 104, 115, 154, 205
encode 4, 121–122, 144, 173, 176, 178–179, 185, 190, 204
error 3, 11, 76, 82–86, 90, 94, 96, 102, 106, 152, 154–155, 185, 193–195
existential 57, 61, 70–71, 164–166, 169, 190, 193
experimental 41, 119, 121–122, 126, 136–137
explicitness 9, 17, 25, 31–32

feminine xv, 146, 188, 190, 193
film 8, 105, 115, 136–137, 205
Finnish 56, 58–59, 62, 67–70
foreign language 75–76, 79–81, 83–84, 86, 90, 93–96
formal ending device 41, 45, 47–48
form-function 5–6, 56–57, 71, 79–80, 95, 167, 170, 175–180, 193–194
French 102, 164–181, 184–199

gender 121–125, 133–137, 146, 148, 188–189, 192–193
generic 77, 81–83, 85–87, 95, 145–148, 154–155, 159–161
genre 39–40, 52, 104, 149, 167, 205
gesture 43, 46, 49, 192, 206–207
Givenness Hierarchy 3, 142–161, 203–205
Givón, T. 56–57, 122–123
global planning 170, 178–180, 189, 191–192
Grice, H. P. 102, 143–145
Gullberg, M. 206–207
Gundel, J. 3, 142–146, 150, 160–161, 203–204

Halliday, M. 2, 41
hearer *see* interlocutor
hearer-new xiv, 100, 113
Hedberg, N. 3, 142–146, 150, 160–161, 203–204
heritage 75–76, 79–81, 83–84, 86, 89–80, 93–96
hierarchy of referring expressions 3–4, 100–101, 143–148, 160, 192
honorific 36, 76–77, 85, 92

identifiability 143–147, 189–190
indefiniteness 56–60, 62–65, 70, 100, 142–148, 150–152, 154–157, 160, 177, 187–188, 190, 192, 194, 197–198
indefinite *this* 43, 45, 48–49, 51–52
infelicitous 3, 6, 49, 83, 102–103, 107–108, 112, 114, 125–126, 129, 151, 173
inference 4, 41, 146, 171, 176, 204
interlanguage 5, 58, 136, 185–186, 190, 194, 198–199
interlocutor xiv, 1, 3–4, 7–8, 40–43, 50, 52, 79, 100, 114, 142–146, 186, 188–190, 199
introductions 43, 49, 58–71, 77, 79, 83–85, 95–96, 100–101, 104, 111–112, 132, 164–180, 192–197, 206–208

language-specific 57, 77, 79
listener *see* interlocutor
locative 167, 170–171
longitudinal 16–17, 30, 32, 58, 100–101, 103, 106, 109, 199
low accessibility marker (LAM) 101, 105–106, 108, 188, 195, 199

Mandarin *see* Chinese
mapping 5–6, 56, 71, 77, 79–80, 95, 100, 108, 142
markedness 18
markedness differential hypothesis (MDH) 68
memory 40, 94, 100–101, 115, 188, 204
metalinguistic knowledge 178, 180
miscommunication 3, 107–108, 112, 118
morphology 40, 120, 179, 189, 191
morphosyntactic 119, 121, 166, 190

narrative data xiv, xv, 6, 8
native-like performance 29, 131, 137, 148, 150–151, 154–155, 159–160, 173
non-count 143, 145, 147–148, 152
numeral 77, 79, 193, 196

omission 58–59, 61, 69, 71, 85, 94, 96, 114, 151, 156, 177
organisation 40, 115, 180, 189–192
over-explicit xv–xvi, 1, 6, 31, 79, 91–92, 102–103, 107, 109, 114–115, 122, 127, 136, 186, 194–195, 198–199, 204
overuse 59, 62–64, 101, 114, 127, 173, 177–178, 180

Index

particles 59–60, 65, 173
passive 59, 101, 168, 172–175, 180
perspective xiv, 49, 186
plural 67, 77, 112–113, 145–148, 154–156, 159
Polish: language 184–186, 189, 193, 198; learners 193–199
possessive 84, 107, 151, 187–188, 192–195, 197–198
postpositional 56, 59, 62, 65, 69–70, 169
Pragmatic Principles Violation Hypothesis (PPVH) 31, 102
pragmatics interfaces 3, 5–6, 76, 129, 131–132, 177
preposition 94, 95, 97, 101, 105, 106, 155, 203, 207
preverbal 26, 179, 182, 183, 185, 191, 192
processing 6, 12, 111, 114, 117, 129, 132
pro-drop 121, 126
pronominal 1, 6, 18, 20, 25, 31, 64–70, 72, 76–78, 82, 83, 101, 103, 108, 109, 125
proposition 56, 59, 61–62, 64, 68, 82, 84, 86, 90, 93–94
pseudo-relative 170, 179

quaestio 81, 185, 189–190
quantifier 64–67, 71, 87, 151, 198
Quantity, Maxim of 143–145, 147, 151

reactivated referents 178–181
Relevance Theory 6, 204
role-play 16–19, 29–34

Spanish: language 75, 119–123, 127–137, 146–148; learners 148, 152–160; second language 102, 119, 121–123, 137
strategies 12, 79, 102–103, 108, 114, 122, 127, 136, 173–177, 180
Swedish: language 56, 58, 67; learners 56, 58–59, 186
switch-reference 77–79, 81–83, 88–89, 93–94, 96
switch-role reference 77–78, 81–82, 92–93, 96
syntax 2, 3, 5, 7, 24, 33, 83–85, 175, 197, 203

target-like use (TLU) *see* native-like performance
teaching 5, 39, 51, 207–208
temporal relationships 40, 45, 48–49, 94, 105, 190, 192
typological accounts xiv–xv, 2, 4–6, 56, 58, 191, 198–199

under-explicitness 31, 64, 101–103, 106–114
universals 1–2, 4–5, 7, 39–40, 43, 50–53, 77, 79, 104, 143, 184, 199, 205

variability 4, 28, 76, 83–83, 86, 88–89, 92–93, 106, 119, 122, 142, 150, 155, 158–159, 171, 188
verb 4, 40–41, 76, 120, 130, 165–167, 169–171

Zacharski, R. 3, 142–146, 150, 160–161, 203–204

Printed in the United States
by Baker & Taylor Publisher Services